Handbook of Themes
for Preaching

Handbook of Themes for Preaching

James W. Cox, Editor

Westminster/John Knox Press
Louisville, Kentucky

Scripture quotations from the Revised Standard Version of the Bible are copyright 1946, 1952, © 1971, 1973 by the Division of Christian Education of the National Council of the Churches of Christ in the U.S.A. and are used by permission.

Scripture quotations marked NRSV are from the New Revised Standard Version of the Bible, copyright © 1989 by the Division of Christian Education of the National Council of the Churches of Christ in the U.S.A., and are used by permission.

Scripture quotations marked JB are from the Jerusalem Bible, copyright © 1966, 1967, 1968 by Darton, Longman & Todd, Ltd., and Doubleday and Co., Inc. Used by the permission of the publishers.

Scripture quotations marked KJV are from the King James Version.

Scripture quotations marked NEB are taken from the New English Bible, © The Delegates of the Oxford University Press and The Syndics of Cambridge University Press, 1961, 1970. Used by permission.

Scripture quotations marked NIV are from *The Holy Bible, New International Version.* Copyright © 1973, 1978, 1984 International Bible Society. Used by permission of Zondervan Bible Publishers.

Book design by Gene Harris

First edition

Published by Westminster/John Knox Press
Louisville, Kentucky

PRINTED IN THE UNITED STATES OF AMERICA

9   8   7   6   5   4   3   2   1

Library of Congress Cataloging-in-Publication Data

Handbook of themes for preaching / James W. Cox, editor. — 1st ed.
    p.   cm.
  ISBN 0-664-21928-4

  1. Sermons—Outlines, syllabi, etc.   I. Cox, James William,
1923–   .
BV4223.H26 1991
251′.02—dc20   91-3324

How to Use
This Book

Let me say, at the outset, that you do not need anyone to tell you how to use this book. Whether you browse through it or plough through it with dogged determination, you will come upon a theme here or there that offers promise of a helpful and interesting sermon. Then you will be off and running, and you will arrive at your destination in your own way, with your usual results, satisfying or not. You may even be bold enough to project a preaching program for an entire year. Notwithstanding, I will indicate some ways to facilitate the use of this volume. First, however, I must deal with a legitimate theological/hermeneutical/homiletical concern.

You have noted that this is a book of themes. For some of us, this will immediately raise a warning flag: Shouldn't we begin with a biblical text? But think about it—it does not really matter where the sermon begins, whether with a text or with a theme; a preacher who is committed to preaching biblically will preach biblically in either case. To be sure, Jesus' sermon in the synagogue at Nazareth sprang from a passage in the book of Isaiah. However, many of Jesus' most pointed teachings were responses to concrete situations, responses that intertwined interpretation of ancient scripture with his messianic authority. The apostle Paul began with local church situations that clearly indicated specific themes and brought these themes to expression in dialogue with the scriptures of the Old Testament. Was not Professor John Knox correct when he described biblical preaching, in part, as "preaching which remains close to the characteristic and essential biblical ideas"? This handbook treats many of those themes. But cannot preaching be biblical also (and Professor Knox does not deny this) when it deals with subordinate themes related to the larger, more comprehensive ones? The *Handbook* provides entry into both types of themes, sometimes through an article that focuses on one large theme, sometimes through an article relating a number of subordinate themes as it discusses a major one.

As you endeavor to meet the needs of your congregation, you discover, no doubt, that questions arise that you cannot answer satisfactorily by sticking to a verse, a paragraph, a chapter, or even an entire book of the Bible. The hearers often need a more systematic or comprehensive view of a teaching. In other words, what is said about the matter at hand in other parts of the Bible?

To be sure, we can make a good case for sermons that present the one-sided message of the chosen text. Eduard Schweizer asserted that a too-well-balanced sermon does not make its point. We can on-the-one-hand, on-the-other-hand a sermon to death! However, we may have to present a truth in its multi-faceted aspects in order to enable our hearers to appreciate one vital aspect of that truth.

And now for "some ways"! As you can see, each article begins with a definition. This gives a quick yet comprehensive general view of the theme. What follows unpacks the meaning or implications of the definition; it expands and extends it; it points to examples of it; it shows its relation to specific biblical texts; it suggests possible approaches to preaching on the theme. Once this scheme is understood, sermons can profit from the reader's seeing a theme "steadily" and seeing it "whole," whether the preacher discusses the major aspects of a theme or some lesser though important single aspect.

You will find that themes treated in this volume are diverse, corresponding to varied concerns you may find in your congregation, your reading, or recommended scripture. These articles represent topics in ethics, theology, spirituality, pastoral care, and biblical studies chosen as important for preaching. In each article the writer, a specialist in the subject, offers his or her most current thinking for your use in bringing God's message to your congregation. These writers are professors, counselors, parish clergy, or religious writers. They represent a wide ecumenical range of religious traditions, from Quaker to Anglican and Roman Catholic, as well as Presbyterian, Southern Baptist, Methodist, Lutheran, and a rich variety of other traditions.

Thanks are due to the editorial advisors: in ethics, J. Philip Wogaman, of Wesley Theological Seminary; in theology, Daniel Migliore, of Princeton Theological Seminary. From Southern Baptist Theological Seminary: in spirituality, E. Glenn Hinson; in pastoral care, Wayne E. Oates; and in biblical studies, R. Alan Culpepper. These advisrs thoughtfully suggested topics and reviewed articles in their areas. Thanks also to the staff of Westminster/John Knox Press: Davis Perkins for help in planning the project and carrying it out; Cynthia Thompson for originating the idea; and Katy Monk for administrative direction and editorial work. Finally, deep thanks are due to the individual writers for sharing their knowledge and wisdom in this volume to enrich preaching from many pulpits.

Contributors

Daniel Aleshire
Associate Director
The Association of Theological Schools in the United States
  and Canada
Vandalia, Ohio
—Education

Bernhard W. Anderson
Professor of Old Testament Theology, Emeritus
Princeton Theological Seminary
Princeton, New Jersey
—Word of God

Glenn H. Asquith, Jr.
Associate Professor of Pastoral Theology
Moravian Theological Seminary
Bethlehem, Pennsylvania
—Decision-making; Faith; Forgiveness; Wholeness; Work

Paul A. Basden
Minister to the University
Samford University
Birmingham, Alabama
—Election

John C. Bennett
President Emeritus, Union Theological Seminary
New York, New York
—Church and State

C. Clifton Black
Assistant Professor of New Testament
Perkins School of Theology
Southern Methodist University
Dallas, Texas
—Ministry

James L. Blevins
Professor of New Testament Interpretation
The Southern Baptist Theological Seminary
Louisville, Kentucky
—Crucifixion

Gerald L. Borchert
J. Rupert and Lucille Coleman Professor of New Testament
    Interpretation
The Southern Baptist Theological Seminary
Louisville, Kentucky
—Resurrection

Georgine Lomell Buckwalter
Chaplain, Westminster Terrace Healthcare Center
Assistant, St. Thomas Episcopal Church
Louisville, Kentucky
—Anger

William R. Cannon
Bishop, The United Methodist Church
Former Dean and Professor of Church History and Historical
    Theology
Candler School of Theology
Emory University
Atlanta, Georgia
—The Ten Commandments

James T. Clemons
Professor of New Testament
Wesley Theological Seminary
Washington, D.C.
—Suicide

Phillip A. Cooley
Pastor
First Baptist Church
Gallatin, Tennessee
—Providence

Martin B. Copenhaver
Senior Minister
First Congregational Church (United Church of Christ)
Burlington, Vermont
—Doubt

James W. Crawford
Senior Minister
The Old South Church in Boston
Boston, Massachusetts
—Envy/Jealousy; Guidance; Idolatry

Hugo H. Culpepper
W.O. Carver Professor Emeritus of Christian Missions and
    World Religions
The Southern Baptist Theological Seminary
Louisville, Kentucky
—Evangelism/Missions

R. Alan Culpepper
James Buchanan Harrison Professor of New Testament
    Interpretation
The Southern Baptist Theological Seminary
Louisville, Kentucky
—Joy; Reign of God; Sacrifice; Wealth

Richard B. Cunningham
Professor of Christian Philosophy
The Southern Baptist Theological Seminary
Louisville, Kentucky
—End-time; Incarnation; Stewardship

John R. Donahue, S.J.
Professor of New Testament
University of Notre Dame
Notre Dame, Indiana
—Parable

Joel F. Drinkard, Jr.
Associate Professor of Old Testament Interpretation
The Southern Baptist Theological Seminary
Louisville, Kentucky
—Covenant

O. C. Edwards, Jr.
Professor of Preaching
Seabury-Western Theological Seminary
Evanston, Illinois
—Scriptures

Dorothy Ashman Fackre
Minister for Pastoral and Group Counseling
South Congregational Church (United Church of Christ)
Centerville, Massachusetts
—Abortion (co-author)

Gabriel Fackre
Abbot Professor of Christian Theology
Andover Newton Theological School
Newton Centre, Massachusetts
—Abortion (co-author)

Reginald H. Fuller
Professor Emeritus of New Testament
Virginia Theological Seminary
Alexandria, Virginia
—Miracles

James Leo Garrett, Jr.
Professor of Theology
Southwestern Baptist Theological Seminary
Fort Worth, Texas
—Image of God

Timothy George
Dean, Beeson Divinity School
Samford University
Birmingham, Alabama
—Sovereignty of God

Catherine Gunsalus González
Professor of Church History
Columbia Theological Seminary
Decatur, Georgia
—Righteousness of God

William L. Hendricks
Professor of Theology
The Southern Baptist Theological Seminary
Louisville, Kentucky
—Children/Youth

Dieter T. Hessel
Visiting scholar
McCormick Theological Seminary
Chicago, Illinois
Former director
Committee on Social Witness Policy, Presbyterian Church
(U.S.A.)
—Environment

E. Glenn Hinson
David T. Porter Professor of Church History
The Southern Baptist Theological Seminary
Louisville, Kentucky
—Discipline; Mystery; Patience

Randall J. Hoedeman
Director of Training and Education
Personal Counseling Service, Inc.
Clarksville, Indiana
—Hope; Love

Edwina Hunter
Joe R. Engle Professor of Preaching
Union Theological Seminary
New York, New York
—Women's Issues

James A. Hyde
Director, Program of Ethics and Pastoral Counseling
Assistant Professor, University of Louisville Department of
    Psychiatry
Louisville, Kentucky
—Depression, Disease/Illness

J. Estill Jones
Seminary Pastor
The Southern Baptist Theological Seminary
Louisville, Kentucky
—Prayer

Patricia Beattie Jung
Visiting Associate Professor of Social Ethics
Wartburg Theological Seminary
Dubuque, Iowa
—Honesty

Robert Kysar
Professor of Homiletics and New Testament
Lutheran Theological Seminary
Philadelphia, Pennsylvania
—Eternal Life

Bill J. Leonard
William Walker Brooks Professor of American Christianity
The Southern Baptist Theological Seminary
Louisville, Kentucky
—Church

John Macquarrie
Lady Margaret Professor of Divinity Emeritus
University of Oxford
Oxford, England
—God

Larry L. McSwain
Dean
School of Theology;
Professor of Church and Community
The Southern Baptist Theological Seminary
Louisville, Kentucky
—Community

Molly Marshall-Green
Professor of Christian Theology
The Southern Baptist Theological Seminary
Louisville, Kentucky
—Mary; Sin

Daniel L. Migliore
Professor of Systematic Theology
Princeton Theological Seminary
Princeton, New Jersey
—Trinity

John M. Mulder
President
Louisville Presbyterian Theological Seminary
Louisville, Kentucky
—Conversion

Cecil Murphey
Presbyterian minister;
freelance writer
Louisville, Kentucky
—Divorce; Heaven

Wayne E. Oates
Professor of Psychiatry and Behavioral Sciences
School of Medicine, University of Louisville;
Senior Professor of Psychology of Religion and Pastoral Care
The Southern Baptist Theological Seminary
Louisville, Kentucky
—Conscience; Guilt; Suffering; Temperance; Temptation

Allan M. Parrent
Associate Dean for Academic Affairs
Clinton S. Quin Professor of Christian Ethics
Virginia Theological Seminary
Alexandria, Virginia
—Ethics/Morality; Violence/War

Basil Pennington, O.C.S.O.
Professor of Theology and Canon Law
Saint Joseph's Abbey Institute of Theology and Monastic
    Studies
Spencer, Massachusetts
—Humility

Karl A. Plank
Associate Professor of Religion
Davidson College
Davidson, North Carolina
—Jewish-Christian Relations

James T. Pollard
Chaplain
Center for Behavioral Health and Neuro-Rehabilitation
Baptist Hospital East
Louisville, Kentucky
—Addiction

Charles P. Price
Professor Emeritus of Systematic Theology
Virginia Theological Seminary
Alexandria, Virginia
—Revelation; Secularism

J. Bill Ratliff
Associate Professor, Counseling and Applied Theology
Earlham School of Religion
Richmond, Indiana
—Family

John P. Reed
Executive Director
Kilgore Samaritan Counseling Center
Louisville, Kentucky
—Eucharist; Inspiration

Earl E. Shelp
Executive Director
Foundation for Interfaith Research and Ministry
Houston, Texas
—Sexuality

H. Stephen Shoemaker
Pastor
Crescent Hill Baptist Church
Adjunct Professor of Preaching
The Southern Baptist Theological Seminary
Louisville, Kentucky
—Blessing; Narrative

Donald W. Shriver, Jr.
President
Union Theological Seminary
New York, New York
—Vocation

Karen E. Smith
Assistant Professor of Church History
The Southern Baptist Theological Seminary
Louisville, Kentucky
—Tradition

Glen Harold Stassen
Professor of Christian Ethics
The Southern Baptist Theological Seminary
Louisville, Kentucky
—Capital Punishment; Peace

Stephen L. Stell
Visiting Assistant Professor of Religion
Austin College
Sherman, Texas
—Absence of God; Creation; Grace; Holy Spirit; Truth

Dan R. Stiver
Associate Professor of Christian Philosophy
The Southern Baptist Theological Seminary
Louisville, Kentucky
—Knowledge of God

George W. Stroup
Professor of Theology
Columbia Theological Seminary
Decatur, Georgia
—Jesus Christ

Marjorie Hewitt Suchocki
Ingraham Professor of Theology
School of Theology at Claremont
Claremont, California
—Evil

David K. Switzer
Professor of Pastoral Theology
Perkins School of Theology
Southern Methodist University
Dallas, Texas
—Grief

Jane M. Thibault
Clinical Gerontologist
Assistant Professor of Family Medicine
School of Medicine, University of Louisville
Louisville, Kentucky
—Aging

Richard L. Thulin
Ulrich Professor of the Art of Preaching
Lutheran Theological Seminary
Gettysburg, Pennsylvania
—Justification

William Powell Tuck
Pastor
St. Matthews Baptist Church
Louisville, Kentucky
—Death

Wayne E. Ward
Joseph Emerson Brown Professor of Theology
The Southern Baptist Theological Seminary
Louisville, Kentucky
—Repentance; Salvation; Theodicy

John D. W. Watts
Donald L. Williams Professor of Old Testament
The Southern Baptist Theological Seminary
Louisville, Kentucky
—Promise

Theodore R. Weber
Professor of Social Ethics
Candler School of Theology
Emory University
Atlanta, Georgia
—Politics

Ernest White
Gaines S. Dobbins Professor of Church Administration and
    Leadership
The Southern Baptist Theological Seminary
Louisville, Kentucky
—Fear/Anxiety

Preston N. Williams
Houghton Professor of Theology and Contemporary Change
The Harvard Divinity School
Cambridge, Massachusetts
—Racism

William H. Willimon
Dean of the Chapel and Professor of Christian Ministry
Duke University
Durham, North Carolina
—Baptism; Discipleship; Marriage; Worship

J. Philip Wogaman
Professor of Christian Ethics
Wesley Theological Seminary
Washington, D.C.
—Equality; Justice/Liberation; Poverty

Eugene L. Zoeller
Theology Department
Bellarmine College
Louisville, Kentucky
—Confession; Obedience

Contents

Handbook of Themes
for Preaching

ABORTION

Gabriel Fackre and Dorothy Ashman Fackre

Abortion, spontaneous or induced, is ending a fetal life before it reaches full term.

Analysis

Key questions in the debate on abortion are: *When* is a fetus a human being? *What* are the circumstances, if any, under which abortion is a legitimate moral choice?

Preaching on this controversial issue requires familiarity with the range of opinion in the church and wider society on the two disputed questions.

Human beginnings. In past and present debate, human origins are placed at:

1. Fertilization—sperm and ovum join to create a zygote with its own genetic code.
2. Implantation—the embryo is implanted in the uterine wall, five to eight days after fertilization.
3. Segmentation and recombination—"twinning" (one egg that becomes two) and "mosaic" (two eggs that become one) are definitive—at fourteen days. (Fertilization, implantation, and segmentation have been variously identified as the point of "conception.")
4. Detectable heartbeat, at three to four weeks.
5. Discernible cerebral cortex, at approximately five weeks.
6. Formation—the fetus "looks human" and ultrasound technology shows movement—at six to seven weeks.
7. Readable brain waves, at eight weeks.
8. Quickening—the mother feels movement—at fourteen to twenty weeks.

9. Viability—survivability outside the womb—at twenty to twenty-eight weeks.
10. Birth—natural life begins outside the womb.

Christian opinion on human beginnings has taken significant shifts, as in the change in the traditional Roman Catholic view from "quickening" to "conception," beginning in the eighteenth century.

A subquestion of political import is, Do human beginnings entail "equal rights"? Some believe fetal personhood proceeds developmentally, rights being determined by the stage of growth, with parity at viability or birth. Others declare for equal rights at conception. Still others defend fetal rights, but give priority to maternal rights under circumscribed conditions.

Reasons for abortion. Perspectives within and beyond the Christian community vary widely.

Roman Catholic moral teaching forbids "direct abortion." However, its "principle of double effect" holds that a pathological organ that threatens the life of the mother can be removed, even though the surgery results in "indirect abortion." Others allow for abortion only when the mother's life is in peril, but do so without the limited rationale of double effect.

An additional reason for abortion offered by another constituency is peril to the health of the mother. Opinion is divided as to whether this includes mental as well as physical health. In close proximity are those who hold that other violations of the mother or breaches of moral law, such as rape and incest, justify abortion.

Still other points of view focus on the perceived consequences to the fetus, mother, family, and wider society. Some believe birth into a dehumanizing socioeconomic setting or a dysfunctional condition warrants termination of fetal life. Others contend that overpopulation justifies selective abortion. Still others hold that the fulfillment of a woman's personal goals takes precedence as a value and legitimates the removal of any reproductive barrier to that fulfillment.

Biblical Instances

Only two verses in scripture refer directly to abortion. Exodus 21:22 (NRSV) requires a fine for persons who, while fighting, "injure a pregnant woman so that there is a miscarriage." (The following verse, Ex. 21:23, exacts heavier punishment for additional hurt: "If any harm follows, then you shall give life for life," implying a distinction between abortion and murder.)

In Hosea 9:14, the author berates the people ("Ephraim") for their sins and entreats God to "give them a miscarrying womb and dry breasts."

As with some other doctrinal and ethical themes, theological reflection on abortion develops by inference from scripture rather than by direct citation. Such texts can include the following:

Genesis 1:26–27 establishes the sanctity of human life as made in the image of God.

Matthew 1:18–23; Luke 1:31; John 1:14; and other passages on the Word made flesh suggest (as in the Orthodox tradition) that human life from conception forward is hallowed by the incarnation. Jeremiah 1:4–5 and Luke 1:15 comment on the consecration of life before birth.

Psalm 90:10; 1 Corinthians 13:12; and other passages on human finitude, and Romans 3:9–18 and other passages on human sin, imply that judgments on moral issues with no explicit directives in revelation should be made with a modesty appropriate to that ambiguity.

Romans 3:21–29 and other passages on justification affirm that Christians live by grace and forgiveness in the midst of the shortfalls and unclarities of human decision making.

Psalm 82:3–4; Amos 4:1; and other passages on the "weak and the needy," or those who "oppress the poor, who crush the needy," call for the defense of the helpless. These suggest the concern for *both* the vulnerable fetus and women whose pregnancies are related to oppressive social circumstances.

Options for Preaching

Commentary should take its orientation from biblical indicators, recognize the variety of perspectives within the Christian community, and have due regard for the insights of human experience—from those most directly affected, from the conscience of the community, and from the state of scientific knowledge. With these reference points in mind a preacher can:

Ground assertions in the biblical warrants for human dignity. Important here is the classical teaching that humans are made in the image of God (Gen. 1:26–27). Sanctity is conferred on each by virtue of this special relation of God to the human order, climaxing in the Word made flesh (John 1:14).

Explore the affirmation of human sanctity in the light of the New Testament's description of the incarnation. As the Holy Spirit brings Christ into solidarity with the human race at conception (Matt. 1:18–23), fetal life is dignified from its beginnings. Yet the angels sing, the shepherds kneel, and the star shines at Jesus' birth (Matt. 2:1–2; Luke 2:6–20). Accordingly, Christmas is the high festival of Christ's coming. This distinction between the days of conception and nativity points to a difference between human being (the fetus) and full human being (birth). So, too, does the Exodus 21:22–23 allusion.

Show the relation of decision-making on abortion to choices made on other moral questions in which reality factors (finitude and sin) regularly qualify the perfect or literal execution of absolutes.

When the life of the fetus is pitted against the life of the mother, abortion is recognized, even by most "pro-life" advocates, as a legitimate choice of the lesser of two evils. Implicit in this judgment is the distinction between human being-ness and full human being-ness.

The church is currently struggling to clarify the conditions under which the sanctity of the bearer might take precedence over the sanctity of the fetus. In addition to peril to the life and health of the mother, rape and incest are increasingly cited as evils of sufficient warrant for a "just abortion." Beyond that, there is no developing "mind of the church." Defense of the weak and oppressed is adduced by both pro-life and pro-choice positions. Partisans also warn about the corruptibility of power by those who wield it over the fetus or over the woman who bears it.

The conscience burdened with a painful abortion choice must hear from the church the word of forgiveness and justifying grace (Rom. 3:21–29) and experience the support of the community of forgiven sinners (Acts 2:42–47).

Make clear the varied opinion in church and culture on the point of human beginnings and the influence of the state of science on the same. (Current data on segmentation and recombination indicate that individual humanness cannot be settled until the fourteenth day after fertilization, which suggests this as the point of conception.) A preacher can also call for modesty in Christian assertions about origins, given their dependence on shifting scientific data.

Show how abortion decisions are inextricable from institutional patterns. As such, Christians have the right and duty to implement their convictions in political action and legislation. (Ex. 21:22–23 is an ancient civil code.) However, in a pluralistic society, they must not force their biblically grounded views on the public but press instead the points of convergence with the community's conscience (as in the civil rights struggle of the 1960s).

Where abortion is widespread, its relation to social, economic, and educational deprivation is unmistakable. The church has a responsibility to address these contextual factors ("creatureliness") and also to avoid a moralism insensitive to predisposing circumstances.

Comprehensive church education in sexuality is a necessary complement to institutional witness.

ABSENCE OF GOD

Stephen L. Stell

This phrase describes feelings of abandonment, solitary helplessness, and despair threatening individual and/or corporate existence. Although such feelings may be widespread, the absence of God is uniquely and acutely problematical for the believer, whose existence and perception of reality centers on God.

Analysis

The phrase "absence of God" is meaningful only in relation to God's expected presence.

The true God is always "absent" in the sense of not being controllable, manipulable, or fully comprehensible. Yet God is not only challenged by false gods but by experiences of evil and the absence of God's loving presence and power. Even mystical union with God is traditionally followed by the abysmal "dark night of the soul."

For Christians this paradox of God's presence and absence is paradigmatically expressed on the cross. Jesus Christ, the very presence of God, experiences forsakenness by God. Christians, too, sometimes tread this path of forsakenness as their own cross, though now being assured of walking with Christ. Christ's redemption of death and despair means the experience of God's absence can itself yield God's presence.

Biblical Instances

Old Testament. The covenant community experiences God's absence both personally (1 Sam. 28:6, 15; Job; Pss. 13:1–4; 22; 42:9–10) and corporately (Ps. 115:2; Lam. 5:20). Tensions are inherent in these experiences of faith: on the one hand, God is faithful and will not forsake God's people (Deut. 4:31; 1 Sam. 12:22; Isa. 49:15; Job 8:20; Ps. 37:25); on the other hand, God does forsake them (2 Kings 21:10–26; Jer. 11:11; Job 30:20; Hos. 1:9).

This abandonment is often explained by the faithlessness of God's people (2 Chron. 12:5; 15:2; Jer. 7:13–34; 11:9–23; Ezek. 5:7–17). Yet a fuller answer perceives abandonment as a moment in God's gracious and everlasting covenant (Isa. 54:7–8). Here abandonment even touches God, who gives up "the beloved of my soul" (Jer. 12:7).

New Testament. This internal tension in God and God's people reaches its peak in the person of Jesus Christ. Fully forsaken by God (Matt. 27:46; Mark 15:34), Jesus nevertheless expressed the fullness of God's presence. This tension continues in Jesus' departure, which enables his presence in the Spirit (John 14:18; 16:7).

Options for Preaching

God in the world. In following and serving Jesus in the world, Christians encounter the very presence of God (Matt. 25:31–46). Yet as Christians share one another's burdens and sufferings and oppose evil and injustice, they simultaneously confront God's absence from the world. In bringing God's presence into this overwhelming absence, Christians follow their Lord and participate in his work.

Finding God while missing God. While the gospel offers no panacea for the depths of human suffering and despair, Jesus Christ has entered into that forsakenness and the fullness of human weakness (Heb. 4:15), thereby assuring believers of God's presence therein. Even in abandonment, then, Christians can encounter God and thus the hope of God's ultimate victory (Rom. 8:31–39).

ADDICTION

James T. Pollard

Addiction is an obsessive or compulsive dependence on a substance, person, or activity, or on a mental or emotional state. It presents itself as a primary identifiable pattern in an individual, family, or culture. The cycle may start with emptiness, emotional pain, guilt, shame, secrets, or substance, then take the form of preoccupation, obsessing ritualization, or compulsive behavior, ending in despair. Addiction is present when a person (1) forms a primary relationship with a substance or activity by surrendering self to the habit, (2) cannot control stopping or starting the activity, and (3) begins to damage self and others. Addictions are supported by negative thinking and an impoverished belief system. All addictions have these things in common: there is no relationship of trust and safety with God, self, and others.

Analysis

Whether addictions are chemical, food, work, spending, saving, sexual, or relational, they all have a common core. The person is separated from self, others, and God. The spiritual connection is missing. The object of desire becomes the god, and it takes on a power of its own. The addictive self is split off from the real self and has little esteem and no self-care. Shame is at the core of the self. Relationships to others are not in balance since the addiction has the power. The core of spirituality is the awareness and experience of being blessed, loved, known, and good. In addiction, the person does not know affirmation and feels empty. The desire to fill the empty space may drive the addiction. In emotional, physical, and sexual abuse, the light of spirituality is blown out. Sometimes even in grief the empty space is too painful to bear. Something is needed to fill this space. In recovery, spirituality replaces the addiction. The person learns that being empty is a part of being human. The person learns that the empty space is a place where God can dwell and yet never be filled completely by God until being transformed in death. In the struggle of recovery, the person admits powerlessness to control the addiction. By discovering hope and help from God, as the secrets, guilt, and shame are shared in honesty with people of similar addictions, a person begins to relight the candle of spirituality.

Biblical Instances

Old Testament. The creation account set a context for an addictive response. God blessed Adam and Eve and saw that they were very good. God told them they could eat fruit from all the trees in the garden except the tree of immortality and the tree of the knowledge of good and evil. The snake told Eve that she would become like a god if she ate the fruit (Gen. 3:5). God creates humans with free will and they respond by trying to be gods.

The First Commandment is: "You shall have no other gods before me" (Ex. 20:3). The history of humankind reflects the need to find its ultimate value in God. Loving God and loving neighbor are the heart of spirituality (Deut. 6:4–25; Lev. 19:18; see also Luke 10:25–37). The addictions that occur in life keep one from reaching this ideal.

New Testament. Idolatry is used figuratively as undue obsession with created things instead of devotion to the Creator. In Paul's writings, obsession with any object less than God is idolatry. Idolatry is a part of every human relationship. Each day of peoples' lives, God gives them grace and calls them to claim God's love. (See Rom. 1:25.)

Options for Preaching

Children of light. Ephesians 5:1–14 asserts that humans are to be imitators of God as "beloved children." One who is covetous has no inheritance in the kingdom. As one brings the shame to the light, it becomes visible and is light. Recovery is learning to name the shame and becoming children of light and love. Anonymous groups are a witness to the light that has come into the darkness of addiction.

"Material Girl." This song was popular a few years ago and is a reflection of Western culture. Philippians 3:17–21 is a reminder of humanity's need to invest in spiritual reality rather than see the earthly existence as an end in itself. Verse 19 speaks of "their god is the belly," meaning gluttony and material things. Paul says that our "commonwealth is in heaven" (v. 20). Citizenship in this commonwealth gives human beings meaning; without meaning people are lonely, insecure, anxious, and without ultimate purpose.

Relationship addiction. John 4:7–25 is a story of a person who had struggled with many relationships in her life. Jesus offers her living water. She is called to worship God in "spirit" and in "truth." She tells her neighbors and friends the truth about her life and meets Jesus in person.

AGING

Jane M. Thibault

To age means to change over the course of time. All things in creation age, though not all things change at the same rate. The maximum length of a human being's life is approximately one hundred and fifteen years, but within the same body, organ systems wear out at different rates so that, for example, a person's eyes age faster than his or her digestive system.

Modern society views aging as a process of deterioration. However, aging can also be seen as an opportunity for development, for a coming to the fullness of being. Not only are human beings physical beings but they also have intellect, personality, and social and spiritual selves. These latter aspects of being can continue to develop until death.

Analysis

Most people fear the aging process because they believe to age is to:

1. grow closer to death,
2. become physically less attractive,
3. lose physical strength, function, and the sense of well-being,
4. lose social status and power,
5. lose independence,
6. lose the very sense of self,
7. become financially unproductive and a burden to others.

The positive aspects of aging, which are not considered to be of special value today, include wisdom, increased ability to adapt and cope with the losses of life, increased freedom of personal time, and fewer social constraints on behavior.

Biblical Instances

The Bible does not attend to aging in great detail. The two themes that relate to age are that old age is a gift of God and that with old age should come growth in wisdom. Examples include Job 12:12: "Wisdom is with the aged, and understanding in length of days"; Job 5:26: "You shall come to your grave in ripe old age, as a shock of grain comes up to the threshing floor in its season"; and Isaiah 46:4: "Even to your old age I am He, and to gray hairs I will carry you."

The New Testament says little about aging. It mentions the advanced age of Zechariah and Elizabeth upon Elizabeth's miraculous pregnancy (Luke 1:18, 36). Timothy 5:1–2 gives brief instructions as to the treatment of older persons.

Options for Preaching

The following themes can be the basis for preaching:

No matter how old a person may be, God calls him or her to a deeper and stronger relationship with God.

There is no limit to potential for growth in wisdom and grace, even though a person may experience physical deterioration.

God has promised to be with God's children, even in their old age.

The losses of old age are the stripping away of all that comes between human beings and God. They can help Christians to identify with Christ in his crucifixion.

Old age and the unstructured time it provides is a gift to be used in service to others via many kinds of volunteer work.

One can pray for others, even if one is confined to a bed or unable to move or talk.

ANGER

Georgine Lomell Buckwalter

Anger is a strong emotional response to any of a variety of stimuli perceived as negative. The feeling itself is a signal and serves a purpose. It is neither good nor bad. It alerts one to the presence of a problem, as in a threat to one's safety or selfhood. However, anger may include the urge for vengeance or the desire for redress. Therefore, it is the behavioral responses to anger that are either constructive or destructive. In the behavioral response lies the challenge to the Christian.

Analysis

Traditionally, the church has seen anger as stemming from the Fall and therefore part of humanity's carnal nature. The feeling itself was thought to be a sin in medieval times, and throughout history, Christians have been taught that anger was wrong.

Certain passages in the Bible present anger in a somewhat less negative sense. Psalm 109 is an example of anger being expressed to God in prayer. The Gospels portray Jesus in anger (Mark 3:5, for example), and Paul gives specific instructions about anger in Ephesians 4:26: "Be angry but do not sin; do not let the sun go down on your anger."

For the most part, however, the church has failed to see anger as a gift of the Creator. Anger, seen as a signal that something is amiss, is a necessity in humanity's emotional equipment (providentially supplied by God for the welfare of humanity). Therefore, anger may be seen as stemming from a creation declared "good." However, like all of creation's gifts, it may be misused.

Theologically redefining the purpose and genesis of anger is important. Once one recognizes its rightful place in God-given humanness, one is freed to examine its causes and appropriate behavioral responses to it. Recent studies in grief, for example, witness to the universal experience of anger in the face of loss. Researchers in the field of chemical dependency agree that the powerlessness of this disease produces anger. Anger rightfully arises when one fails to mend what is broken or to right what is wrong.

It can be said, then, that the feeling of anger is "in order that." It calls people to some action. In the face of injustice, it may stir one to redress. In the face of loss, it may move one to acceptance. Destructively, it may become wrath when nourished, explosive fury when past anger goes unresolved, and vengeance, with its calculated intent to harm. Anger *may* prompt these negative responses, but anger presents choices. What one does with it is what matters.

Biblical Instances

Part of the church's misunderstanding has been due to its propensity for citing those biblical passages that deal exclusively with descriptions of anger, not with those that deal with root causes or redemptive responses. "Wrath is cruel, and anger is outrageous" (Prov. 27:4, KJV) mixes feelings and actions in ways that mislead. Descriptions are not sufficient for understanding the "whys" or for answering the ethical questions of what to do with anger.

Passages that deal with the results of mishandled anger are far more helpful. Anger in the face of loss is seen in Saul's feelings at Yahweh's abandonment of him in favor of David. The sin occurs in Saul's destructive *behavioral* response. He heaved a spear (1 Sam. 18:11). Also helpful are those passages that reveal injustice as the source of anger, as in David's response to Nathan's story or Jesus' response to the disciples' disregard for children (Mark 10:13–15). Anger in the service of love and truth may be seen as Jesus sets out to right wrongs, whether it is healing on the Sabbath (Mark 3:1–5) or driving out the Temple money changers (John 2:13–16).

Perhaps the most frequently quoted and misunderstood passage is the one in which Jesus says one is liable to judgment if angry with a brother or sister (Matt. 5:22). Misinterpretations have equated anger with murder, but careful exegetes stress the original verb tense. Accurately translated, one is liable to judgment if one keeps the anger going or is continuously angry. In the overall context of the ministry of reconciliation, chronic anger sabotages the will of God and invites judgment.

The majority of passages regarding anger refer to God. The human capacity to feel anger, particularly at injustices that impede the reconciliation of creation, may well be part of the *imago Dei*.

Options for Preaching

While responsibly casting anger in a more balanced light, one cannot ignore that the Bible portrays it as an occasion for sin. Truthful preaching recognizes it as part of being human without overlooking its destructive potential. The consummate pastoral theologian, Paul, offers the best preaching theme: "Be angry but do not sin" (Eph. 4:25–27).

Options within this overarching theme include:

Tempted as we are. Stress is on the humanity of Jesus, who was tempted to sin by anger but instead responded redemptively to injustice, idolatry, and unrighteousness (John 2:13–16, Mark 3:1–5).

Ministry of reconciliation and right worship. Anger interferes with the human relationship with God when it is not dealt with promptly or appropriately, as in that which cooperates with reconciliation (Matt. 5:23).

The sin of nursed anger. Simple anger can become behavioral wrath when it is nursed (Eph. 4:25–27 as complementary to Matt. 5:22–25). Discuss possible positive responses.

The sin of mishandled anger. Destructive behavioral responses to understandable anger or jealousy are made by Saul in 1 Samuel 18:11 and Cain in Genesis 4:3–7. Discuss possible positive responses.

Forgiveness, forbearance of others in charity, and ridding oneself of bitterness are all complementary themes in Paul that emphasize constructive responses to anger. Sermons that present anger as a double-edged gift of the Creator may release hearers from the psychological tyranny of the past and challenge Christians to responsible choice making in the future.

BAPTISM

William H. Willimon

The word "baptism" is derived from the Greek and means "to immerse or dip in water" (Mark 7:4). Baptism, performed either by immersion or by application of water to the head, is the rite of initiation into the new covenant. Thus baptism is compared to circumcision (Col. 2:11–12).

Analysis

Baptismal meaning is as rich as the gospel, as multifaceted as the demands of discipleship. Paul compares baptism to Israel's exodus through the sea (1 Cor. 10:1–4). Baptism is compared to Noah's escape from God's wrath (1 Peter 3:21). A primary Pauline image for baptism is death and resurrection. The Christian dies to sin in order to rise to new life (Rom. 6:1–4) so that to be baptized is to be reborn (John 3:4–5). Christian baptism means almost everything that the human experience of water means—death, birth, cleansing, refreshment, life.

Biblical Instances

Throughout the Old Testament, water is associated with ritual and moral purity (Ex. 40:12–15; Lev. 16:4, 24; Isa. 1:16–17). By the time of Jesus, Jews apparently baptized proselytes to Judaism.

The Gospels begin with John the Baptist's prophetic call to repent (Mark 1:4). John's baptism signals radical preparation for the new kingdom.

Jesus submits to John's baptism, not because he had sinned (Matt. 3:13–15) but as revelation of his identity ("This is my beloved son") and of his work (Mark 1:10–11). Jesus links baptism with his own death (Mark 10:38; Luke 12:50). The risen Christ tells his disciples to go into all the world baptizing (Matt. 28:19).

Options for Preaching

Baptism as initiation. Baptism is a sign of the creation of a new family out of nothing (1 Peter 2:4–5, 9–10). God created a world out of nothing. Even as circumcision created a family, Israel, out of a group of nomads, so baptism is a sign of the calling of a new people based not on race, nationality, or class (Gal. 3:27–29).

Baptism and rebirth. The world emerged from water (Genesis 1). Humans are conceived in the waters of the womb. Humans can be called Christian, not through their own efforts, but through the creative grace of God who does for them what they cannot do for themselves. Rebirth as a Christian is a gift, grace (John 3:4–5). Baptism is the beginning of our lives as Christians, not the end.

Baptism as death. God's grace is offered to people as they are. But God's grace does not leave them the same as it found them. Something must die in order to be reborn. All who "have been baptized into Christ Jesus were baptized into his death" (Rom. 6:3). God destroys one's old, sinful self so that a new self might be born. That destruction may be painful, but its goal is birth of a new person in Christ.

BLESSING

H. Stephen Shoemaker

Blessing is the daily providential power of God that supplies and sustains life; life-force and spirit-force, it causes all creation to flourish. Blessing is also the power of affirmation bestowed by one human being upon another, most powerfully by parent onto child, through the gift of delight and the gift of encouragement. Blessing bestows vitality, potency, creativity, health, well-being, peace.

Analysis

Blessing is one of the two spheres of God's salvation. Christians tend to emphasize *salvation as deliverance* (e.g., the exodus, the cross) to the neglect of *salvation as blessing*. The latter has to do with the everydayness of God's salvation, the ordinary but not really ordinary gifts of God that bring health and peace.

Blessing has to do with the birth and the receiving and nurture of children, with the gifts of the earth that call humans to gratitude and responsible stewardship, with the miracles of everyday health and well-being, with the gift of food and table blessings, with the gift of family, friends, and community. Blessing is inherent in words of greeting and goodbye and is in the spiritual gifts of communion with God.

Biblical Instances

"Salvation as blessing" puts in a new light the whole expanse of scripture.

Old Testament. The meaning of blessing changes and develops here. In the earliest stories it is only the fathers who bless (e.g., Isaac)—and in an almost magical way. Later others are given the power to bless; finally the God of the universe blesses all. At first it is only the first son who gets the blessing, then other sons and daughters receive it; finally, all children of earth are blessed. Blessing itself undergoes transformation. At first it is the threefold blessing of fertility: babies, crops, flocks. Later it is expanded to include all good things, material and spiritual.

New Testament. Blessing is seen as the goodness of God bestowed on all people (Matt. 5:45) and as a spiritual gift offered to those who wish to receive it (Matt. 5:1–10; Ephesians 1). God blesses Jesus at baptism and confers the Spirit. Jesus blesses children and disciples and all who follow; he heals sickness of body, mind, and spirit. Paul speaks of the spiritual blessings of God through Jesus Christ. In Revelation, John is given a vision of the final blessing. Prophecy and Apocalyptic are infused with the imagery of blessing.

Options for Preaching

In a series of sermons the preacher can create a biblical theology of blessing from Genesis to Revelation.

God's original blessing of creation (Genesis 1).

Isaac's blessing of his children (Genesis 25–27).

God's blessing on those who spread faith (Gen. 12:1–3; Matt. 28:19–20).

Human powers of blessing and cursing (Numbers 22–24; Eph. 4:29–32; Luke 6:27–28).

Jesus and blessing (of children, at the table, in calling and sending, in healing, and in resurrection commissioning).

Spiritual blessing in the life of the church (Paul's epistles).

The final blessing (Isa. 65:17–25; Rev. 21:1–5).

CAPITAL PUNISHMENT

Glen Harold Stassen

Capital punishment, punishment by death for a serious crime, gets its name from the Latin for decapitation. In the

United States, South Africa, Iran, and the Soviet Union, it is execution by poison gas, electric chair, hanging, shooting, or poison injection as punishment for some murders. Other Western industrialized nations do not practice it. In the United States those executed are 99 percent males, 100 percent of low or moderate income, and disproportionately nonwhites whose victims were whites.

Analysis

Almost all major denominations have voted to oppose capital punishment for several reasons: cruelty; irreversibility when the wrong person was convicted; race, class, and gender discrimination; cancelation of the chance for late-in-life repentance; failure to deter.

Scientific studies (e.g., the sophisticated study in *Minnesota Law Review*, May 1977) show it does not reduce homicide rates and may increase them. They also show what *does* reduce homicides: catching and convicting murderers more efficiently, governmental example in opposing killing (homicides increase when governments kill, make war, or spread guns), a culture that opposes violence (as opposed to a culture shaped by television violence and ready access to guns), remedial justice for society's outcasts, developing neighborhood communities rather than depersonalized cities.

Biblical Instances

Old Testament. Life is a sacred gift of God. God has compassion for the powerless and oppressed, and all persons are created in God's image—still true *after* the fall (Gen. 4:9–26; 9:6; Matt. 25:40).

The Torah, however, authorized the death penalty for murder (Ex. 21:12), sorcery (Ex. 22:18), kidnapping (Deut. 24:7), doing any work on the Sabbath (Ex. 31:14; 35:2), sacrifice of a child (Lev. 20:2), adultery (Lev. 20:10), a stubborn child's disobedience (Ex. 21:15, 17; Lev. 20:9; Deut. 21:18–21), blasphemy (Lev. 24:15–16), and other crimes. In practice, however, Judaism made these almost impossible to carry out in the Mishnah (200 B.C.–200 A.D.).

New Testament. Jesus confronts the death penalty in John 8. Sinful accusers may not so condemn a fellow sinner (cf. Romans 8).

In Matthew 5:38–48 Jesus rejects retaliation and says, "Do not resist violently/vengefully an evil person" (a more accurate translation; cf. Rom. 12:19). Instead, he urges initiatives to cure the cause of the enmity.

He himself was the victim of capital punishment. Crucifixion was state terrorism against slaves and rebels. Jesus prayed his crucifiers be forgiven for they knew not what they did.

The Greek in Romans 13:4 refers to the dagger carried by police accompanying tax collectors, like a billy club, not the sword used for capital punishment or war. Paul is urging Christians to make peace, pay Nero's new tax, and not rebel.

Options for Preaching

Jesus not only taught against retaliation but pointed to constructive alternatives. Preaching *against* is not enough. Capital punishment is like the ancient practice of bloodletting to cure disease: ineffective; but society, angered by homicides, probably will not give it up until they see a more effective cure. Preaching should make contact with this anger, and ground the *effective* alternatives (see Analysis section) in biblical passages on justice.

For example:

A culture pro-violence or anti-violence? (Rom. 12:17–21; Isa. 60:17b–20).

A people whom the Lord has blessed, doing remedial justice for the outcasts (Isa. 61:1–4, 8–11).

Not by shedding blood, but by justice and righteousness (Jer. 22:1–5 or 22:13–17).

Seek the welfare of your city's neighborhoods, not false escapes (Jer. 29:4–9).

CHILDREN/YOUTH

William L. Hendricks

A child is a young person, not fully grown or mature; youth is the last stage before adulthood.

Analysis

Contrasts between ancient and contemporary views of childhood/youth are: (1) the biblical world thought much more of the connectedness and corporateness of the family than the modern world does; (2) comparatively little attention was given to the specific needs or characteristics of children in the ancient world because education was more by observation, experience, and verbal memory. In the modern world, children are singled out as consumers, isolated by age, and educated by written documents and media productions.

Similarities between ancient and modern views of childhood and youth are: (1) love and concern for the human young as the extension of the family and as the future of humankind; (2) an awareness that value formation, ethical guidelines, and religious education are best accomplished and are most fruitful among the young.

Biblical Instances

The Old Testament posits God as creator of all that exists. The propagation of the species is a divine behest (Genesis 1–2). The sanctity of human life is guarded by the various Old Testament guidelines for sexual conduct. The obligation for safeguarding the stories of origin and God's mighty acts of deliverance is required of Israel in the first injunction following the *Shema* (the confession of faith, Deut. 6:5).

The Old Testament reflects a preference and compassion for the young. Children are perceived to be the blessing of God. Having a child means the continuation of the parents, the tribe, and the nation through a kind of collective immortality.

A special use of the idea of childhood is found in the adoptive-covenant bond of God with Israel. Through Abraham, Isaac, and Jacob—the patriarchs—and through Jacob's sons, the tribes of Israel are brought into being by a special covenant, which brings about the adoptive status, children of Israel, the children of God (Hos. 11:1).

In the New Testament, childhood is given its highest and most definitive representation by the sonship of Jesus Christ to God, the divine parent. The choice of these familial terms as a description of the interrelatedness of God is a testimony of God's estimate of worth of the parent-child relationship. Jesus, born as a child and maturing through youth to adulthood, is perceived as a paradigmatic child who, though favored, is permitted to suffer for others (Heb. 5:8). Jesus' teaching valued children (Matt. 19:14) and made childhood simplicity a model for the faith of discipleship. The compassion of God is extended to all humankind who, through God's son, Jesus, are invited into the household and family of God (John 3:16).

Options for Preaching

Children and youth can readily assimilate good religious instruction. Humankind's natural affection for the young desires for them the best religious instruction possible.

God does not reserve attention for adults. God called children, such as Samuel and David, and required of them special qualities.

Children are equal sharers in God's kingdom, not second-class citizens (Matt. 19:13–15). They are valued both for their potential—as the future of humankind—and for the qualities they possess in their youth, such as simplicity and trust.

The coming of Jesus as the Son of God is clearer to children in stories of his infancy (Luke 2) than in a summary of his ministry (John 1:9–14).

CHURCH

Bill J. Leonard

In its most basic sense, the church is a historical community that originates with God and is founded on Jesus Christ. Through its mission in word and deed the church points beyond its own existence to Jesus Christ. Without Christ there is no church. The church represents Christ and extends his work in the world. To be "in Christ" is to be in the church.

Analysis

The church bears certain marks that inform its past, present, and future. These marks include unity, holiness, universality, and apostolicity. Unity means that all Christians are one in Christ. Diverse churches and traditions are united in the one body of Christ. The church is holy, set apart in dedication to God, who is the foundation of holiness. The church is universal—catholic—because Christ's presence extends throughout the whole world. Local congregations share the universality of the one church. The church is also apostolic. The church is "built upon the foundation of the apostles and prophets, Christ Jesus himself being the cornerstone" (Eph. 2:20). Like the first apostles, the church is a "messenger" of Christ, bearing witness to the good news.

Biblical Instances

The church itself has many beginnings. Biblically, it is rooted in the covenant that God made with Israel. Like Israel, the church is a covenant people chosen by God and related to God. The New Testament writers linked the church to covenants old and new (2 Cor. 3:5–6; Heb. 9:15; Gal. 3:23–29). Yet the church itself begins with Christ's incarnation, his calling of the twelve and his teachings as recorded in the Gospels. It rests in the cross event and in the resurrection. The experience of the Holy Spirit at Pentecost marks another of the church's beginnings. The church originates, not in one specific event but in God's complete activity in Jesus Christ. Jesus is the church's servant (Phil. 2:7–8), its savior (Eph. 5:25), its model (Rom. 8:28), and its head (1 Cor. 3:11).

The New Testament uses numerous words to define the nature of the church. They provide one way of understanding the church's life and work. Two of the most familiar words are *ekklesia* and *koinonia*.

The word *ekklesia* is most frequently used for church in the New Testament. It is a Greek translation of the Hebrew word *qahal,* meaning "to call out" the assembly of faithful people. In the New Testament, *ekklesia* is the new assembly of Christ, a visible community of faith. While *ekklesia* refers primarily to local congregations, it should not be interpreted as promoting the absolute independence of each church. Indeed, *ekklesia* is inseparable from *koinonia.* That word, sometimes translated as "fellowship," is better understood as a partnership or "to be in communion with" (Acts 2:42; Rom. 15:26; 1 Cor. 10:16–17). The church, therefore, is a communion of persons in relationship with Christ and each other. *Koinonia* knows no national, social, racial, or economic boundaries. Without it, there is no church.

Scripture presents numerous images or word pictures that expand our ideas about and relationships to Christ's church. The image "people of God" bridges both covenants, old and new. The people of God existed long before the church. They were delivered from bondage and led to the Promised Land, and they heard God's word through the prophets.

The New Testament writers said the church was heir to the covenant as the new people of God. Like Israel, they were to remain faithful or face judgment (1 Cor. 10:1–13). To the beleaguered Christians, such a promise gave great courage. "Once you were no people, but now you are God's people" (1 Peter 2:10).

Options for Preaching

The body of Christ is one of the most significant of the church's images (Rom. 12:5; 1 Cor. 12:27; Eph. 4:12). Through Christ the entire people of God are united. The church does not symbolize the body of Christ; it *is* Christ's body: There is no church apart from him. Neither are there various bodies of Christ but one complete body in him (1 Cor. 12:12). Christ alone, however, is the head of his body, the church (Col. 1:18; Eph. 1:22–23). Thus the church still seeks the wholeness of the one who is its head (Eph. 4:13). Baptism and the Lord's Supper are the faithful "signs" of incorporation into the body of Christ (1 Cor. 12:13, 10:16–17).

The household of faith. Family is bound, not by flesh and blood, but by faith (Gal. 6:10; Eph. 2:19). The family analogy occurs throughout the New Testament. The church is composed of those who know God as *abba*, in parental relationship (Rom. 8:15; Gal. 4:6–7). In it, those once illegitimate (Gentiles) are brought into God's family through Christ (Rom. 9:30–33; 11:17–19; Eph. 2:13). In Christ, all are children of God (Gal. 3:26). Personal faith has familial implications (Rom. 12:15).

The church as a fellowship of the Holy Spirit. Only through the Spirit is *koinonia* possible (2 Cor. 13:14; Phil. 2:1). Through the power of the Spirit the church receives spiritual gifts by which it ministers in the world (1 Cor. 1:7; Rom. 1:6; Eph. 4:11). The unity of the church is the work of the Spirit (Eph. 4:2–7).

CHURCH AND STATE

John C. Bennett

The state is the political structure of a national community. A democratic state recognizes the freedom of both individuals and institutions, including churches, who live within the community. The church is both local and international ecumenical community. Its international experience and its faith in God who loves the people of all nations give Christians a global perspective as they view the policies and behavior of their states.

Analysis

A democratic state makes laws binding its citizens and also itself. The churches seek to influence law making, and within them there is strong awareness of the sinfulness of their own nation. Both the state and the habits of people are responsible for the neglect of millions in poverty and for the persistence of racism.

Biblical Instances

Churches, when they are true to their mission, should never allow states to have full authority over them. Consider two biblical examples from very different situations: Nathan saying to King David, "Thou art the man" (2 Sam. 12:7, KJV), and Peter saying in behalf of the apostles, "We must obey God rather than men" (Acts 5:29). Many prophets, such as Elijah and Jeremiah, followed Nathan's example. Amos saw his own nation condemned by God's judgment (Amos 2:4–8).

Jesus set the example of confrontation with the political powers. The cleansing of the Temple was a symbolic act of religious resistance against the Jewish authorities. His saying about Caesar's coin (Luke 20:24–25) indicates that while Rome may have legitimate interests, their legitimacy depends on their consistency with the things of God. While he was not an active rebel against Rome, Jesus was crucified by Rome as a subversive.

Two New Testament passages coming from very different historical situations reflect opposite attitudes toward the state: Romans 13:1–6 and Revelation 13. The former expressed Paul's hope that governing authorities would be God's agent for good. The latter expressed the experience of Christians who were persecuted by an evil state. Romans 13 has often been used in churches to prevent needed criticism of states or resistance to them. Christian preaching should strengthen a state's humane commitments in a religiously pluralistic nation.

That humane spirit is reflected in the American civil religion at its best. It is civil religion that is emphasized on national holidays, and civil religion is what presidents often invoke in times of crisis. For example, there is a witness to it when, on July 4, the nation celebrates the Declaration that says that "all men are created equal, that they are endowed by their Creator with certain unalienable Rights." This means that such rights are not a gift of the state.

Civil religion is often used in the spirit of a narrow nationalism and of national self-righteousness. One may be thankful that the American civil religion is itself corrected by the biblical vision of Abraham Lincoln, who was a witness to the God who transcends all states and nations, to God's judgment upon national sins, and to God's calling of nations to reconciliation.

Options for Preaching

A number of sermon topics can be culled from the discussion above.

A Christian view of patriotism contrasts Romans 13:1–6 with Luke 20:24–25 and Acts 5:29.

God's vision for peaceful foreign policy between nations is expressed in Micah 4:2–5. Jesus warns against the self-righteousness that leads a nation to have a false view of the world in Matthew 7:3.

COMMUNITY

Larry L. McSwain

Community is the gathering together of persons for the sharing of common commitments, relationships, and goals. The community of faith is a gift of God known in the experience of deliverance from bondage and participation in God's mission of righteousness and justice.

Analysis

Community arises in the freedom granted by a graceful God. Its model is the personal experience of the God who frees from bondage, covenants to bless a new order of righteousness, and empowers followers to function as agents of *shalom* in a disordered world. Community has a remnant quality as believers live out the radical implications of true equality, prophetic change of the social order, and expectant waiting for God's hopeful community of realized justice and mercy.

Biblical Instances

Old Testament. The creation of humanity forms a community of intimacy with God and between persons (Genesis 1–3). In covenant, the family of Abraham is called to be a community guided by moral precepts with a universal mission (Genesis 12–39). Such a community lives in pilgrimage from the bondage of slavery through an exodus of release to the struggles of building a society (Exodus 1–15) that requires just and merciful laws as guides for living together (Ex. 20:21–23:19). The presence of God preserves the true meaning of community even in the face of the most desperate human experiences, whether famine (Joel), exile (Jeremiah 29), religious corruption (Amos), or individual treachery (Joshua 7).

New Testament. Community in the New Testament is the creation of Jesus, who calls persons to follow in obedience to the kingdom of God (Mark 1:14–20). Its fullest meaning is discovered in the postresurrection gathering of persons infused by the Holy Spirit to share all they have with one another (Acts 2:43–47). In community arises courage to proclaim the reconciling message of community with God through Christ as Lord (Rom. 1:8–17).

Options for Preaching

Possibilities for preaching on the multiple meanings of community include:

God is the creator of true community. The call of Abraham (Genesis 12), Jesus' call to the disciples (Mark 1:14–20), and the creation of the church at Pentecost (Acts 2) provide textual examples.

Threats to meaningful community may arise from multiple directions, including the threat of internal disharmony (Numbers 16; 2 Timothy 2), the threat of external pressure (Jeremiah 29; Acts 16:19–40), the threat of false allegiance (Exodus 32, 2 Peter 2), and the threat of moral breakdown (Joshua 7; Acts 5:1–11).

The meaning of true community is to be found in relationship with God through Christ (2 Corinthians 5).

The mission of the church is the creation of true community in the world (Matt. 18:16–20; Ephesians 3).

CONFESSION
Eugene L. Zoeller

The classical definition of "confession" comes from Augustine: "Confession is either a matter of praising God or of being repentant in the presence of God."

In the Septuagint translation of the Hebrew scriptures, the

Greek word *exomologesis* (Latin: *confessio* or *confiteri*) describes the repentance of famous men as well as of Israel's enemies. Frequently, such confession of guilt is inspired by awareness of God's mighty deeds and an expectation of God's imminent judgment.

Analysis

Western theology and many treatises on spiritual life have held the two aspects of confession—praising God and confessing publicly before God one's sins in prayer—together as inseparable elements of Christian life. Nowhere is this unity more carefully forged than in the Psalter (Pss. 8:12–17; 32:3–6).

From a biblical viewpoint, confession begins with the person and the human condition embraced by the unrelenting, gracious presence of God manifest in creation, in God's mighty deeds, in the person of Jesus, and in signs of the times (1 John 4:15–16). Meditation on such a graced human condition and on guidance offered by God's word leads to wonder and conversion. Wonder finds proper expression in prayer, acclamation, song, and profession of faith (James 5:13–16; Pss. 5:11; 32:11). Conversion is expressed in the personal and corporate abandoning of sin and idolatry, of all that opposes God's plan for salvation and liberation (James 5:16).

Biblical Instances

The Christian scriptures contrast explicit belief in Jesus as God's Son with the denial and derision of unbelievers: "every one who acknowledges me before men, I also will acknowledge before my Father who is in heaven; but whoever denies me before men, I also will deny before my Father" (Matt. 10:32–33; see also Luke 12:8–9).

As Jesus' words indicate, confession of faith in Jesus as God's Son is both public and corporate in character. The Christian is obliged to speak this faith openly and before all (1 Tim. 6:12), anticipating great opposition. Though proclaimed by one individual, this confession is the treasure and proclamation of the church.

1 Timothy 6:13 shows a true confession of faith: Jesus stands before a questioning Pilate, proclaiming the truth from God and willing to accept the consequences of such a confession.

Options for Preaching

Contemporary preaching must interpret the confession of faith broadly. Confessions of the Christian scriptures, such as "Jesus is Lord," are obviously to be included, as are the ancient creeds of Nicaea, Constantinople, and Chalcedon. One should note that use of the confession of faith continues to develop with the 1934 Declaration of Barmen, foundation confession of the "Confessing Church," and with liberation theology of the 1970s and 1980s, which insists that there can be no authentic orthodoxy apart from a living orthopraxis.

Confession of sin must not be limited to sacramental confession as practiced in the Roman Catholic, Orthodox, and some Episcopal churches. Ecumenical sensitivities would require the meaning to include moments of private prayer inspired and sustained by the Psalms as well as the invitation to confess one's sins and repent. The World Council of Churches suggests that confession of sin is an integral part of every Christian celebration of the Eucharist.

Within celebration of the sacraments of baptism and the Lord's Supper, there is a public confession of sin, and the Christian identity as *peccator* (sinner) is explicitly expressed. Likewise, a confession of faith is expressed in the Trinitarian formula of baptism and in the Eucharistic prayer and Jesus' words at the Lord's Supper, and the Christian identity as *justus* (justified) is explicitly declared.

Biblical insights, the experience of Augustine, the theology of Martin Luther, and the Christian identity as *simul justus et peccator* suggest the necessity of holding together the dynamic unity of the word "confession."

CONSCIENCE

Wayne E. Oates

Conscience means inward knowledge, one's inmost consciousness or mind; it involves a person's internal convictions as to what is right and wrong.

Analysis

Conscience involves having the law of Christ written on one's heart. Thus conscience "bears witness and their conflicting thoughts accuse or perhaps excuse them on that day when . . . God judges the secrets of people by Christ Jesus" (Rom. 2:12–16). Conscience is far more than the sum total of the prohibitions, inhibitions, and compulsions that result from one's upbringing. This is the unconscious superego of the psychoanalytic theory. Conscience is a function of the consciousness in evaluating a given behavior according to one's knowledge of Jesus Christ and of human life.

Biblical Instances

The term "conscience" is not an Old Testament concept. It occurs one time in the Septuagint in Ecclesiastes 10:20. It occurs in 2 Chronicles 1:10–12, where it simply means "knowledge." On the whole, in the Old Testament conscience merely means the "mind," or the inner secret place of thought.

The New Testament speaks clearly of *different kinds* of conscience. In Acts 23:1 Paul speaks of having lived in "all good conscience." In referring to the idolatry of some Corinthians, he says the conscience is "weak and defiled" (1 Cor. 8:7–13). In 1 Timothy 4:2, false teachers are spoken of as "liars whose consciences are seared" (RSV) or "branded as though with a red-hot iron" (JB). In 2 Timothy 1:3 Paul thanks God whom he serves "with a clear conscience." By this he clearly means that he was not "disobedient to the heavenly vision" (Acts 26:19). This may well have been a direct reference to his conversion experience on the road to Damascus.

Options for Preaching

Clarity of conscience before God (2 Tim. 1:3). This clarity can be expressed in terms of a person's having convictions that give him or her confidence, which is derived from fellowship with God in ethical decision making.

Peer pressure and conscience (1 Cor. 8:12; 1 Tim. 4:2). This text can also be related to 1 Corinthians 8:12 in the weakness of conscience of the Corinthians in buckling under to the pressure of their neighbors' practices. The most nefarious of these practices was the Corinthians' participation in pagan religious rites. An excellent example of this is found in 1 Corinthians 10:6–14.

The marks of a good conscience (1 Tim. 1:5). The text supplies the marks of a good conscience: (1) a sincere faith in Christ Jesus as Lord; (2) a pure heart, which means one is not double-minded, halfhearted, or always fantasizing evil deeds; and (3) a love that is humanity's charge from the Lord Jesus that people love one another as he has loved them and given himself for them.

CONVERSION

John M. Mulder

The term "conversion" literally means "to turn" or "to turn around," and the Christian understanding of conversion involves a threefold turn—away from sin (repentance), to God (forgiveness), and to service (new life in Christ). The experience of conversion thus lies at the heart of what it means to follow Christ.

Analysis

While not unique to Christianity, conversion experiences are incredibly diverse, shaped by differences in personalities, theological traditions, sociological factors, and historical settings.

Because of its centrality in Christian faith, conversion has been the source of lively theological controversy. One debate has centered on the divine and human roles. Does God control every turn toward faith, or is a decision by the individual a critical part of conversion? Another debate focuses on the doctrine of the church. Shall church membership be restricted to those who can demonstrate an experience of conversion, or shall the church be defined by a confession of faith? Are the sacraments the channels of grace and thus ordinances of conversion, or are they symbols of God's grace in the community of faith? Other debates involve the nature of conversion itself. Is it gradual, instantaneous, moral, aesthetic, intellectual? Is there only one conversion, or can there be multiple conversions?

Despite these debates and the diverse traditions within Christianity, three themes characterize the Christian understanding of conversion: repentance, release in forgiveness, and discipleship. In this sense, conversion is very similar to the biblical understanding of vocation, where a confrontation with God becomes virtually indistinguishable from a call to mission. First is a turn away from self; next is a turn toward God; and finally comes the turn back to the world in discipleship and obedience.

Biblical Instances

The Hebrew and Greek texts of the Bible scarcely use the words for conversion. Instead, the scriptures are filled with images and metaphors of the root meaning of conversion—to turn. In the Old Testament, a common image is the prophets' and psalmists' call to the people of Israel to return to the true worship of God. They implored Yahweh to turn toward them and restore them to health and salvation (e.g., Isa. 55:7; Ezekiel 18–30; 32; Hos. 14:2; Psalms 6; 32; 38; 51; 102; 130; 143).

In the New Testament, Jesus preached new life through the gospel. As he began his ministry, he declared, "The time is fulfilled, and the kingdom of God is at hand; repent, and believe in the gospel" (Mark 1:15). Although conversion through repentance and forgiveness in Christ becomes the hallmark of life in the gospel, the New Testament is remarkably cryptic about the actual details of conversion—in marked contrast to modern fascination with conversion accounts. The most dramatic story is the "conversion" of Paul, which some interpret as an experience of Paul's commissioning as an apostle, rather than as a conversion. What is striking is that Paul never directly recounts the story in the Pauline letters. Instead, there are three accounts by Luke in Acts (9:1–19; 22:1–21; 26:1–23). In 2 Corinthians 12, Paul even seems to suggest the danger of overemphasizing one's own experience at the expense of relying upon the power of God's grace in Jesus Christ.

A counterpoint to Paul's dramatic conversion are the more gradual and subtle changes in individuals like Zacchaeus (Luke 19:1–10), Matthew (Matt. 9:9; Mark 2:13; Luke 5:27), Lydia (Acts 16:14), and Timothy (Acts 16).

Today the most prevalent image of conversion is the "born again" or "born anew" experience, taken from the confrontation between Nicodemus and Jesus in John 3. But the New Testament uses many more images to describe the new life in Christ—moving from darkness to light (1 Peter 2:9; Acts 26:18) or from impurity to purity (Titus 2:14), turning from Satan to God (Acts 26:18), shedding an old humanity and taking on a new one (Col. 3:9), dying to self and rising in Christ (Rom. 6:2–8); and so on. Paul even refers to a continuing process of dying to the flesh and living by the Spirit for those who walk in faith (Rom. 8:13).

The final mystery of conversion is not captured even in the story of Christ and Nicodemus. When Jesus tells him he must be "born anew," Nicodemus presses Jesus on how this happens. Jesus responds, "The wind blows where it chooses, and you hear the sound of it, but you do not know where it comes from or where it goes. So it is with everyone who is born of the Spirit" (John 3:8, NRSV).

The threefold pattern of conversion can be seen in the call of

Moses (Exodus 3–4), Jeremiah (chapter 1), and Isaiah (6:1–8) or in the accounts of the conversion of the apostle Paul (Acts 9:1–19; 22:1–21; 26:1–23). In each case, there is a terrifying sense of God's power and human weakness and frailty, a liberating turn toward reliance upon God, and a movement outward to the world to bear testimony to the God who loves and redeems the world.

Options for Preaching

Ideally all Christian preaching should have conversion as its goal—the proclamation of good news that results in repentance, forgiveness, and discipleship and service. The theme of repentance is crucial to avoid portraying a Christianity of "cheap grace." Without the theme of forgiveness, Christianity becomes a religion of guilt, rather than the source of joy and freedom. Discipleship and service are essential elements of the understanding of conversion. Without them there would be no community of faith or doctrine of the church; without them there would be no witness of the church in the world and to the world.

Diversity of conversion. Preaching "for conversion" should recognize the manifold ways in which people have experienced the grace of God throughout the history of the church and therefore the diverse ways in which people experience conversion today. The dramatic, datable type of conversion is perhaps the most familiar because it is the most interesting. William James called these people "the twice born" and devoted most of his *Varieties of Religious Experience* to them. But he conceded that there were "the once born" as well— those whose lives are nurtured in faith and who seemingly go "from strength to strength" (Ps. 84:7). Their lives are marked not by radical disjunctions but by growth in spiritual maturity.

Resistance is characteristic of those called by God. For example, Sarah laughs when told she will bear a son in her old age (Gen. 18:12); Moses protests that he cannot proclaim God's word because he is "slow of speech and tongue" (Ex. 4:10); Isaiah declares that his lips are unclean (Isa. 6:5); Jeremiah protests that he does not know how to speak, for he is only a youth (Jer. 1:6); and Paul is warned not "to kick against the goads" prodding him to recognize Jesus whom he is persecuting (Acts 26:14). In each case, the theme of human resistance is both a realistic insight into the frailty of human nature and the majesty of God's saving power.

God selects unlikely people to be "turned" for divine purposes (e.g., Sarah the barren woman, Moses the murderer, David the adulterer, Jesus the carpenter from Nazareth, Paul the persecutor). These and other instances demonstrate God's sovereignty and the ways in which divine providence confounds human expectations and the world's wisdom (e.g., Isa. 55:8; 1 Cor. 1:23).

God's love is mediated through human beings—most notably in the incarnation of God in Jesus Christ. This is an important insight into the Christian understanding of conversion. When Annanias visits Paul and lays his hands upon him, "something like scales" falls from Paul's eyes, and he regains his sight (Acts 9:18). Just as God became known in Jesus Christ, so also the saving love of God becomes real through the continuing ministry of the witnesses to Christ. They become the agents of God in interpreting the work of the Holy Spirit in the lives of those who have been turned.

COVENANT

Joel F. Drinkard, Jr.

The word "covenant" refers to an agreement that is usually formal, solemn, and binding. In the Bible, whether a covenant was formal or informal, the legal and judicial basis was always in the background of its use.

Analysis and Biblical Instances

The covenants between God and God's people are treated in the Bible much like treaties between nations: the covenant had witnesses (Josh. 24:22), stipulations (Ex. 20), and blessings and curses dependent on fidelity or infidelity to the covenant (Deuteronomy 27). Copies of the covenant were put in safekeeping (Ex. 25:26; Josh. 24:26). Most biblical covenants were conditional, like the one between God and the Hebrews at Sinai; if Israel was disobedient, the consequences would be severe. Israel's prophets called on the people to repent from their sins, specifically those involved in breaking covenant, lest God bring the judgment decreed in the covenant upon the people.

In contrast, God's promises to Abraham and David seem to be unconditional covenants. In the Abrahamic covenant (Genesis 12; 15; 17), repeated for Isaac (Genesis 26) and Jacob (Genesis 28), God promised land and descendants. The only stipulation on Abraham was circumcision, but that is described as a "sign" of the covenant rather than a condition. David was promised a descendant on the throne in perpetuity (2 Samuel 7; Psalm 89). Yet the Sinaitic covenant was overarching and influenced the perception of all Old Testament covenants.

Even the Sinaitic covenant needed to be renewed periodically, for instance by Moses (Deuteronomy 27), Joshua (Joshua 24), Josiah (2 Kings 23), and Ezra (Nehemiah 8). Biblically, covenant defined the relationship that existed between God and the people. Through covenant, God became *their* God and they became God's people (Ex. 20:2; Jer. 31:33). Covenant was the basis of biblical faith and preaching.

The New Testament understanding of covenant grows out of Old Testament usage, especially Jeremiah 31:31–41. The word "testament" is a translation of the Hebrew word for covenant. The new covenant is a renewed covenant, for the old covenant was still in effect. Yet there is newness as well: this renewed covenant is internal, written on the heart (see also Heb. 10:10–17). Christ's self-giving sacrifice institutes the new covenant ("This cup is the new covenant in my blood," 1 Cor. 11:25).

Covenant is always a matter of God's grace. He takes the initiative in offering covenant. A human faith-response is necessary to enjoy the blessings covenant offers.

Options for Preaching

As elaborated in the discussion above, four options provide the preacher an opportunity to explore covenant:

Covenant is God's grace reaching out for relationship (Ex. 20:2; Jer. 31:33).

Faith and obedience are the necessary human response to covenant (e.g., Deuteronomy 27).

The prophetic call to repentance was based on covenant and was a call to return to covenant faith.

The new covenant in Christ completes the old and brings an emphasis on individual response.

CREATION

Stephen L. Stell

Creation is the belief that this universe arose from the creative power, love, and will of God. This affirmation of faith stems from historical encounters with God's creative goodness: in the deliverance and creation of a covenant community; in the self-giving life of Jesus Christ; in the creative power of God over death; and in the re-creative working of the Spirit. The meaning of creation is thus inseparable from the past actions, present life, and future hope provided by God.

Analysis

The world created by God is not simply the stage upon which human drama takes place but is integral to the life that God gives. Thus creation defines human existence by establishing relations among God, humanity, and the world.

One such relation, "creation out of nothing" (*creatio ex nihilo*), insists that God as the ultimate source of all reality is totally other than the world and is not simply the highest part of it. Similarly, nothing in the world can be equated with God; thus the prohibition of idolatry and the relativity of all human constructs.

This conception of creation also means that God is not inherently (necessarily) related to the world. Rather, God graciously forms that relationship in creation and continues it in covenantal faithfulness. Knowing God as Creator is thus inseparable from knowing oneself as God's creature, utterly dependent upon God for life and salvation. This recognition gives humanity the role of steward, rather than lord, in creation.

Finally, the universal dependence upon God in creation points toward community—humans are co-creatures organically related to the world. From this perspective, God's redemptive love applies to all creation (Rom. 8:18–25), and the goal of creation is not simply individual salvation, but the kingdom of God. This kingdom accordingly represents a transformation of heaven and earth by the same creative power and love that gave it birth.

Biblical Instances

The scriptures have considerable continuity concerning the meaning of creation for God's people.

As the Creator of all things, God's power and wisdom are radically different than the world's (Isa. 40:26, 28; Jer. 10:12–16; Job 38:4–40:2). Thus in creation, something of the nature and character of God is displayed (Rom. 1:20). Accordingly God not only created this good world through God's word (Genesis 1; Ps. 33:6, 9; Heb. 11:3), but this affirmation of goodness and power affirms God's speech as right and true (Isa. 45:18–19).

Creation as the expression of God's steadfast character suggests that God's action is continuously expressed in the world (Isa. 44:24–28; 45:12–25). Because the same power and love of creation finds expression in the covenant, God's people seek and expect God's creative activity in their midst (Neh. 9:6–37; Acts 4:24–25, 29–30). As the ultimate expression of God's relationship with and for humanity, Jesus Christ was not only active in creation (John 1:3, 10; Col. 1:16–17; Heb. 1:2) but also represents God's continuing involvement therein.

Finally, biblical creation not only tells about God's character and action but also explains the human response demanded. Although the Creator does not require human aid (Acts 17:24–31), creation and covenant entail a call to righteousness. God who freely gives life also creates and preserves a people to spread that life to the needy and downtrodden (Isa. 42:5–7). God's relationship with humanity in creation is thus inseparable from God's judgment (Amos 4:11–13) and forgiveness (Isa. 64:8–9) of sin.

Options for Preaching

Creative faithfulness. Unlike many human commitments, God's originating faithfulness in creation continues unbroken. In Exodus 4:11–12, when Moses laments his speaking capabilities, God replies that the One who created his mouth can surely help him speak and teach him what to say. Likewise, the New Testament insists that the One who began a good work in the Christian shall surely complete it (Phil. 1:6). Here God's creative power, wisdom, and love are promised for one's concrete daily life.

God: king or pal? Many people today perceive God at one of two extremes. Either God is the transcendent, otherworldly ruler whose fatalistic control oppresses the spirit or damns the soul, or God is a warm, but powerless, experience or feeling. Biblical creation, however, insists that the God who is transcendent, free, and sovereign is also the one in whom "we live and move and have our being" (Acts 17:24–28). Jesus Christ, in whom all things "hold together" (Col. 1:17), uncovers the transcendent yet immanent creative work of God in the world.

God's continuous creation. The Old Testament prophets make it clear that the effects of God's gift in creation apply today (Isa. 42:5–25; 44:24–28; Jer. 10:12–16; Amos 4:13). The fact that God created the world and gives life to its people entails a claim: the righteous God calls creation to righteousness; the loving God creates a covenant relationship; the self-giving God claims other selves for God's redemptive work in the world. Such claims are also promises to which Christians respond (Acts 4:24–30).

CRUCIFIXION

James L. Blevins

Crucifixion was an instrument of punishment and torture for criminals of various kinds in the ancient world. The practice included the use of a sharpened stake implanted in the ground or various pieces of wood tied or nailed together. The oldest form, traced back to the ancient Persians, may have been simple impalement on a piece of sharpened wood. Later the punishment included being tied or nailed to an upright beam (capital T shape).

Crucifixion as practiced by the Romans in the New Testament world was a horrible and degrading thing. Roman citizens thus could not be crucified; the penalty was reserved for brigands and thieves.

Biblical Instances

The extreme brutality of the cross and its shame come to light in many sermonic sections of the New Testament. In 1 Corinthians 1:18, Paul stated: "For the word of the cross is folly to those who are perishing, but to us who are being saved it is the power of God." The Jews could not conceive of a Messiah figure ending up on a Roman cross. The Messiah, when he came, would be in the glorious tradition of King David and would establish the Jewish nation in a preeminent position. For Paul and other early Christians to preach a crucified Christ made no sense to the majority of Jews who heard the proclamation.

The gospel writers make the cross the central proclamation of the early preaching. In Mark's Gospel, one cannot know Jesus unless one stands at the foot of the cross. The messianic secret in Mark is that messiahs do have to be crucified (Mark 8:31–33; Matt. 26:2). Only the demons and a few others state the false Christology of a glorified messianic role (Mark 1:2, Luke 4:34). In fact, the only person who recognized Jesus in the second Gospel was the centurion standing at the foot of the cross (Mark 15:39).

Options for Preaching

The offense of the cross. Today the cross has been made into an ornament, jewelry to wear about the neck. In view of its degrading nature in the first century, the equivalent today would be to wear an electric-chair charm on a necklace (see 1 Cor. 1:23).

The "folly" of the cross and crucifixion as a basic tenet of the Christian faith. Sermons on the cross and crucifixion should stress this folly, yet emphasize that within this position of folly rests the great spiritual truth of God's love for humankind. A theology of the cross also shifts one's eyes from all the glory and thoughts of the next world to the suffering and pain of this world (see 1 Cor. 1:28; Phil. 2:5–11).

The cross as reminder that defeat can be success. From the world's point of view Jesus was a failure. In this very failure, however, salvific success came into being (see John 11:25; Rom. 3:25).

DEATH

William Powell Tuck

Death is the termination of life in this world. All life forms reach the end of their organic existence. Unlike other organic life forms, however, human beings are aware of their own mortality. This awareness produces a variety of responses. Death may be the universal fear that lies behind all human fears.

Analysis

Many live out their lives by denying the ultimate reality of death with "an illusion of immortality." These persons cling to the illusion that by eating the right food, getting proper exercise, using the best medicines, or by disguising, camouflaging, or ignoring death, they can elude its grasp. Others view death as the great scandal. Having to live with the consciousness of their mortality negates life's meaning and produces despair, hopelessness, and dread for them. The awareness of finitude strips away their purpose for living.

But there are still others who believe that the reality of death enhances the significance of life. The fact that a person knows that life has a termination point forces each individual to take seriously the significance of time and therefore to use time wisely and carefully.

Not only does each person have to struggle with the reality of his or her own death, but everyone has to face his or her grief at the struggle with pain, suffering, and eventual death that one sees one's relatives or friends bear. This grief often produces feelings of shock, denial, depression, guilt, or anger, which may cause physical or emotional reactions. Elisabeth Kubler-Ross and others have suggested normal stages through which a person passes when confronting his or her own dying or the grief at the death of a loved one. The awareness that these feelings are normal human reactions can help a person adjust better to grief.

Biblical Instances

In the Old Testament the subject of death is approached from several perspectives. From one vantage point, death is viewed as a normal end to life (Gen. 25:11; 27:2; Eccl. 12:6). When human beings reach the end of life, they die like the rest of nature (Josh. 23:14; Job 30:23). If a person lives to an old age, he or she is "gathered to his [or her] people" (Gen. 15:15; Judges 8:32; Job 42:17).

Yet the Old Testament declares that death is not a natural part of life but a contradiction. After the Fall, as recorded in Genesis 3, death overshadows the life of man and woman, even to the woman's childbearing and the labor of man. Death is the result of the entrance of sin into the world (Gen. 3:2, 7). Death is not merely a biological fact but a moral issue. Death is depicted as an enemy, not a product of orderly nature but of disorder.

The basic way to understand life after death was through one's heirs (Gen. 30:1). The concept of Sheol as the region of the dead passed through an evolution in the Old Testament: a place where the person who dies is cut off or annihilated from God (Ps. 6:5; Isa. 38:18), a place where the dead enter into a realm of sleep (Job 14:10–12; Ps. 3:5), and finally the writers project life out of death (Job 19:25–27; Ps. 16:8–11; Isa. 25:8; 26:19; Dan. 12:2–3).

The New Testament affirms that death is the result of sin. Paul wrote: "Sin came into the world through one man, and death came through sin, and so death spread to all because all have sinned" (Rom. 5:12). "The sting of death is sin" (1 Cor. 15:56). "The last enemy to be destroyed is death" (1 Cor. 15:26).

The belief in life after death in the New Testament, however, is posited in the resurrection of Jesus Christ. "If Christ has not been raised, your faith is futile and you are still in your sins" (1 Cor. 15:17). Christ was seen as "the firstborn of the dead" (Rev. 1:5). The Christian hope for life after death is grounded in the risen Christ (Rom. 6:9; 1 Cor. 15:12–28). He has the keys of death (Rev. 1:18), freeing the Christian from the power of sin (Rom. 7:4–6) and assuring the believer of life everlasting (John 11:25).

Options for Preaching

Using key texts on death. A minister might want to develop expository or doctrinal sermons based on key texts, such as 1 Corinthians 15:12–58. The emphasis could be placed as follows: (a) the resurrection of Christ gives the believer hope; (b) life in Christ, (c) the spiritual body, (d) the mystery of death. Romans 8:18–39 might be examined under the headings: (a) the liberation of nature; (b) cooperating with God's spirit; (c) the love from which the believer can never be separated.

Living with dying. A series of sermons could focus on: (a) the fear of death, (b) learning how to meet grief, (c) helping a friend in grief, (d) death and the meaning of life, (e) the mystery of death. A physician, nurse, pastoral counselor, funeral director, and lawyer could be asked to speak out of their various disciplines on death, and following each presentation, the congregation could engage in dialogue with the speakers.

The stages a person goes through when death is imminent—denial, anger, bargaining, depression, and acceptance—could be the basis of another series.

Individual sermons could focus on passages such as:

Death: The last enemy to be destroyed (1 Cor. 15:26).

Living with Christ (Rom. 6:5–11).

Never to die (John 11:25).

The God of the living (Mark 12:26–27).

Eternal life, a present possession (John 17:3; 2 Cor. 4:10–11; John 4:9).

No more night (Rev. 21:22).

DECISION MAKING

Glenn H. Asquith, Jr.

The word "decision" comes from a Latin verb that means "to cut short" or "to cut off." Thus the act of deciding is a conclusion or a termination of a process. There is a finality in the act of making up one's mind, arriving at group consensus, or receiving a legal judgment that cuts off any further discussion, deliberation, or options.

The term "decision making," however, implies the process that precedes such a final choice. Various elements are included in this process, such as gathering data, analysis of prior related decisions; consideration of alternatives; the application of one's values to the emotional, spiritual, and ethical implications of the decision; and the amount of time available for such a process.

Analysis

Decision making is a central theme for preaching because it occurs so regularly in all aspects of life. Levels of decision making range from small, individual choices, such as what to wear on a given day, to life-changing decisions, such as selection of a mate or occupation. Historically, effective preaching calls for some kind of decision of faith, ranging from the basic choice of committing one's life to Christ to making a new decision of discipleship or service. Preaching may call for an ethical commitment to certain values or behavior within the Christian life. In general, sermons should stimulate some kind of decision.

Many persons have difficulty with decision making, especially those who have trouble with endings or terminations. Indecisiveness is one of the criteria for diagnosing major depression or depressed mood. Inability to make everyday decisions without advice or reassurance from others or allowing others to make one's major life decisions are signs of a dependent personality. The obsessive-compulsive person avoids or delays decisions due to excessive rumination about priorities and fear of making a mistake. For such persons, decisions are often made by default due to the passing of time; while making no decision is still a decision, the person feels less responsibility for it.

Thus one goal of preaching on decision making is to enable and empower persons to both take risks and assume responsibility for their decisions. Decisions are acts of faith, requiring trust in a gracious God to guide and redeem human actions. This leads to trust in one's self and the attendant feelings and values involved in the decision. All major life decisions have both a rational and a nonrational dimension. There are the logical, objective approach and the subjective feelings or mystical revelations that one has about the decision. Both are to be trusted because both capacities can be gifts from God; overdependence on one at the expense of the other makes for a less complete process of decision making.

Because decisions are made by human beings, there can be no "perfect choice." The risks involved in making decisions cause varying degrees of stress, which can also be addressed by preaching in the context of the community of faith. There is a dependent person in everyone who needs reassurance and moral guidance for the tough choices of life. Acknowledging one's dependence upon God makes such decisions easier. Further, making decisions public in the community of faith can strengthen one's commitment and responsibility for those decisions. Public declarations of faith at the time of baptism or confirmation solicit the continuing support of the community as one grows in the faith. Announcements of engagement and a public wedding ceremony involve the community's expectations for commitment and fidelity in a relationship. Ordination or consecration adds the important public dimension to one's individual vocational decision for spiritual leadership.

Biblical Instances

Old Testament. King Solomon was perhaps one of the most famous decision-makers in the Old Testament. The story of the conflict between two women over the maternity of a living child in 1 Kings 3:16–28 is given as an example of Solomon's wisdom in judgment, which came from an astute awareness of human character. This enabled his decision-making ability to have some very concrete and practical applications.

The casting or drawing of the lot was a widespread practice in ancient Israel as a method of discerning the divine will. It was used to apportion land among the tribes in Numbers 26:55 and in Joshua 14:2, to determine Jonathan's guilt in 1 Samuel 14:42, and to uncover Jonah in his flight from the Lord (Jonah 1:7). First Samuel 10:20–21 describes how King Saul was chosen by lot. Proverbs 16:33 affirms the belief that the lot was not a magical practice but resulted in a decision which was "wholly from the LORD."

Joel 3:14 speaks of the valley of decision as one of the prophet's images of the last judgment. As the day of the Lord approaches, multitudes of the wicked will be trapped in a final time of reckoning from which there will be no escape and no possibility of moral compromise. This, again, implies a negative and terminal nature to moral decision and judgment, which leaves no further room for discussion or change.

New Testament. The Synoptic narratives of Jesus in Gethsemane (Matt. 26:36–46; Mark 14:32–42; Luke 22:39–46) portray Jesus in a time of anguished moral struggle as he faces crucifixion. While there is scholarly debate as to the exact nature of this struggle, this dramatic encounter with God reflects the deepest dimensions of the decision-making process. A person's prayerful struggle with the will of God for his or her life is ultimately an isolated, lonely process with which even the most trusted human companions cannot help (e.g., Mark 14:37). Further, all such struggles have an end time in which "the hour comes" (e.g., Mark 14:41) for decision and action.

In Acts 15:1–16:5 the council of the elders and apostles of the Jerusalem church, prior to the second missionary journey, decided whether to admit Gentiles to the church. While there was "sharp contention" within the church during this time (15:39), the church was strengthened in the faith and increased in numbers following that important decision (16:5).

Options for Preaching

Risk and redemption. Philippians 2:5–11 states the primary Christian theme of the redemption which comes from taking risks. By taking up his cross and "emptying himself" in obedience to the will of God, Jesus redeemed all of humanity. The image of Christ as the humble servant, giving his life for others, becomes a guiding image for Christians in the throes of decision making. Instead of holding onto the status quo, taking risks in decision making through faith in God results in newness and fullness of life.

The valley of decision. This image in Joel 3:14–15 suggests that decision making can be a lonely, threatening process that often has life-changing impact. These decisions often involve a test of one's will and values and must be made in a limited time. The story of Jesus in the wilderness in Matthew 3:13–4:11 is illustrative of the "wilderness" one is placed in when certain life decisions based on one's values must be made at the threshold of new beginnings in life.

The search for truth. Pilate's questioning of Jesus in John 18:33–38a illustrates another key issue in decision making: the need for accurate information. Pilate's desperate question "What is truth?" indicates the need for all the data—the true story—before a right decision can be made. In this case, Jesus bears witness to the importance of the true knowledge of God in all of our life actions.

Therefore choose life. The Gospel narratives of Jesus' encounters with people frequently involve a choice of discipleship. The rich man went away sorrowful at the invitation to sell all that he had and give to the poor (Mark 10:21–22). The reluctant disciples in Luke 9:59–62 were not ready to follow Jesus because of family obligations. On the other hand, in Luke 10:38–42, Jesus answers Martha by praising Mary's choice of the "good portion" of setting aside worldly concerns to become his disciple.

DEPRESSION

James A. Hyde

Depression, which literally means "to be pressed down," is a sustained change in mood that ranges from mild to moderate to severe. A figurative definition is "low spirits, gloominess, dejection, or sadness." Depression is not a new emotional illness. It has been written about for centuries and occurs in all races, sexes, and faith groups. Today depression is referred to as the "common cold" of mental illness. It may be caused by situational or biological factors or a combination of both. Clinical depression interferes with a person's functioning in daily life and requires professional help. In clinical depression there is a significant change in one's interests or pleasurable activities; a significant weight gain or loss accompanied with an increase or decrease in appetite; sleep disturbance; restlessness; fatigue; isolation from friends; inability to express anger, guilt; feelings of worthlessness; poor concentration; impaired judgment; indecisiveness; and recurrent thoughts of death, which may include suicidal ideas.

Analysis

Depression can become a crisis of one's religious values and sense of self-worth. Often those experiencing depression will use religious language to describe their situations. They feel as if they have sinned away the days of grace (see Hebrews 6:4–6) or committed the "unpardonable sin" (see Mark 3:29).

In the Bible, the depressed person is almost always met by a loving God. Psalm 88 is the sole exception. It is an exceptionally precise description of what is today described in psychiatric diagnosis as a major depression.

In extreme cases of depression a person may take literally a passage from the scriptures such as Matthew 5:29, "If your right eye causes you to sin pluck it out and throw it away." Professional intervention is important in cases of major and severe depression.

Most depression is treated without hospitalization, and the majority of people suffering from depression live relatively normal lives once the depression is brought under control. To prevent recurring bouts of depression, clinicians encourage regular exercise, good eating habits, adequate sleep, and structured involvement in activities with friends and acquaintances.

Biblical Instances

The Bible is quite descriptive of those suffering with various levels of depression. For example, King Saul became so disturbed and depressed that he took his own life. The Bible reports that the Spirit of the Lord departed from Saul and he was troubled by an evil spirit (1 Sam. 16:14–15). He had mood swings, sleepless nights, and impaired judgment. His colleagues, family, and friends were constantly on guard due to Saul's behavior. Upon the news of his son's death Saul killed himself. In contrast, although David is described as depressed in his grief over the death of his son, he did not kill himself. It was an expected behavior for David to grieve and be "low in spirits" over the loss of Absalom. He eventually moved back into the duties of his daily routine.

Women in the Bible are also described as depressed. Sarah and Hannah (1 Sam. 1:7–11) grieved because they were unable to conceive children. Their level of depression is conveyed in the descriptions of their relationship to their husbands, friends, and priests.

As in the Hebrew scriptures, the New Testament considers depression an illness. The early Christian church leaders called it the "noonday sickness" and "the spirit of acedia" (compare Psalm 91). Depression was treated with certain rituals, which included the eating of unleavened bread for seven days as "the bread of affliction" and fasting in sackcloth and ashes (see Ezek. 3:15). The application of Paul's teachings in 1 and

2 Thessalonians was to encourage the sufferer by praise, appreciation, guidance in personal affairs, and self-reflection. In the Bible, depression is not considered a sin but an affliction that is inherent in the human predicament. Although no one biblical word is used for depression, several terms describe it: affliction, desolation, discouragement, despairing, despondency, mourning, pining, sadness, sorrow. The New Testament provides the insight that anger can be expressed openly. Ventilation of feeling in constructive ways is encouraged (Matthew 19). Since suppressed anger can lead to depression, this New Testament injunction is prescriptive.

Options for Preaching

Awareness of both the biblical and psychological manifestations of depression creates an atmosphere of empathy and care. Preaching becomes the vehicle of empathy, instruction, encouragement, and encounter for persons afflicted with depression. Dynamically, the minister is able to affirm and appreciate the sufferer as a person of worth in God's sight as well as the church's and community's.

The following themes emerge for the minister:

Depression is not a sin, but inherent in the human condition.

Humans have a place of value in a world of facts because they are wondrously made by God.

The cry of absence is always met by a loving God (e.g., Psalms 5; 6; 22; 28; 38; 39; 41; 69; 77; 102; 103; 116). Psalm 88 is the only exception.

Depression happens in community, and friends and acquaintances need "to sit where they sit." Sunday school and church services of worship provide a structured community of faith to prevent withdrawal and isolation.

Depression leads to distorted thinking and impaired judgments, which are confronted by the Christian community of faith thinking straight in a crooked world.

Feelings of abandonment are met by the incarnation, the Word made flesh.

DISCIPLESHIP

William H. Willimon

A disciple is an apprentice or student who is attached to a teacher, usually a teacher who is part of some distinct movement. The word comes from the Greek for "learner."

Analysis

To speak of Christianity as discipleship is to emphasize that Jesus worked like a rabbi, handing over the truth of Israel's tradition in a creative way to his followers, helping them to see new significance in that tradition (Matthew 5–7). It is also to stress the uniqueness of Jesus' teaching. Jesus' way was different and demanding. His challenge was not one of simple intellectual assent but also demanding, converting obedience to a way that was not popular. His call was not the simple "Do you agree?" but the more engaging "Will you join me?"

Biblical Instances

Following rabbinic custom (Isa. 8:16), most New Testament references to the followers of John the Baptist or Jesus as disciples designate those who were closest to Jesus, those who had committed to follow his teaching and way. Sometimes the designation is applied to his closest followers (the Twelve) while other times it is applied to a larger number who responded to his teaching (Luke 6:17). The Gospels frequently portray the disciples of Jesus as not fully understanding him, at times forsaking him, but always actively in relationship to him.

Options for Preaching

Disciples are disciplined. To be a disciple is to be someone who disciplines life in accordance with the dictates of the master. Stressing discipleship as the chief characteristic of a Christian means stressing the necessity of discipline. A Christian is not merely a member of a church, someone who has had some momentary religious experience, one who intellectually affirms Christian belief; a Christian actively lives as Jesus lived. "If any man would come after me, let him deny himself and take up his cross and follow me" (Matt. 16:24).

Disciples are sent out. A Christian disciple is one who is commissioned by the Master for service. Disciples are not only those who are gathered to the Master, but also those who are sent to do the work of the Master in the world. Jesus has entrusted his disciples with life-giving work and empowers them to do that work (Luke 10:1–12).

Disciples have different tasks to do. Each disciple has a special task assigned, based upon the needs of the church (Acts 6:1–7) and upon the gifts of the individual disciple

(Rom. 12:3–9). The church has its duty to "equip the saints" (Eph. 4:11–16), giving disciples the equipment they need to fulfill the duties of discipleship.

DISCIPLINE

E. Glenn Hinson

Discipline refers to the training that develops self-control and character or the result of such training. In Christian usage it is practiced both privately and corporately. In Roman Catholic churches it is exercised through the rite of penance. The most noteworthy practice of discipline, however, is in monasticism with its system of rules for living the devout life.

Analysis

Christian discipline includes a variety of elements, the most basic being prayer, fasting, and silence. Prayer is the chief means for listening and speaking to God, discovering God's will. Fasting serves as a preparation for prayer and thus is a key discipline. Silence sensitizes. Inner, psychic noises must decrease in order to hear the "still, small voice" of God.

Biblical Instances

In the Old Testament, God is the chief disciplinarian. God enters into covenant with a people and expects obedience, as in Deuteronomy 4:36: "Out of heaven he let you hear his voice, that he might discipline you." God instructs the people personally (Ps. 32:8; Isa. 28:26) through the Spirit (Neh. 9:20). From the human side, obedience necessitates prayer and fasting. Happy are those who meditate day and night on the law (Ps. 1:2) and attune their ears constantly to God. Fasting, called for especially in times of crisis (1 Kings 21:9; 2 Chron. 20:3; Ezra 8:21; Isa. 58:3–6; Jer. 36:9), deepens prayer.

In the New Testament, Jesus, warning about the cost of discipleship, called people to deny themselves, take up a cross, and follow him (Mark 8:34). Following would require severing all ties—even those with fathers, mothers, sisters, and brothers (Mark 10:29–30). The community of the faithful were to "instruct and admonish" one another (Col. 3:16). Obviously the church should care enough about its own to discipline them, even by exclusion in rare cases (1 Cor. 5:3–5), but it must always balance judgment with forgiveness (2 Cor. 2:5–11). Because spiritual growth will not come easily for most, the faithful must "train" themselves for godliness (1 Tim. 4:7) and develop a sense of things that matter (Phil. 1:10).

Options for Preaching

Preaching about discipline should emphasize the positive aspect, that is, that discipline is a voluntary response to God's searching love.

God's watchful eye. Old Testament texts such as Psalm 32:8 tell of "God's watchful eye," which may keep the faithful on their toes and reassure them that God cares.

Train in godliness. For a generation of physical-fitness buffs a call to train in godliness with at least as much zeal as physical training should catch the ear of some.

A sense of things that matter. In Philippians 1:9–11 the apostle Paul outlines a trajectory for spiritual growth, the centerpiece of which is the ability to recognize things that really matter.

Ready forgiveness and reaffirmation of love. In a situation requiring corporate discipline, Paul offers wise counsel about these themes in 2 Corinthians 2:5–11.

Developing discipline (1 Tim. 4:6–16).

The relationship of discipline and grace (2 Cor. 9:8).

DISEASE/ILLNESS

James A. Hyde

Illness is a state in which the body or mind is not functioning properly. Degeneration or perversion of physical or mental structures or functions can cause illness. Disease may be caused by organisms or viruses that attack the body, and illness may result from mental stress that creates physical changes within the body. As people age, decay of the body causes sickness and ultimately death.

Analysis and Biblical Instances

Modern medicine and behavioral sciences have made discoveries regarding illness that seriously challenge early biblical attitudes about causes, particularly of illnesses previously thought to be punishment from God or caused by demons. Some, for instance, have been revealed as infections or resulting from poor mental and physical care.

In the Hebrew scriptures, disease was sometimes considered sent by God to punish wrongdoing. Disease could be regarded as a divine response to one's disobedience or sin. Yet God could heal diseases as well as forgive iniquity (Ps. 103:3). Satan, the adversary, was also a tempter of human beings and had the power to cause illness. Job's painful sores were caused by Satan (Job 2:7). Illness was also understood as the result of the sins of one's parents. In general, the words in the Old Testament for disease, sickness, and illness are primarily translated "to be weak or feeble." Illness could be caused by improper living habits and might result in feebleness and weakness of the body (compare Ex. 15:25b–26 to Leviticus 11–15).

Mental or emotional illness was generally related to some specific organ of the body. Jesus healed people with physical problems but clearly connected the illness with their spiritual well-being. Illness was not just a physical phenomenon but related to the nature of one's spiritual relationship with God.

Jesus regarded disease as one manifestation of evil within the human predicament. For him, disease was not a part of the divine order. Illness was the result of evil, creating suffering in the body and mind. Jesus confronted the earlier belief that illness was the result of parental sin and shifted the focus to one's relationship to God (John 9:1). Jesus chose not to explain illness but moved with compassion to minister to and heal the weak and ill. He never supported the idea that illness was a punishment sent by God. Because illness was considered abnormal or unhealthy, the key to health was not just a properly functioning body but a right relationship with God, others, and oneself.

Options for Preaching

Illness is not a punishment from God. It is not a cross that one must bear as a result of God's response to sin. Jesus denied the concept of punishment and focused on the relationship of God within the human predicament (John 3:16). God is present in every person's life and joins in the struggle with illness and suffering. As mentioned, the blind man in John's Gospel was not blind because of sin. Nor was the crippled man at the pool of Bethesda being punished because of sin. The focus of each narrative was on the relationship to God.

Personal responsibility. Many people believe that illness is caused by evil or demonic forces. Essentially, that theme is "the devil made me do it." This is frequently the case with mental illness. Distorted religious thinking allows or encourages sufferers not to take responsibility for themselves. This is a common theme for those who abuse alcohol. "Demon rum" has been blamed for many illnesses and destructive behavior. The issue of personal responsibility for behavior is essential for mental and physical health (John 5:13–14). People are responsible for their bodies as the temple of God (1 Cor. 3:16–17). Placing responsibility for illness on Satan finds no support in the New Testament.

The responsibility of parents for health. Any time parents violate the laws of nature and put their bodies at risk, the danger of passing disease on to their children must be considered. Drug use, smoking, and alcohol affect the fetus. It is every person's responsibility to attend to his or her body, observe good health care, and teach children how to care for themselves. Health codes in the Old Testament and New Testament provide clear guidelines for physical and mental hygiene (Leviticus 11–15). These codes cover sexual behaviors as well as drinking or eating behaviors (1 Cor. 6:12).

God's power is healing. God as creator of human bodies and minds offers power for maintaining health and recovering from illness. Even when cure is not possible, God's care can comfort people, for not even physical death can separate them from God's love.

DIVORCE

Cecil Murphey

Divorce is the legal ending of marriage.

The mutual commitment of a man and a woman was the standard of marriage set forth in Genesis 2:21–24. Divorce, although allowed, cut across Jesus' statement that "what God has joined together, let no one separate" (Matt. 19:6).

Analysis

God's unfolding biblical revelation expressed humanization and compassion. It sought to control social practices dealing with human failure. The Bible especially advocated justice and fairness; a constant theme throughout the Bible is a concern for the oppressed, the hurt, and the wounded.

When people cannot live harmoniously, their situation comes into tension with God's redemptive intention, that is, forgiveness and redemption. Divorce stands as one among many instances of human failure. There is no biblical justification for looking upon divorce and remarriage as more sinful than other human acts.

God's redemptive purpose has always been to forgive, and that forgiveness includes divorced people, who are loved and accepted by God. Having been forgiven, divorced people may have another opportunity to achieve the goal of marriage in a new relationship.

When marriage fails to further the total well-being of the two parties involved, divorce is a realistic solution. Unrealistic restriction on divorce can result in the destruction of human personality (especially in cases such as physical and sexual abuse). Which is more important and more loving—continuing a legal marital bond or furthering the happiness and nurture of the two persons involved?

Biblical Instances

The single Old Testament provision for divorce occurred in Deuteronomy 24:1–4. This did not command divorce, but permitted it if a husband "found some indecency" in his wife (v. 1, RSV). He gave her a bill of divorce and dismissed her from his house. She was then free to marry another man. Because God permitted divorce, the law imposed no civil or ecclesiastical penalty.

To guard against hasty divorce, the law provided that if she divorced a second time, under no circumstance could a woman ever remarry her first husband.

The teachers of the law debated the statement "he finds something objectionable about her" (v. 1, NRSV). While the school of Shammai restricted the term to mean nothing except unchastity (or adultery), the school of Hillel asserted that if a wife displeased her husband in any way, no matter how trivial, he could divorce her.

Jesus reaffirmed God's purpose for the institution of marriage (see Matt. 19:3–10) by saying that the divorce law of Deuteronomy 24 was a concession to human weakness ("for your hardness of heart," Matt. 19:8).

The situation in which Jesus made his one-exception pronouncement came in answer to a question from some Pharisees who wanted to test him. They asked, "Is it lawful for a man to divorce his wife for any cause?"

Instead of discussing the validity of divorce "for any cause" (Matt. 19:3), as they asked, Jesus focused on God's purpose expressed in the creation account that a husband and wife were to become a spiritual unity.

Jesus cited one exception to no-divorce marriage: "except for unchastity" (Matt. 19:9). In Greek the word is *porneia*, which originally meant prostitution, but later it took on the sense of "to be unfaithful." *Porneia* could refer to a prostitute, a betrothed, or a married woman. Using the same term, biblical writers also equated the Jewish nation's unfaithfulness to apostasy.

The dispute over the statement in Matthew 19:9 ("except for unchastity") has arisen in relation to the silence concerning an exception in Mark 10:11–12 and Luke 16:18. A few scholars have alleged the words in Matthew are an editorial addition.

Matthew's Gospel provided two reservations about the indissolubility of marriage. First, the injured party could put away an unfaithful mate. Second, the injured party was then free to remarry. The other Gospels mentioned no such exception. Quite likely Mark and Luke, wanting to stress the continuity of marriage, simply did not record Jesus' exception.

After Jesus responded to the question of the Pharisees, Matthew recorded the response of Jesus' own disciples to his answer. They asked whether, if that was the only way a man could divorce his wife, it might be better not to marry (see Matt. 19:10). Their words showed how lightly they considered the state of marriage.

Paul was the only other writer of the New Testament to mention divorce. His two references appear in Romans 7:1–6 and 1 Corinthians 7. In the Romans passage he used marriage as an analogy. Since the marriage vows are dissolved only by death, Jesus fulfilled the Mosaic law and put it to death. Now believers are free to belong to Jesus Christ.

While Paul reaffirmed the permanency of marriage (1 Cor. 7:10–11), he also pointed out that simply being married to an unbeliever did not constitute grounds for a divorce (v. 12). He summarized his position by writing, "A wife is bound to her husband as long as he lives" (v. 39).

Despite that strong statement, Paul did express one exception to the prohibition against divorce: If the unbelieving partner desired a divorce, the Christian spouse should allow it (v. 15).

Using marriage as the normal human relationship, Ephesians 5:21–33 compared the husband-and-wife commitment to Christ and the church. Marriage emphasized self-giving and mutual caring.

While Jesus permitted dissolving a marriage because of adultery, Paul allowed dissolution when an unbeliever wanted out of the relationship. It can then be argued that Paul did not understand Jesus' words to be taken as an absolute restriction. He apparently viewed Jesus' exception as guidance for human welfare, because no human beings fully live by the ideals presented in the Bible.

Paul's position opens the door to understanding and acceptance of those who choose divorce when they encounter circumstances that forbid them to live together in peace. Both Jesus and Paul contended that where there was a violation of God's intention by human failure—sin—God's love is there to pardon.

Options for Preaching

Marriage—a spiritual union (Matt. 5:31–32; 19:3–9). God provided for human need by instituting marriage. The purpose of God was for male and female to "become one," that is, to enter into spiritual union. One way to think of Jesus' divorce regulation is to view it as intended more to nurture the concept of spiritual unity than to deny the possibility of divorce.

Living the ideal (Mark 10:2–12). Throughout the Bible, God presents a realistic picture of humanity. While the ideal is set up for human beings in many ways (e.g., no lying, no stealing, no murdering), they are still sinful creatures. Who among them lives up to God's standard of perfection?

Jesus viewed the indissolubility of marriage as the ideal. He also implied that the ideal will not always be realized when he cited adultery as a cause for divorce. The human propensity for distorting God's intention is too vast for Jesus not to recognize that marital breakdowns had occurred and would continue to occur.

Spiritual oneness (Gen. 2:18–24). Spiritual unity is both a divine gift and a human achievement. A good marriage is too complex to assume that unity is obtained strictly by human determination. People also need divine assistance.

Spiritual oneness is a dynamic process and not a state miraculously experienced by two people. Nor is it a state that, once achieved, can never be lost again. It is a relationship of mutual sharing of personhood.

DOUBT

Martin B. Copenhaver

In a religious context doubt refers either to uncertainty about God or to lack of trust in God. In the former sense doubt can be as basic as uncertainty that a God exists. Doubt in this sense can also refer to uncertainty that God has certain qualities; for example, someone can believe that there is a God but remain unconvinced that God is able to answer prayer. Doubt in the latter sense, as lack of trust, refers not to a lack of belief in God but to an inability to entrust oneself to the care of God.

Analysis

Doubt arises from the twin realities of God's majesty and human limitations. God is a being of such power, magnitude, and mystery that God cannot be fully grasped by the limited intellect and feeble imagination of humankind. When Moses asked to see God, he was told that no one can see the face of God—that is, see God fully and directly—and live. Instead, Moses was given a brief glimpse of God's back, a revelation that, as incomplete as it was, is unique in Hebrew scriptures (Ex. 33:20–23).

Even when God comes to be seen and known in the person of Jesus Christ, God is a reality that escapes many of those Christ encounters. The disciples seemed unable to understand the miracles that they themselves had witnessed because the power of God that was revealed through the miracles was too great to comprehend and the subsequent claim on their lives was too far-reaching to accept (Mark 8:14–21). Even when the risen Christ appeared to the disciples, some responded with doubt (Matt. 28:17). Doubt here, and elsewhere, is both a failure of comprehension and a failure of trust.

Doubt about the existence of God is a relatively modern concern. Proofs of the existence of God are not found in scripture; the existence of God is assumed. Even when Jesus asked his hearers to consider the lilies of the field (Matt. 6:25–34), he was not—as has sometimes been supposed—using the mysterious and beautiful design of nature as evidence for the existence of God. Even if such evidence were irrefutable, as no such evidence ever is, it would only lead to the kind of detached belief in God that profits little. Instead, Jesus was referring to the way God cares for even the smallest parts of God's creation in order to prompt humans to put more trust in God's love. He was posing the rhetorical question, If God cares so magnificently for the creatures that seem most insignificant, is it not obvious that those who are God's very children can entrust themselves to that care through faith?

Human doubts give testimony to the scale of what people affirm. That is, human doubts actually give God a backhanded compliment: God is too mighty to be encompassed by certainty. In response to this kind of God, humans both reach for faith and leave themselves open to doubt.

Biblical Instances

Old Testament. The Old Testament literature assumes that only a fool will conclude there is no God (Psalm 53). Nevertheless, the people of Israel do exhibit doubt in the ability and willingness of God to fulfill the covenant promises. Yahweh demonstrated power and faithfulness to the people of Israel when they were led out of slavery in Egypt. But when Moses left them to ascend Mount Sinai, they doubted a God who could not be seen and touched, so they immediately turned to the worship of an idol (Ex. 32:15–24). At other times the people of Israel doubted that Yahweh is the one true God. When the people began to worship Baal, Elijah had to call upon the power of Yahweh in a contest with the prophets of Baal to demonstrate that there is only one God, a God who deserves their exclusive allegiance (1 Kings 18:20–40). More generally, the Old Testament is the story of a people who reach for faithful trust in God and yet exhibit a continual struggle with doubt through their unwillingness to fully trust in the promises of a God who is bound to them in covenant.

New Testament. It is not belief in certain ideas about God but trust in the person of God that is central to the gospel. The writer of the letter of James makes it clear that what is important is faith in God, not mere belief (James 2:19–20). James assumes that even a demon cannot fail to believe in some kind of God. But if nothing in the way of action or relationship flows from that belief, it is worthless. The fear of the disciples on the Sea of Galilee during a storm is interpreted as doubt in the faithfulness of God (Mark 4:35–41).

The powerful pull of doubt is evident in John the Baptist, who, though he was the first to recognize Jesus as the promised Messiah, later expresses uncertainty (Matt. 11:2–6).

At the resurrection Thomas demonstrates the inability to believe in a God who cannot be seen and touched, the same inability that is found in idolaters. Jesus blesses those who do not doubt the unseen Christ (John 20:24–29), a theme that is picked up by the author of Hebrews (11:1–3).

Doubt and faith are often found together, a mixture that need not be debilitating (Mark 9:14–29). Nevertheless, the power of doubt is clearly recognized. It is only doubt that prevents human beings from being able to move a mountain with a simple command (Mark 11:22–23).

Options for Preaching

Believing is seeing. The followers of Jesus on the road to Emmaus did not recognize that the one who traveled with them was the risen Christ (Luke 24:13–35). It was only later, when he sat at table with them, that they could see that their fellow traveler was none other than Jesus himself. It is when people come to believe that Christ is risen that they can see that he has been with them all along. Doubt can keep a person from seeing God. In many instances, believing is seeing.

No doubt about it? The father who brings his son to Jesus also expresses doubt (Mark 9:14–29). He believes and does not believe, an almost universal mixture. But he does not wait for his doubts to be resolved before he seeks out Jesus. Indeed, he is doubting the very one he is looking to for help. Before his doubts are resolved, before he can claim any certainty about God's nature and God's power, before he can affirm without reservation that God can heal and, more to the point, that God can heal through Jesus, the father entrusts himself and his son to the care of Jesus.

What you see and hear. In this scientific age, people frequently express skepticism about anything that cannot be seen and measured. Naturally, this skepticism extends to Christian claims about that great unseen reality called God. Nevertheless, though one cannot see God, one can see the ways in which God is at work in the world. When the disciples of John the Baptist conveyed John's doubt that Jesus is the promised Messiah, Jesus did not respond with abstract claims or a learned dissertation. Rather, he told them to report only what they had seen and heard (Matt. 11:2–6). It was enough.

EDUCATION

Daniel Aleshire

Education for faith involves the activities of learning and teaching that are part of a Christian's responsible participation in the purposes of God.

Analysis

Christian education is a broadly inclusive enterprise. It includes the activities that occur in the education rooms of a church building, but it also includes the busyness of the workplace and the idleness of a wakeful night. Learning for faith embraces all the ages of life. Experiences that accrue over time refract an individual's perception of scripture and the human condition into different understandings. Education for faith also includes many kinds of learning. Faith needs both the learning that leads to new knowledge and the learning that produces mature feelings and faithful actions.

Biblical Instances

Old Testament. Perhaps the most central affirmation about religious education in the Hebrew scriptures is that learning for faith begins in the home. The Deuteronomist teaches Israel to write the story of Yahweh's actions "on the doorposts of your house and on your gates" (Deut. 6:9), and to tell it in the form of answers to questions the children have been instructed to ask (6:20–25). The Wisdom literature teaches that knowledge embraces more than the head, "for wisdom will come into your heart, and knowledge will be pleasant to your soul" (Prov. 2:9–10). Learning for faith is a way of knowing that invades lives and touches hearts. The prophets admonish people to "learn to do good" (Isa. 1:17a). Responsible faith requires appropriate behavior, and behavior requires tutoring.

New Testament. The New Testament associates learning with Christian discipleship. Jesus invited people to "take my yoke upon you, and learn from me" (Matt. 11:29), and told the eleven disciples at his ascension to make disciples of all nations, "teaching them to observe all that I have commanded" (Matt. 28:19–20). Teaching and learning are thus normative aspects of the Christian life. (See also Acts 2:42; 1 Cor. 15:3; Phil. 3:17; 2 Tim. 1:13–14; 2:1.)

Options for Preaching

Family and faith. The family has a central role in religious instruction. Parents make good teachers of young children because they are their parents. Teaching children requires attentiveness to the religious dimensions of their questions, and a readiness to share the story of faith. The Old Testament entrusts its most central affirmation to teaching that occurs in the home (Deut. 6:7–25).

Learning and community. The pastoral writer encourages Timothy to "continue in what you have learned and have firmly believed, knowing from whom you learned it" (2 Tim. 3:14–26). The text makes an important point about the process of education in faith. Teaching is a gift people give to one another. Faith is transferred from generation to generation, from person to person, like a communicable blessing.

Learning and discipleship. Learning is neither optional nor merely an intellectual exercise for Christians. Christians learn because they are followers of Christ (Matt. 11:29). A part of love of God is expressed through learning that leads to faithful actions and thoughtful love.

ELECTION

Paul A. Basden

Election in the Bible means "choice" or "selection." It is often identified with other biblical concepts, such as predestination, calling, or foreknowledge. The word "election" itself, however, while related to these other terms, stands alone in naming a significant concept that describes God's sure and gracious choice of a person or a group of persons to fulfill God's sovereign purpose.

Analysis

By the fourth century, the biblical doctrine of election had been hardened into the speculative philosophical notion of predestination. Augustine of Hippo (354–430) taught that God eternally predetermined to save some humans from the eternal damnation that they deserved because of Adam's sin. This absolute, irresistible choice of a fixed number of persons to eternal salvation, and the consequent passing over of the rest, is called single predestination. John Calvin (1509–1564) went beyond Augustine by stating that God not only elected some for salvation but also predestined some for damnation. This is called double predestination. In the twentieth century, Karl Barth (1886–1968) has revolutionized the doctrine of election by reinterpreting it christologically. Barth saw in Jesus Christ both the electing God and the elected man, chosen to suffer and to die for the sins of humankind.

Biblical Instances

The primary Old Testament reference to election concerns God's electing of Israel for the specific purpose of blessing the surrounding nations (Ex. 19:3–6; Deut. 7:6–8). God's choice depended upon nothing in Israel; it was based solely upon God's desire to make it "my own treasured possession."

In the New Testament, Jesus is referred to as God's elect Son, chosen by the Father to redeem the lost human race from sin (Matt. 12:18; Luke 9:35). God elected Jesus to this sacrificial ministry "before the foundation of the world" (1 Peter 1:18–20). Jesus became the savior of humankind not by divine afterthought but by sovereign appointment. Following Jesus' death and resurrection, some Christians believed that the church had replaced Israel as the elect people of God, chosen to bring glory and praise to the Father through the Son (Eph. 1:4–6; 1 Peter 2:90).

Options for Preaching

The doctrine of election, when rightly understood as God's gracious and sovereign choice to save all who are in Christ, reminds the preacher of God's eternal purpose to love his fallen creation. Consider the following sermon possibilities.

Election of Israel (Ex. 19:3–6; Deut. 7:6–8; Rom. 11:1–6). God chose Israel to be a "blessing" to other nations; that is, to mediate the divine message to all peoples. Israel's election was to mission.

Election of Jesus Christ (Matt. 12:18–21; Isa. 42:1–4; 1 Peter 1:18–21). God chose his beloved Son to mediate the divine nature and message "to the nations." The message was redemption, the method was sacrifice. Jesus' election was to suffering and glory.

Election of the church (Eph. 1:3–14; Rom. 8:28–30; 1 Peter 2:9–10). God chooses all who are in Christ to be "holy and blameless in his sight" and to "declare his praises." The church's election is to sanctification and worship.

END TIME

Richard B. Cunningham

The end time refers to the final events of human history initiated by the return of Jesus Christ and consummated by the entry of human beings into their eternal destinies. The end time is one part of eschatology, which means literally "the study of last things." It focuses upon the future reign of God over all creation and the possibility of the inbreak of God's rule into the present historical process.

Analysis

New Testament eschatological thought is complex and varied about such topics as the kingdom of God and the Son of man, and whether the kingdom is future, fully present, or proleptically present. Diverse traditions and developments are found in the New Testament.

Variations are also found in the New Testament pictures of the events of the end time and how they are to be interpreted. Scholars generally agree that a widely consistent New Testament pattern includes three dominant events—the return of Christ, the resurrection of the dead, and the final judgment. Detailed eschatological schemes often include such things as the appearance of the Antichrist, a rapture of the church, a millennial reign, two resurrections, and other events. In general these are not central to the primary intention of the major symbols of the end—the manifestation of Christ's sovereignty over history, the resurrection of believers to eternal life, and a final judgment that consummates the historical process and initiates the fullness of heavenly life.

Scholars dispute how to interpret the major symbols of the end time. Some interpreters insist they are intended only to underline the seriousness of one's existential decision in the present moment. Others think they symbolize the events at the individual's death in which one is spiritually resurrected into the timeless eternal presence of death. Others interpret the symbols literally. Still others maintain that the symbols stress important theological points about Christ's manifestation of lordship over history but think that the events themselves are unimaginable in our finite understanding. Despite this diversity, one can preach with confidence the critical theological truths of the end-time symbols about the return, resurrection, and final judgment.

Biblical Instances

The return of Christ. The return of Christ underlines that historical life and eternity turn upon our response to the resurrected, exalted Jesus, who is the present reigning lord of the universe and human history. At the consummation of history, he will manifest that lordship to every human being who has ever lived. Depending upon how one has responded to Jesus as personal lord, the future return is either a hope or a warning. The unexpected nature of the return stresses the importance of living as though every night might be the world's last night.

The resurrection of the dead. This idea is affirmed widely in the New Testament. It grows out of the Hebrew holistic view of the person as a unity of body and spirit. Thus only when one is reunited with a spiritual body will one stand as a whole person again before God. The resurrection of the dead indicates that one cannot escape responsibility for one's life, even by the simple device of dying.

The most extensive treatment of the nature of the resurrection is 1 Corinthians 15. Other major passages include Romans 6:5–11; 2 Corinthians 5:1–5; Philippians 3:20–21; 1 Thessalonians 4:13–17; and Revelation 20:4–6.

The final judgment. The final judgment symbolizes God's assertion of sovereignty over creation and history, with the promise that good will ultimately defeat evil. The final judgment underscores that historical decisions have eternal consequences, with the righteous being taken into the eternal presence of God and the wicked separated from God.

Options for Preaching

The following selection of preaching texts provides a comprehensive interpretation of some of the most important themes relating to the return of Christ:

The promise of Christ's return gives Christians hope—Colossians 3:1–4.

The unexpected nature of the return requires constant preparation—Matthew 24:3, 27–31; Luke 12:35–40.

The return provides a stimulus to Christian living—1 Corinthians 1:7; 1 Thessalonians 5:1–11.

The return initiates the last judgment—2 Timothy 4:1–8.

The return leads to the glorification of the saints—1 Peter 5:4.

The following passages are key preaching texts for some of the important themes relating to the resurrection of the dead:

The hope of the resurrection is founded in Jesus—John 11:17–27.

The Holy Spirit is the guarantee of the believer's resurrection—2 Corinthians 5:1–5.

Both believers and unbelievers are to be resurrected—John 5:21–29.

Believers will receive a spiritual body on resurrection day—1 Corinthians 15.

The following texts focus on important themes related to the final judgment:

All people will face the judgment—Romans 3:19; 14:10–12; Acts 17:31.

All sins are to be judged—1 Timothy 5:24–25.

Jesus is the judge of whether people obey his words—Matthew 7:21–27.

Caring for needy people will be a basis for judgment—Matthew 25:31–46.

Christian works will be the basis for reward for the righteous in the judgment—1 Corinthians 3:10–15.

ENVIRONMENT

Dieter T. Hessel

Environment is the milieu of life, the natural setting for creaturely existence in the world. It refers to the whole earth as a dynamic community of living and nonliving entities, as well as ecosystems within continents and oceans. Modern environmental concern focuses on appreciating nature and preserving ecological integrity while using natural resources carefully and distributing benefits equitably. It challenges any human activity that would undermine healthy natural processes.

Biblical writers, though prescientific, reflect implicit ecological wisdom and affirm the intrinsic value of nature as God's good creation. The Creator-Deliverer is understood to be actively concerned for the well-being of all living things and a utilizer of natural processes to set things right. Biblical prophets warn of environmental disasters resulting from social injustice. Both Testaments envision a harmonious community of life in which natural places and all creatures are redeemed.

Analysis

There are both ancient and modern reasons for humanity's failure to do justice to all of God's creation by caring for ecology and equity together.

The ancient (perennial) barrier to eco-justice is carelessness or greed. In the language of the Genesis story, humans, though charged with "keeping" the creation, have failed to "till" the garden with care and to distribute fairly the fruits of tilling. Many local environmental disasters today have the same origin: People in positions of power have abused the environment for short-term gain or situated toxic wastes among the powerless. So it has always been. The larger scale and increased toxicity of environmental abuse today are newer facets of an old story.

Human activity that degrades the environment can cripple any region's capacity for life support and intensify natural calamities (e.g., species extinction, ruined fisheries, devastating floods, rapid desertification). Consider the startling pattern of deforestation on every continent to obtain "cheap" lumber. This is caused in part by greater demand for housing and fuel as population grows. Thus Nepal is deforested and Bangladesh experiences increasing floods. But the role of rich corporations and government allies is at least as big a factor in destroying the rain forests that are crucial to avoiding a disastrous greenhouse effect. A similar combination of demand and greed undermine land stewardship, as soil erosion and toxic pesticide runoff result from modern agriculture's dependence on heavy machinery and dangerous chemicals.

Pride of mastery and fascination with technological prowess have become partnered with greed and carelessness—for example, in efforts to harness the atom for national defense and development. Both capitalist and socialist societies were blind to the long-term hazardous effects of using plutonium in making nuclear weapons and were stunned by power plant accidents at Three Mile Island and Chernobyl.

This exposes the distinctly modern reason for the environmental crisis—the unexpected, ecology-destroying consequences of developing well-intentioned technologies. Modern economics valued industrial processes and products that reduce labor and move goods without regard for cumulative ecological effects. Now ozone depletion and global warming—accelerated by widespread human use of technologies such as gasoline and diesel engines, air conditioning, and convenience packaging—reveal that ecologically destructive human enterprise can threaten earth's health as a whole and human existence itself.

Biblical Instances

God loves and cares for the whole creation (Ps. 145:5, 16). God "who made heaven and earth, the sea, and all that is in them; . . . who executes justice for the oppressed" (Ps. 146:6–7) demands environmental stewardship coupled with social justice. The prophet Hosea (4:1–3) warns that social injustice produces environmental disaster, with severe effects on wild animals, birds, and fish (see also Jer. 9:4–11). In Nehemiah 5:3–19, the people lament being powerless tenant farmers.

Covenant theology and statutes expect eco-justice. Every seven years, the land is to lie fallow (Deut. 15:1–11; Leviticus 25), and on the fiftieth year (jubilee) debts are to be forgiven and land redistributed according to need. Land, rather than being a commodity traded for personal gain, is a community trust with appropriate landmarks (Deut. 19:14; compare the tale of Naboth's vineyard in 1 Kings 21). When the land is apportioned equitably (Ezek. 47:13–48:29), it will be restored to productive harmony (Hos. 2:21–22). But Hebrew history is a long story of land coveting and defilement, symbolized in Solomon's order to cut down the beloved cedars of Lebanon to aggrandize Jerusalem (1 Kings 5:10–11; Ps. 104:16).

Psalm 104 reflects ecological wisdom in describing God's work as Creator and Tender of all earth's creatures. Humanity has the role of ruling deputy, following the ideal of just kingship depicted in Psalm 72:1–3, 16. In this light one may reread Genesis, where God breathes life into earth (1:1–2) to make it perennially productive (Mark 4:28). "Dominion" or earth-caring should enable all creatures, not just humans, to "be fruitful and multiply" (Gen. 1:22, 28). Humanity has earthy origins (from humus) and is to become steward of the garden with acute awareness of humanity's own limited knowledge and dependence on divine guidance (Gen. 2:15–25).

After carrying out the first endangered species project, God covenants with Noah and every living creature (Gen. 9:8–28). But the reality of global warming and ozone depletion, plus the possibility of nuclear winter, make it impossible to count, as did the Noah story writer, on unceasing "seedtime and harvest, cold and heat," or reliable seasons (Gen. 8:22).

In the New Testament the creation groans in travail, waiting for redemption (Rom. 8:22). The Son was sent to save the cosmos (John 3:17). Christ, the firstborn of all creation, reconciles all being (Col. 1:15–20). Revelation 4:11 praises the Creator and 22:2 portrays the New Jerusalem as a restored garden with tree leaves "for the healing of the nations."

Wilderness is as important as garden in the biblical story. The people are bonded to God in the wilderness and learn the life-style of sufficiency (no hoarding of manna!). Jesus clarified his vocation while being tested and renewed in the wilderness. He encouraged a life-style of sufficiency, appreciative of nature, in solidarity with "the least" (Luke 12:22–34; Matt. 25:31–46).

Options for Preaching

Modern people, whether secular or religious, have almost forgotten that the processes of natural history and the ecological contexts of human existence both precede humanity's historical project and are essential to its continuance. The culture of "developed" societies has valued mastery of nature for human convenience and profit. Rather than respecting natural being as a whole and valuing human life within nature, it views human culture as a domineering project requiring an instrumental, mechanistic view of nature. The result is a destructively anthropocentric worldview.

Prevailing Christian theologies from "conservative" to "liberal" have intensified this cultural crisis by celebrating human dominion of nature and emphasizing selfish doctrines of human redemption, to the detriment of creation spirituality. Nature became a vast stage. North Americans inherited a large, resource-rich natural environment and have used it unreservedly, contrary to the wisdom of native peoples. Other northern hemisphere countries have plundered their economic colonies. Now large southern hemisphere nations also are racing to use renewable and nonrenewable resources. The world cannot long sustain the overdeveloped way of life. North Americans thus have special responsibility to change social policy and personal practice to reduce luxury consumption, to use resources in a sustainable way, and to achieve sufficiency for the poor.

Models for living. Preaching can contrast the affluent way of life with Jesus' stewardship stories (e.g., Luke 12) and his promise of "abundant" life (John 10:10).

The meek shall inherit. Preaching can also consider his teaching that the meek—who exercise power disciplined by respect and love—shall inherit the earth.

God's great economy. An alternate term for kingdom of God might be "God's great economy," which brings together sound economics, ecology, and ecumenics (*oikos* is their common root) in an ethic for the planetary household.

ENVY/JEALOUSY

James W. Crawford

The words "envy" and "jealousy" come from the Greek word for "zeal." The Greek root serves as the base for *zealot* as well.

The common understanding of envy is chagrin at the good fortune of another. It bears a grudge. It generates resentment.

Jealousy emerges from a "zealous" devotion to something that may fall into the hands of another. It suggests obsession with an object whose possession by another breeds mistrust, resentment, covetousness.

Analysis

The biblical faith focuses on how people treat one another; it encourages trust, good faith, integrity, outgoing encouragement, mutual support, and gracious community. Envy and jealousy warp the heart, threatening community. Envy and jealousy, seeking satisfaction at the expense of another person's good fortune or dignity, spell breakdown of community. In some cases, the community can be broken irreparably, the resentment gaining such intensity as to lead to the humiliation, the denigration, the removal of the other.

Biblical Instances

Old Testament. Two of the Hebrew Bible's classic references lie in the sagas of Joseph (Genesis 37) and David (2 Samuel 11). In the case of Joseph, the harmony and toleration of a family is broken by resentment generated by favoritism of a father for his son. The reaction of Joseph's brothers to Joseph's favored position illustrates how far envy and jealousy may go to satisfy their passion: murder.

In the second story, David's envy of Uriah's marriage to Bathsheba compels him to design a death trap for Uriah so he might gain his desire, Bathsheba.

New Testament. The New Testament makes reference to envy as one of the "sins," subverting the good will among congregations (Phil. 1:15). Paul accuses preachers of covering their envy by using the name of Christ.

Options for Preaching

The key to confidence. The willingness to celebrate and embrace the good fortune and achievements of others sustains and deepens community. Envy and jealousy kills community. When King Saul begins to envy David's popularity and becomes jealous of what he perceives to be David's authority, the first step to a lethal relationship is taken (1 Sam. 18:6–9). What was once a glorious friendship turns into a struggle for life itself. Close ties mean good faith, magnanimity, mutual celebration.

The transforming power of the gospel. When people surrender to Christ, their lives change, their ethics alter, their treatment of others takes on a new dimension. Paul confirms this when he writes to his colleague Titus (3:3), the leader of a missionary church in Crete. Outside the saving impact of the gospel, life expressed itself in malice, envy, jealousy. Now, embraced by the love of Christ, a compassionate and service-oriented life becomes evident. The gospel transforms an old self to a new.

EQUALITY

J. Philip Wogaman

Equality is the state of being regarded or treated as having the same significance or value as comparable persons.

Analysis

Human beings clearly are not equal in all respects. They manifest rich diversities in age, temperament, external physical characteristics, physical and mental abilities, upbringing, handicaps, experience. They also vary widely in wealth, power, and social status. The question is, which forms of inequality should be accepted or even celebrated and which forms of inequality should be contested in light of the gospel. Christians find their value to God to be more basic than any human differences.

Biblical Instances

The rich diversities of human gifts and experiences are portrayed throughout the Bible. Paul celebrates humanity's different gifts in noteworthy passages, such as 1 Corinthians 12, where he speaks of the "varieties of gifts" and refers to the church as the "body of Christ," in which the members, though different in gift and function, contribute alike to the good of the whole. These differences, thus, do not detract from the underlying equality—they accent it. The New Testament, from the proclamation of the Magnificat (Luke 1:51–53) to the stern admonitions of James (1:9–10; 2:1–7; 5:1–5) is deeply egalitarian. Paul makes the point quite explicitly: "There is neither Jew nor Greek, there is neither slave nor free, there is neither male nor female; for you are all one in Christ Jesus" (Gal. 3:28).

Biblical egalitarianism is deeply rooted in the Old Testament. The great prophets confronted kings who showed disrespect for the rights of their subjects (2 Sam. 12:1–14; 1 Kings 21:1–24) and challenged the arrogance of the rich in the face of the suffering poor (Jer. 21:12; Micah 2:2–5; Amos 2:6–7; 4:1; 5:11–12). The laws of Torah protected the poor, the widows and orphans, even the sojourners, so they, too, might have their portion in Israel (Lev. 19:9–15; 25; Deut. 15).

Options for Preaching

The parable of the vineyard (Matt. 20:1–15) conveys the sense of human equality in the grace of God, challenging the conventional wisdom that God's gifts are dependent upon how much time and effort different people have contributed.

New Testament realism about sin is also a great equalizer. All have sinned and fallen short (Rom. 3:23). No one should judge himself or herself better than others. "Then what becomes of our boasting?" asks Paul. "It is *excluded*!" he answers (Rom. 3:27).

Wealth and power often are based upon sin and greed, not upon deserving. Biblical realism recognizes this fact.

"Preferential option for the poor." This Latin American expression means that the poor and disinherited need special attention, not because they are more deserving but because their plight represents the most important breakdown of God's gracious purposes for humanity.

ETERNAL LIFE

Robert Kysar

Eternal life is the gift of a relationship with God that exceeds the boundaries of time. It refers to a timeless relationship that reaches beyond death and transforms the present life of believers. The expression has roots in the Greek for "life of the age."

Analysis

Eternal life is the existence that God alone bestows, since God is eternal (e.g., "from everlasting to everlasting," 1 Chron. 16:36; Ps. 90:2) and the source of life (Gen. 2:7). It is not a natural attribute of the human being ("the immortality of the soul") but solely a gift from God given in raising the dead to life (Rom. 6:23). Eternal life is associated with the decisive act of God in the future in which the divine age is inaugurated. Since the earliest Christians believed the new age had dawned in Christ, it is the New Testament that speaks of eternal life. The Christ event made possible a relationship with God, the quality of which exceeded the limitations of time. To become identified with Christ's resurrection is to accept the promise of eternal life.

Biblical Instances

Old Testament. The expression "eternal life" is used only in Daniel 12:2. However, the Hebraic view of God is the taproot for the concept of eternal life. Yahweh can bestow that which is everlasting (the covenant, Isa. 24:5). Moreover, one's relationship with God is the difference between life and death (Deut. 30:19–20), and Yahweh gives life and delivers one from death (Ps. 9:13; 16:10; 56:13).

New Testament. God grants eternal life to believers (Luke 18:29–30) at the resurrection of the dead (1 Cor. 15:51–53) as a result of faith (Acts 13:46; 1 Tim. 1:16) and faithful behavior

(Matt. 25:31–46). The expression denotes salvation and is a synonym for kingdom of God (Mark 10:23–30). In Paul's writing eternal life usually refers to life beyond death (Rom. 2:7; 5:21; 6:22; Gal. 6:8), but in the Johannine writings it also includes the quality of the believers' present lives in this world (John 3:36; 5:24; 10:28; 1 John 5:20).

Options for Preaching

Investing for the future. The man was eager to learn what was required to inherit eternal life but shocked to hear that it comprised a total commitment to a relationship with Christ in the present life. That was more of an investment than he cared to make (Mark 10:17–22).

Beyond the boundaries. God's love and faithfulness reach beyond the limits of time and space (Jer. 31:3) and all human boundaries. In Christ God has demonstrated that limitless love and faithfulness in abolishing death and giving life (2 Tim. 1:10).

Life in a time warp. Belief in Christ transports one into the future, where eternal life is a present experience and the passage from death to life a completed journey, so that those are no longer a dreamed-for future but a here-and-now reality (John 5:24).

ETHICS/MORALITY

Allan M. Parrent

Ethics has been usefully defined as the critical study of morality, or as reflection on human moral actions from some critical standard of excellence. Ethics (from *ethos*) refers to what underlies and accounts for a community's customs, attitudes, practices, behavior patterns. Morality (from *mores*) refers more to the actual behavior itself, a group's folkways that are generally accepted as normative. Morality is therefore the subject matter upon which the discipline of ethics reflects. Christian ethics is systematic reflection, from a theological perspective, both on the moral actions and practices of those in the Christian community and on the character traits, virtues, dispositions, and intentions out of which those actions and practices come. From the same perspective, it reflects also on the practices of broader human communities and applies such reflections in both critical and normative ways to those communities.

Analysis

While ethics and morality are important, indeed essential, themes for preaching, they are better considered as general, underlying, pervasive elements of the preaching task rather than as specific topics or themes. Ethics is in fact a discipline, like systematic theology, that one brings regularly to the homiletical task, and to address the ethical implications of a biblical text or theme for the Christian moral life is an appropriate component of almost any sermon.

Sermons dealing with ethics and morality might on occasion be helped conceptually by some attention to Henry David Aiken's four levels of moral discourse. At the "pre-ethical level" the preacher might identify a spectrum of prevailing attitudes on a contemporary ethical issue, for example, abortion or the environment. The second or "moral level" would examine the relevant moral teachings of the Christian community, that is, the primary community that shapes Christian moral identity and preserves the historical Christian moral tradition. The third or "ethical level" would ask the question, Why should this particular moral guidance be accepted as normative? or, Can this prevailing morality continue to be justified in the light of new theological or ethical insights, facts, experience or scriptural interpretations? The fourth or "meta-ethical level" (usually assumed) asks why one should be concerned about morality at all, leading to the basic question of faith commitment on which the whole Christian enterprise is based.

Dangers lurk in addressing moral questions. One is the tendency to think too narrowly about what biblical materials count as ethically relevant. The most obvious texts of moral exhortation are not necessarily the most helpful way to get to the particularities of the Christian moral life. A second is selectivity, that is, the failure to take the whole canon into account, risking thereby a distorted understanding of God's word and will for the moral life. The discipline of using a lectionary can help to avoid this danger. A third is the danger of reductionism, or reducing the meaning of Christian ethics and morality to one theme or virtue. Love, for example, is central to any understanding of Christian ethics, but it is not the sum total of the matter. A fourth danger is the temptation to translate morally relevant biblical materials too directly from the first to the twentieth century without taking sufficiently into account the profoundly different contexts involved.

Biblical Instances

The biblical resources available for preaching on ethics and morality are almost limitless in both Old and New Testaments. There are, first, some explicit moral exhortations and rules, clear normative standards for right behavior and good character traits. The most obvious and frequently quoted are doubtless the Ten Commandments (Ex. 20:1–17) and the Sermon on the Mount (Matthew 5–7). In the same category are such passages as Jesus' "new commandment" (John 13:34), Micah's summary of the Lord's requirements (Micah 6:8), Jesus' double commandment (Matt. 22:37–40), and Amos's exhortation to let justice roll down like waters (Amos 5:24). Second, specific teachings relate to specific moral issues, for example, marriage and divorce (Matt. 5:31–32; Luke 16:18); sexual practices (Rom. 1:26–27); killing (Ex. 20:13); dishonesty (Acts 5:1–10); self-righteousness (Luke 18:10–14); greed (Jer. 22:13–17); treatment of the poor (Deut. 14:28–29). Third, more general ethical themes are interwoven throughout scripture—love, justice, moral obligation, stewardship, forgiveness, reconciliation, compassion, righteousness, covenant loyalty.

Finally, a host of biblical narratives tell stories of all sorts of persons doing all sorts of things. As often as not, it is such stories of biblical characters and their moral or immoral behavior, their admirable or disreputable character traits, the exemplary or unworthy intentions behind their actions, that provide the most vivid and rich biblical material for preaching on ethical themes or moral issues. Stories about such very human characters as David and Bathsheba (2 Samuel 11–12); Jacob and Esau (Genesis 27); Abraham and Sarah (Genesis 16); Peter (Mark 14:66–72); the other disciples (Mark 9:33–37); the good Samaritan (Luke 10:29–37), and a host of other characters from the parables can all serve as vehicles for biblically based preaching on ethics and morality, on virtues and vices, and on character traits that are pleasing or displeasing to God. The character of Jesus and the virtues illustrated in his life and works (e.g., love, eschatological hope, obedience, faithfulness, humility) are, of course, prime sources for such preaching as the preacher focuses on the imitation of Christ as a model for the Christian life. But all four types of biblical materials can provide images and concepts that help to form the moral orientation of the Christian, and all can be used to teach conduct that is consistent with Christian character and commitment, at both individual and social levels of human existence.

Options for Preaching

Christian faith versus social mores. Jesus disregarded or questioned some of the details of the prevailing code of morality of his own religious community and tradition. For example, he chose to heal on the Sabbath (Mark 3:1–5; Luke 13:10–17) and to eat with sinners (Mark 2:16). Similarly, ethical reflection may bring into question today some aspects of the prevailing moral practices or social arrangements of contemporary Christianity and the culture in which it exists. Martin Luther King, Jr., did precisely that on the issue of racism in modern times. Conversely, ethical reflection may also reaffirm and reinforce traditional Christian moral norms, perhaps an increasingly important task in a secular society increasingly disconnected from its own moral traditions and reluctant to accept any moral discipline that might interfere with the "good" of self-actualization or self-gratification.

Quandary ethics. Sermons may be structured so as to focus on a significant moral dilemma in which Christian moral norms seem to be in conflict (the problem of the "perplexed conscience"). Such an approach has been called quandary ethics. One example is the conflict between environmental concerns and the need for industrial development that provides jobs for the unemployed. The goodness of, and God's intention for, the created order, and the human responsibility to tend it, are fundamental themes of Genesis 1 and 2. The responsibility of a society to provide opportunities for material livelihood and the expression of human creativity in work are clear implications of the biblical theme of justice as found especially in the prophets.

The Sermon on the Mount. Matthew 5–7 has always held an important place in Christian ethics. Even though it is not a self-contained summary of Jesus' ethical teachings and makes no reference to such ethically relevant themes as the double commandment or justification, the preacher's understanding of the import of the Sermon on the Mount will have a significant impact on how he or she addresses ethics and morality in general. Is the Sermon to be understood literally and applied absolutely? As intentional hyperbole used for dramatic effect? As general principles illustrating the quality of Christian actions? As an indication of proper inner attitudes and intentions for

Christians? As a call to repentance after bringing humans to a realization of their inability to live in obedience to its teachings? As teaching applicable only to those who withdraw from the world where they can supposedly live by such counsels of perfection? As relevant for one's spiritual life only and not for one's life in the temporal sphere? As an interim ethic based on the conviction that the end of history was near at the time and that mundane concerns were therefore unimportant, making the Sermon irrelevant for today?

The Christian community and the civil community. Romans 13 implies that a "good" state is one that is "a terror" to bad conduct and not to good conduct. Mark 12 implies that there is always some tension between loyalty to God and loyalty to Caesar. What is a "good" state or political order and what is the nature of the Christian's responsibility for shaping and maintaining it? The church-state issue has been a perennial one for Christians since New Testament times, and clarity on that issue is fundamental before clergy and the institutional church can address in a coherent and faithful manner specific moral issues arising in the public arena.

EUCHARIST

John P. Reed

The Eucharist, also called "Communion" or the "Lord's Supper," is the Christian rite or sacrament commemorating Christ's Last Supper with his disciples. In its nontechnical usage, the word means "thanksgiving," or in its Greek verb form, "to bless." The term "Eucharist," applied to the sacred meal, derives from the central ritual act of thanksgiving for the bread and wine (e.g., "And he took a cup, and when he had given thanks he gave it to them, and they all drank of it," Mark 14:23).

Paul once referred to the rite as "communion" (1 Cor. 10:16), but his most unambiguous designation is "the Lord's supper" (1 Cor. 11:20). The Eucharist and baptism constitute the two foundational sacraments or symbolic rites of the church.

Analysis

The Eucharist pulsates with the Christian motif of "incorporation." In the ritual act of eating the bread and drinking the wine, the believer incorporates Christ—that is, receives into himself or herself and participates in Christ's crucified and saving body. Furthermore, this eating and drinking involves a consciousness of inclusion in the church, Christ's collective or corporate body in the world. In a profoundly spiritual sense, in the Eucharist the believer incorporates that which incorporates him or her, Christ, and Christ's embodiment, the church.

This incorporative act has a deep psychological significance for the formation of self. Human beings build a sense of self, in part, by incorporating the significant others around them. But in a sinful world, much that gets incorporated is destructive and foreign to true selfhood in its original goodness. Every individual internalizes life experiences of rejection and interpersonal hurt. Everyone is more or less psychologically wounded in a sinful world.

In the Eucharist, individuals and their corporate community reenact the incorporation of the Absolute Good, the perfect love that casts out fear. The Eucharist, symbolic of the full extension of the incarnation, symbolizes in ritual act the spiritual corrective to the psychological consequences of sin, which comes as a result of the Christ event. The traditional liturgical statement, "Feed on him in your hearts with faith," captures in stunning religious metaphor the incorporative saving power of the good news of Christ, as does the phrase "the medicine of immortality," which the early church fathers ascribed to the meal.

The disciplined and regular reenactment of the Eucharist nourishes and strengthens both the communion of the believer with Christ and with the community that incorporates him or her. The Eucharist is reenacted in public worship. It is a corporate matter of a shared memory. Christ instituted it as a communal act. The celebration of the Eucharist points up the fact that participation in God's kingdom does not occur for the individual in isolation. As the simultaneous act of the many, the individual consciousness of its benefit is accompanied by a sympathetic awareness that the same thing is happening to others in the fellowship. The realization that at that moment one's fellow participants are also being drawn closer to Christ has the effect of more closely uniting the participants in a coordinated feeling of their collective embodiment of Christ.

Biblical Instances

The Bible stresses three major themes surrounding the celebration of the Eucharist: (1) the new covenant, (2) participation in Christ's body, and (3) the idea that love, expressed in

Christian unity, is the precondition for authentic Eucharistic celebration.

The new covenant. In the Synoptics, Jesus is portrayed in the Last Supper as proclaiming a new covenant during the passover meal with his disciples. "And he took a cup, and when he had given thanks he gave it to them, saying, 'Drink of it, all of you; for this is my blood of the [new] covenant, which is poured out for many for the forgiveness of sins' " (Matt. 26:27–28; cf. Mark 14:24; Luke 22:20). The Lord's Supper was to be a sign of the new covenant between God and humanity, one sealed in Christ's atoning death and resurrection. In the phrase "poured out for many," Jesus interprets his impending death as an expiatory sacrifice for the sins of the world. The wine, conceived of as blood, is an obvious reference to the blood of the old covenant in Exodus 24:8.

Participation. In two rhetorical questions, Paul reminds the Corinthians that, in the Eucharist, they participate together in Christ's body and blood (1 Cor. 10:16). To join in the Eucharist is to participate in the reaffirmation of the mystic union between the believer and Christ, and between all believers with one another.

Jesus, who proclaimed himself the living bread (John 6:51), must be received through the active participation of believers. Such participation gives life. "Jesus said to them, 'Truly, truly, I say to you, unless you eat the flesh of the Son of man and drink his blood, you have no life in you; he who eats my flesh and drinks my blood has eternal life, and I will raise him up at the last day. For my flesh is food indeed, and my blood is drink indeed' " (John 6:51–55). It is through such participation that one abides in Christ (v. 56).

Love versus idolatry and selfishness. Authentic participation in the Eucharist occurs in a spirit of Christ-centeredness and with an attitude of love. The participant should come in a mood of gratitude and contrition with an inward longing for communion. Paul warns the Corinthians not to contaminate the celebration of the Eucharist with idolatrous meanings (1 Cor. 10:14). He indicates that it is possible to participate unworthily in another sense, that of selfishness (1 Cor. 11:17–22). Such participation is unworthy because it has lost its connection with the purpose of the rite; without a lively sense of personal relationship to Christ, there can be no true remembrance of him as he presented himself in the Lord's Supper (1 Cor. 11:23–26). Furthermore, without a discerning awareness of one's participation in the body, the important experience of unity is undermined (1 Cor. 11:27–32).

Options for Preaching

Shared reminiscence, proclamation, and anticipation. Instructing the Corinthians in the proper approach to the Eucharist, Paul said, "In the same way also the cup, after supper, saying, 'This cup is the new covenant in my blood. Do this, as often as you drink it, in remembrance of me.' For as often as you eat this bread and drink the cup, you proclaim the Lord's death until he comes" (1 Cor. 11:25–26). The Eucharist looks backward in memory and forward in hope, yet it is also rooted in the present awareness of Christ's presence in the present proclamation of his death. Memory is an important medium of inspiration and revelation. The gospel is available in the present in no small part because it has been remembered and remembered and remembered throughout the ages, one generation remembering it on behalf of the next through Word and sacrament.

Celebration of the Eucharist invariably leads to the future. While reminding the community of faith of its historical foundation, it simultaneously looks forward to the consummation of what was begun in Christ.

Dining on living bread. The Eucharist is rife with oral symbolism, which is of extreme relevance in an age in which psychosomatic eating disorders like anorexia nervosa and an array of oral addictions abound. Something is seriously deranged with regard to the human psyche's attempts to assuage deep emotional and spiritual hungers. Jesus said he was what human beings hunger and thirst after (John 4:1–15; 6:48–51). An addiction is a compulsive, repetitive internalization of a substance which enslaves its victim. The Eucharist, also repetitive, is a freely embraced ritual which enables its participants to dramatize their incorporation of the bread of liberation.

Grace and gratitude. Among other things that it symbolizes, the Eucharist is always a thanksgiving meal. Just as Jesus blessed and "gave thanks" for the bread and wine (Mark 14:22–24), so now the community of faith, in remembering Christ's sacrifice, expresses its gratitude for this unmerited gift. The Greek word for "gratitude," which is the root word for Eucharist, also means "grace." When the congregation gathers to celebrate the sacred meal, it gratefully remembers that God abounds in grace. Gratitude is the appropriate response, as well as an humble recognition that at the Lord's Table there are no self-made or self-sufficient persons.

EVANGELISM AND MISSIONS

Hugo H. Culpepper

Evangelism is the proclamation of the gospel of God's gracious love for all people. To evangelize is to herald good news or preach good tidings. It may be with or without an object. The object may be either the persons who receive the good news or the good news itself. The good news sometimes is expressed as a person, as in Acts 5:42.

Missions is the implementation of or the means by which the church accomplishes its mission to glorify God by leading persons to know him through faith in Jesus Christ. Missions is what a church does to achieve its mission in areas of human need that are on the growing edge of the church's confrontation with the non-Christian world.

Analysis

The nature of evangelism is personal rather than propositional. It is personally to introduce others *to* God rather than to teach others propositions *about* God. Evangelism is not only a matter of verbal communication. It is not effective to talk to a hungry or suffering person about God without first feeding him or her or ministering to relieve the suffering. One large Christian denomination discovered that the social ministry department of its home mission board produced more confessions of faith than the evangelism division. However, preaching that is the focus of demonstrated love produces decisions and commitments.

The Bible tells people "to do all to the glory of God." The word "glory" means a manifestation of the true nature of God. Therefore, to glorify God means to reveal him or to make him known. That is the ultimate purpose of the work of missions. This work takes place in areas of human needs, all kinds of need: spiritual, physical, social, and intellectual.

"Growing edge" is a metaphor taken from the biology laboratory: a piece of living tissue placed in a culture bath will grow by adding cells around its edge. Where the church confronts the non-Christian world and God is made known, the church grows by adding new converts and new local congregations.

The origin of missions is ultimately to be found in the heart of God. Since God is love, God has been involved with people from the beginning. It makes a difference to God what happens in the world. As the creator and sustainer of the universe and of all life within it, God has been involved throughout time with the condition of people in history. The spirit of God in the life of William Carey began the modern missionary movement some two centuries ago. It is such persons as missionaries who become close to people and do the work of missions.

Biblical Instances

Old Testament. Although "God saw everything that he had made, and behold, it was very good" (Gen. 1:31), later on sin entered into the world. Death came through sin. Sin is self-centeredness that causes people to rebel against God and miss the mark in life. They are alienated from fellowship with God and have no hope in themselves in this life or for eternity. This is the predicament of all persons when left to themselves.

After God had demonstrated concern for people of all nations (see Genesis 1–11), God began working toward their redemption through a particular people. God called Abraham to become the father of that people. After this people had fallen into captivity in Egypt, God took a second great step in redeeming activity. God sent Moses to the pharaoh so as to lead the children of Israel out of Egypt (Ex. 3:7–10). Moses went up into Mount Sinai, where God gave him a message for the people: God had brought them unto himself; if they kept the covenant, they were to be a priest-nation (Ex. 19:6). Because they would come to know God experientially as their God, they were to live among the peoples of the world and serve as a priest to introduce others to God.

New Testament. "When the time had fully come, God sent forth his Son" (Gal. 4:4) into the world. Jesus went to John for baptism. When John was reluctant, Jesus said, "It is fitting for us to fulfil all righteousness" (i.e., redeeming activity; Matt. 3:15). He intended to carry on to completion the redeeming activity God had begun with Abraham. Jesus was tempted just as other persons are, yet he was able not to sin (Heb. 4:15). Because of this quality of life, he was able to teach with authority (Matt. 7:29), that is, "out of his being." When the Greeks came, he responded, "A grain of wheat falling into the ground abides alone, if it does not die; but if it dies, it brings forth much fruit" (John 12:24, literally translated). Then he came to the existential choice: self-preservation or self-sacrifice. He chose self-sacrifice so as to glorify God. That was his purpose in life—and must become his disciples' purpose (John 12:23–28). Paul gave the best exposition of God's eternal purpose (Eph. 3:1–13, especially Eph. 3:11). In Matthew 28:18–20 the going, baptizing, and teaching are circumstantial participles; the only imperative is "disciple" the nations (by glorifying God). "Christ in you" (Col. 1:24–29) is the hope of God's glory—of God's being made known.

Options for Preaching

The exposition of many biblical passages and verses given above provides suggestions and insights for sermon series and separate occasional sermons. The definitions are basic to correct the popular theological misconception that revelation is propositional and salvation is legalistic and judicial. One's view of evangelism and missions is essentially different when understood as productive of personal relations between God and people throughout history. In the context of this perspective, a preacher can put together various combinations of key scripture passages with descriptive sermon titles.

In a series of sermons on evangelism and missions, the introductory sermon could well be on theological foundations for evangelism and missions. In this connection, before considering the definitions of evangelism and missions, two prior definitions would be needed: first, *revelation* is the coincidence of divinely guided events with minds (of the prophets as persons of God) divinely illumined (by the Holy Spirit—and therefore inspired) to interpret those events in the light of conditions of their time for their contemporaries and for people of later generations; second, the *Bible* is the record and interpretation of the mighty deeds of God and of the experiences of his people in relation to them. Then follows the definitions of evangelism and missions.

In preaching on the theme of this article, key topics and scriptures are aspects of its development.

Hope for sinners. The predicament of people, individually and corporately, is that they are *sinners* (Rom. 3:22–23). Their only hope is that "God is love" (1 John 4:9). God has graciously made himself known through Jesus Christ who "became flesh and dwelt among us" (John 1:14). In response, whoever *believes* (trusts) will be saved (John 3:16).

"Father, glorify thy name." After having demonstrated concern for all peoples (Gen. 1:11), God turned to a particular people (Gen. 12:1–3), establishing a *priest-nation* (Ex. 19:6). From this nation came Jesus, who saw that through death

comes life. This was expressed in the *grain of wheat* passage
(John 12:23–28). "Father, glorify thy name" (John 12:28) was
the meaning of life, and of his disciples' lives, and of the lives
of Christians through the centuries. "To glorify" is to manifest
or make known the character of God, whom to know is eternal
life.

Eternal purpose. It was Paul who was given the insight that
God has realized (literally "made") in Christ Jesus (Eph.
3:1–13, especially v. 11) an eternal purpose. Paul further emphasized that "Christ in you" is the hope of God's glory
(Col. 1:24–29).

The Great Commission (Matt. 28:18–20) is the *climax* of
Christ's exposition and emphasis on evangelism and missions.

EVIL

Marjorie Hewitt Suchocki

Christians have understood evil in three categories: (1) natural evil, sometimes called metaphysical evil, or the problem of
violence and destruction originating in the nonhuman world;
(2) physical evil, or the problem of illness, pain, and death for
human and other sentient beings, and (3) moral evil, also called
sin, or the problem of unintentional or intentional violation of
that which is good, or ordained by God.

The existence of evil entails four closely related themes.

Origins, or why evil exists. Responses emphasize either creaturely freedom or the necessary conditions of finitude, or some
combination of both as the cause of evil.

Theodicy, or the problem of how it is that a God who is pre-
sumed to be all-powerful and all-good created a world in which
evil arises. Responses typically stress the vital importance of
creaturely freedom to a good universe, or modify the meaning
of divine power, seeing it as relational rather than as unilateral,
and hence as limited by creaturely freedom.

Interrelationship of the categories of evil, or whether one
form precedes and is causative for the others. The dominant
(but not sole) Christian response places moral evil as the fundamental cause of physical and natural evil.

Resolution, or what one might hope with regard to any ultimate end of evil. Most Christian responses require a twofold
solution: historical possibilities of addressing evil, and a post-
historical resolution in the life of God.

Analysis

While the biblical presentation of evil is in dramatic form, the subsequent Christian tradition employed a philosophical or theological approach. Most contemporary responses to evil still reflect positions first developed in the early church, particularly by Augustine. Thus a contemporary analysis requires some understanding of at least the Augustinian tradition.

Augustine developed a threefold answer to evil, the most fundamental of which turned on creaturely freedom. He held that all evil is the result of sin and its punishment, and the first sin developed when created beings chose not to cling to God as their source of life but to turn instead to their own resources. This is also phrased as a turning of the will from unqualified love of God, to love for finite things in and of themselves. In either case, since God is the source of life, to turn from God is necessarily to turn away from life. Hence sin is a move toward death, bringing about evil. Furthermore, there is a solidarity of all human life, so that the sin committed by one has an effect upon all. The human condition is one of brokenness, inherited from generations of misused human freedom.

In answering why God would create creatures with the freedom to bring about so calamitous a reality as sin and evil, Augustine argued that freedom was itself a great good, bestowed by a good God upon creation, and that even its misuse tended toward the good inasmuch as it contributed to the fullness of existence. The excellence of creation includes all possible orders of existence, even that order which freely chooses sin and evil. Punishment of temporal and eternal death balances the evil, resulting in a perfectly ordered harmony of creation in its fullness.

Finally, Augustine contributed the notion that evil is a privation of being and not a solid thing in and of itself. Evil is the absence of good, or a parasite presupposing the good. A contemporary example is the illness of cancer: its consuming of the life of its host is at the same time the destruction of its own basis for existence.

Whereas for much of Christian history creaturely freedom was considered to be the source of evil, twentieth-century views tend to understand evil as resulting from some combination of finitude and freedom. Finite existence is sufficient to explain natural and physical evils such as earthquakes, fires, illness, and death, whereas moral evil results from the misuse of one's freedom. The forms combine in instances such as freely choosing to use the environment in such a way that ecological disasters occur, or choosing to abuse one's body so as to invite sickness or death.

Biblical Instances

Recent scholarship in the Hebrew scriptures uncovers layers of the tradition whereby early interpretations of evil portray a primordial chaos, a deterrent to creation over which the creator God prevails (Ps. 74:12–17; Isa. 51:9–11). This watery chaos is personified as Leviathan, a sea monster with analogies to the Babylonian goddess Tiamat. Progressively (Psalm 82; Genesis 1; Job) the chaos is projected, first as controlled, and then as created by Yahweh. The complexity of evil in the Hebrew scriptures includes a pervasive perception of creation as an ongoing drama in which human participation in righteousness, or the law of God, is essential to the completion of creation through order, and the final overcoming of chaos. Creation presumes an ultimate completion in which chaos and evil shall be no more, and God shall reign supreme. This completion involves human participation, both ritualistic and moral.

The New Testament texts presuppose Hebrew scriptures, the writings of later Judaism, and the speculative/mythic thinking of the Hellenistic world. Evil is primarily moral evil—disobedience to the divine command—and, as in the Hebrew scriptures, moral evil affects the whole creation negatively (Romans 8). In the Gospels, the issue is presented primarily in terms of the reign of God, or the complete realization within the human community and therefore the cosmos of God's righteous order. In the epistles, human righteousness is necessary for the completion of creation, and this righteousness is presented as accomplished by Jesus of Nazareth on behalf of all creation. His death as expiation for moral evil is offered for all, and his resurrection is God's re-creation of the world, into which all may enter. The theme of creation and re-creation through Christ is emphasized particularly in Pauline literature through the parallel of Jesus Christ with Adam. Thus the New Testament story is not discontinuous with the themes of the Hebrew scriptures, but rather presents a variation that becomes foundational for Christianity.

Both Testaments reflect a fundamental ambiguity with regard to the relationship of moral to physical evil. A pervasive strain emphasizes a cause-effect relationship between the two: "on the day that you eat thereof, you shall surely die." Suffering and death are associated with sin. The theme is reflected in the New Testament in John 9, where the disciples ask Jesus who sinned, "this man or his parents," that he was born blind. The connection is challenged in Job and Habakkuk in the Old Testament, and by Jesus' response to the disciples in the New. Job illustrates that personal calamity befalls even the righteous. Habakkuk notes that the sufferings experienced by Israel through military invasions were visited upon them by a nation far more unjust than they; therefore, there is no exact correlation between sin and misfortune. In the New Testament, Jesus responds to the disciples' query by stating that the man's blindness was the fault of neither the man nor his parents, but was "for the glory of God." There is, then, a mystery to evil. The profound response given in Job is an experience of the majesty of God; the final answer in the New Testament is in the book of Revelation, where the completion of creation takes place when God will wipe away every tear, and the "leaves of the tree of life" are given for the healing of the nations.

Options for Preaching

Repercussions of evil. The contemporary sensitivity to the interrelated nature of all existence heightens the awareness that evil in any sector of existence has repercussions on all others. The clearest example is that a nuclear disaster in one portion of the world has negative effects to varying degrees throughout the world, but the connectedness holds for the smallest as well as the greatest of evils. The ancient perception of the solidarity of human beings among themselves and with nature once again speaks forcefully to experience.

Mystery and hope. As noted above in John 9, Jesus says that the man's blindness was the fault of no person but was "for the glory of God." Evil is couched in mystery and, as the books of Job and Revelation attest, can ultimately be faced with hope for healing.

Working with texts. Classic texts for preaching on evil include Genesis 2 and 3; Job; Romans 5, 6, 7, and 8; and Revelation 21 and 22. However, there is no text that does not in some way address itself to the issue of evil and God's redemptive answer. The following questions are suggested for use as one works with a scripture text on the issue of evil for the purpose of preaching.

A. The problem:

1. What is the human predicament portrayed in the text?
2. Within the text itself, are there a variety of ways by which that predicament may be interpreted?

3. Is there a connection between the human predicament and the wider world of nature?
4. Is the issue related primarily to personal or societal suffering?
5. How does the predicament in the text relate to contemporary experience?

B. The resolution:

1. Does the text portray a way out of the predicament?
2. Is this form of redemption partial or complete?
3. Does this form of redemption take place in history? When?
4. Does the text suggest a resolution beyond history?
5. Does the resolution in the text have any bearing on contemporary experience?

C. The means of redemption:

1. What needs to happen in order for redemption to take place in this text?
2. Is there human as well as divine action?
3. What must God be like, in order to accomplish this redemption?
4. What are the personal and social implications of this redemption?
5. How does God as portrayed through this text speak to present issues?

Theological issues to bear in mind concern the personal *and* social dimensions of all evil in this interconnected world; the role that free will plays in evil; and the power of God for redemption. A biblical fact to keep in mind is that scripture is not particularly concerned with the question of the origin of evil; it is fundamentally concerned with the overcoming of evil through the power and empowerment of God.

FAITH

Glenn H. Asquith, Jr.

Faith normally refers to belief, trust, or confidence in something or someone. It can connote an expression of loyalty, as in "faithful to a cause." It can refer to a specific system of belief such as "the Catholic faith." Hebrews 11:1 defines faith as the "assurance of things hoped for, the conviction of things not seen." Thus, faith is a transcendent awareness based on religious experience. In Christianity, God is the object of faith, which is professed through belief in Jesus Christ, the Son of God, as Lord and Savior.

Analysis

In the psychology of religion, faith is based on the subjective experience of the presence of God in one's life. While not devoid of a rational dimension (such as creedal statements), it is primarily nonrational. While systematic confessions of faith have been necessary in preserving the basic tenets of the church, it is the mystical perception of God's providence and intervention in one's life that provides vitality and fidelity to a given belief system. Worship is a collective expression of faith in which the common sacramental symbols of water, bread, and wine, along with prayers, liturgies, and scripture, become reminders and signs of the action of God in human life. In the context of worship, preaching is a living and contemporary statement of faith that is based on the scriptural witness to God's action in human history.

In pastoral theology, faith is the opposite of fear and anxiety. Søren Kierkegaard speaks of the "leap of faith" that is taken when a person feels secure enough in his or her relationship with God to plunge into the unfamiliar, to renounce old patterns and habits and accept a new way of life. As with Abraham and Sarah in Hebrews 11:8–12, faith enables one to respond in obedience and trust to the call of God into new and unknown places of discipleship and service. Thus, while faith is a source of stability in one's life, it is not static; one's relationship with God changes and evolves in the same way as human relationships.

Biblical Instances

Old Testament. A primary theme of faith in the Old Testament is trust in God in the midst of adversity. This is portrayed in the story of Job, where fear of the Lord provides a sense of security and confidence (Job 4:6), and the sovereignty and purposefulness of God is acknowledged in contrast to humanity's finite nature (Job 42:1–6). This is also the message of many of the psalms, especially songs of trust such as Psalm 23 and Psalm 130.

In a broader sense, faith in the Old Testament is portrayed in the covenant relationship between God and Israel. This was initiated with Abraham (Gen. 12:1–3) and established through Israel's deliverance from bondage in Egypt (Ex. 13:17–14:31), followed by Israel's sojourn at Sinai, where the Ten Commandments were given to Moses (Ex. 20:1–17) and the covenant code was established. The covenant theme is restated in Deuteronomy 6:4–9.

New Testament. The Synoptic Gospels portray the positive results of the response of faith in Jesus Christ. Faith is a source of healing for the woman whose hemorrhage ceased when she touched the fringe of Jesus' garment (Mark 5:24b–34; Matt. 9:20–22; Luke 8:42–48). Faith led to salvation for the woman who anointed Jesus' feet with ointment (Luke 7:50).

In his postresurrection encounter with Thomas in John 20:24–29, Jesus proclaims that, in the future, saving faith will come to those who can believe in the unseen Christ. Paul reflects this truth in Romans 8:24–25.

Based on the gospel message, Pauline theology asserts that one is justified through faith in Jesus Christ and not through works (Rom. 3:21–31). Ephesians 2:8–10 states that good works are the result of faith, not the cause of salvation. Thus faith is the essential foundation for living the Christian life.

Options for Preaching

Faith versus anxiety. Jesus' discourse in Matthew 6:25–34 calls for a transcendent view of life, which trusts that basic life needs will be met when one lives in faith to the glory of God. This is also addressed in Jesus' assertion in Mark 8:35 about saving and losing one's life. When Jesus' disciples awaken him in fear during a storm at sea, Jesus asks, "Why are you afraid? Have you no faith?" (Mark 4:40; Matt. 8:26; Luke 8:25).

The unshakable kingdom. Hebrews 12:25–29 asserts that, while heaven and earth may be shaken, the kingdom of God will remain, even in the midst of tremendous change and upheaval. The steadfast love of God and the redeeming power of Jesus Christ are two constants upon which the people of God can always depend.

The greatest legacy. In 2 Timothy 1:3–7, Timothy is reminded of the "sincere faith" of his grandmother Lois and his mother Eunice, a faith that he has now inherited. This great gift is to be rekindled into Timothy's own unique expression of faith in a spirit of power and love.

FAMILY

J. Bill Ratliff

The family is the basic unit of society. "Family" usually refers to a mother, a father, and their children. Broader definitions include people living under the same roof, all of one's relatives, and finally the human family. Some churches have begun to define family as including single persons (families of one), blended families, single-parent families, and other variations.

Analysis

The Bible presupposes the family. Although the Bible shows wide diversity in its approach to the family, certain themes recur throughout. (1) In the family, deep feelings are engendered and a legacy passed down through generations. (2) Children should honor their parents. (3) The circumstances of early family life help set the course for adult life. (4) While the family is important, God is most important. (5) Following the will of God may mean one must leave one's family.

Biblical Instances

Old Testament. The Fifth Commandment, to honor one's father and mother "that your days may be long" (Ex. 20:12), implies that someday children will become old and will need the same kind of treatment in order to live long.

The flawed nature of families is revealed in Cain's jealousy and murder of his brother Abel (Gen. 4:8) and in Hosea's marriage to a prostitute (Hos. 1:2).

New Testament. The New Testament takes the family seriously but not ultimately so. Jesus at age twelve stayed at the Temple to do God's will, although he remained obedient to his parents (Luke 2:49–51).

The Gospels—especially Luke—assert the priority of the realm of God over every human allegiance, including the family (see Luke 8:19–21). Luke 14:26 leaves no room for divided loyalties.

The early church believed that all believers are members of the household of God (Eph. 2:19). Providing for one's family was a demonstration of faith (1 Tim. 5:8).

Options for Preaching

Family roles. Paul's writing has often been used to reinforce traditional roles for husband and wife. However, a close reading of 1 Corinthians 7:2–5 and Ephesians 5:21–33 shows a real mutuality of respect and love.

Secrets. All families face difficulties. The fact that one of Adam and Eve's sons murdered his own brother can help Christians accept that no family is perfect (Gen. 4:1–16). But, as with Cain, God seeks out those who hide from God or from one's family. God is a God of openness, confession, and forgiveness, not of secrets.

Honor and "hate" your father and mother. Juxtaposing the Fifth Commandment with the Lukan verse (14:26) points up the importance of parents without making them of primary importance. One can honor one's parents while still being one's own person and placing God first.

Hospitality. Hospitality to the stranger is a major value espoused by scripture (Gen. 18:1–15; 1 Kings 17:9–24; Luke 24:13–35). Strangers can bring a family new life and gifts from God. Hospitality is the mark of a family's healthy openness to others and to the world.

FEAR AND ANXIETY

Ernest White

Fear is an unpleasant emotion of anticipation of, or awareness of, some kind of nameable threat. Anxiety, by contrast, is an often unfocused sense of apprehension.

Analysis

Though intimately related, fear and anxiety differ. Fear has an identifiable source, whether the threat is real or not. The object of fear can be pointed to as something (imagined or physical) in the environment of the person who fears.

Anxiety is more murky and less identifiable. Anxiety is a free-floating feeling of uneasiness that has no specific object. Anxiety brings a certain fogginess with it that keeps objects threatening but not quite visible. Sometimes the anxious fog itself is the source of dis-ease.

In many ways, fear and anxiety connect. Sometimes anxiety

settles on an object or situation with which a person must live. That results in fears of open spaces (agoraphobia), heights (acrophobia), and so on. Managing one's fear and anxiety can be challenging. The preacher who can help listeners with these ghosts invites the Christ who calms the seas for frightened disciples.

Biblical Instances

The Old Testament word *yirah* carries the meanings "to be afraid," "to fear" or "to reverence," with many other nuances. Human beings are the subjects of fear from the beginning: Adam speaks for humanity and the generations that follow him when he confesses, "I was afraid . . . [so] I hid myself" (Gen. 3:10).

Other instances of fear abound. Isaac is afraid to identify Rebekah as his wife because he fears envious men will kill him (Gen. 26:17). Moses, after killing an Egyptian, feared the wrath of the pharaoh (Ex. 2:14). Psalm 55 is an anguished plea from one distraught and terrified of violence and death; the writer turns to God to assuage those fears: "men of blood and treachery shall not live out half their days. But I will trust in thee" (55:23).

Very often it is God who is feared, as in Isaiah 8:12–22: "let him be your fear, and let him be your dread" (v. 13). Exodus 15:11; Deuteronomy 28:58; and Psalm 96:4 put forth similar messages.

Phobos is the major word for fear in the New Testament. Among its other meanings are those of "running away" or "fleeing." Jesus generated fear by his miraculous deeds, as Luke notes in 5:26; 7:16; and 8:37. In this regard, fear appears as an aspect of faith.

Jesus also addressed the issue of anxiety, using the word *merimnao*, in Matthew 6:25–34. If God takes care of the birds of the air or the grass of the field, surely God will take loving care of the faithful.

Fear and anxiety appear in both positive and negative light. Fear (reverence) for God is the basis of true wisdom, as emphasized in Job (28:28), Psalms, and Proverbs and throughout the Old Testament. Positive fear includes both concern for righteousness (Ps. 38:18) and concern for others.

Negative fear, the more familiar kind, focuses on fear of other people who may hurt or persecute. But the Bible discourages negative fear and anxiety, such as anxiety about material things and the forces of nature. John presents a picture of love free from fear.

Options for Preaching

Preaching on fear and anxiety can be approached from many angles. The few options spelled out here scarcely exhaust the possibilities but do demonstrate the variety of needs.

Fears and anxieties can expose idols. Jesus spoke pointedly about this when he warned about being "anxious about what we shall eat or what we shall put on." He confronted the admirable young man with his idolatry when he asked him to sell all and come to follow him. The young man's grief resulted from his anxiety about keeping his "many things." In Luke 12, the man anxious to get everything coming to him in the inheritance led Jesus to identify covetousness as idolatrous anxiety. James points to anxiety as the source of destructive competition, in which people fight to get as much or more than the next person (4:1–4).

Managing fear and anxiety. This is a major theme of the Psalms (23) as well as of Jesus' teaching. Management begins with getting in touch with and owning one's fears and anxieties. They can often control a person from out of sight.

The next step in fear management comes when one names it and refuses to run from it. Containing fear and anxiety requires courage; the Bible is rich as a courage resource (2 Chron. 15:7; 2 Cor. 5:6–21; 1 Thess. 2:2; 1 Cor. 16:13).

The soul's need for serenity. Fear and anxiety create need; they attack and destroy peace and serenity of life. Hence, offering sources of peace for the center of a person's life meets a frequent need. Quietness of soul is a most potent antidote for the infections of fear and anxiety. Preaching can squeeze people or it can help them find space in which to find *shalom.* Paul's word (Rom. 8:15) is needed.

Trust vanquishes fear. With trust, the believer can triumph over fear and anxiety. Jesus' basic message on the subject was that it required learning to trust so well that fear and anxiety are pushed out. Perhaps few spiritual challenges are so great. A connection could be made between the forces of trust and love against fear: "There is no fear in love, for perfect love casts out fear" (1 John 4:18).

Positive kinds of anxiety. Eu-anxiety—good anxiety—is translated "care." The Bible encourages people to be anxious. To be fully Christian, it is necessary to be anxious for good and for the good of others. Preaching can direct anxiety into productive paths while helping people overcome its more destructive effects.

FORGIVENESS

Glenn H. Asquith, Jr.

In human terms, forgiveness refers to pardoning or being pardoned for transgressions or offenses between persons. It can also refer to a disposition or willingness to forgive. In biblical understanding, forgiveness is an act of God's grace that allows for restoration of a relationship with God. In the Old Testament, forgiveness for sin is part of the covenant relationship with God that comes after human acts of sacrifice and repentance. In the New Testament, Jesus establishes the covenant of forgiveness through his atoning act on the cross; forgiveness comes from repentance and confession of faith in Christ, thus reconciling humanity in a right relationship with God.

Analysis

In biblical theology, forgiveness is the removal of barriers between God and humanity. The words used for forgiveness in both Hebrew and Greek mean literally "to send away." God has the power to remove sin and thus restore or establish a relationship with humanity.

However, this removal of transgressions requires effort on humanity's part. First, as Jesus instructs his disciples in the Sermon on the Mount (Matt. 6:14–15), one will not be forgiven unless one is willing to forgive others their trespasses against one; only a forgiving heart can receive the gift of forgiveness.

Second, this implies that forgiveness should be received with gratitude; it is a gift of grace, which God did not have to give. When humans are grateful for this gift, instead of taking it for granted, they are more likely to extend this precious gift to others who have offended them.

A third, and perhaps more difficult, condition for forgiveness is that people must be able to forgive themselves. When they feel deep and massive guilt for their own shortcomings, mistakes, and transgressions, they are unable to hear any word of forgiveness from God or others. Sometimes they cripple themselves with this guilt because, oddly enough, to accept forgiveness could result in the necessity to move on from a current, comfortable place.

Confession is necessary before forgiveness can be received, and before one can accept the unacceptable parts of oneself. For example, willingness to have God remove one's defects in character is number six in the Twelve Steps of Alcoholics Anonymous. In these steps, readiness for forgiveness comes only after admitting one's powerlessness over alcohol, expressing faith and obedience to God, and confessing to God, self, and another human being the exact nature of one's wrongs.

Biblical Instances

Old Testament. The conclusion of the Joseph story in Genesis 50:15–21 provides an important commentary on the nature and source of forgiveness. While Joseph could forgive his brothers for their evil deeds against him, he asserts that ultimately only God can forgive and transform humanity's transgressions to a good end.

Numbers 15:22–26 describes cultic regulations regarding how a corporate sin offering is to be brought before the Lord and says that the congregation shall be forgiven as the priest makes atonement on their behalf.

Daniel's prayer of confession on behalf of Jerusalem in Daniel 9:4–19 becomes a model for the attitude and form of contrition before the Lord. Daniel seeks forgiveness not "on the ground of our righteousness, but on the ground of thy great mercy" (v. 18).

In a cry for help for personal trouble, the author of Psalm 130 finds hope in the assurance that there is forgiveness with God (v. 4).

New Testament. Following his instruction to Peter in Matthew 18:21–22 that forgiveness of one's brother is beyond calculating, Jesus tells the parable of the king and his servants in verses 23–35 to state that God will not show mercy to anyone who does not forgive others.

The account of Jesus' forgiveness and healing of the paralytic in Mark 2:1–12 causes the scribes to raise the point made in the Joseph story (Gen. 50:15–21) that only God can forgive sins. The physical healing is added to the forgiveness of sins in order to demonstrate Jesus' identity and authority as the Son of God.

At Pentecost, Peter issued a call to repentance, that all be baptized in the name of Christ for the forgiveness of sins (Acts 2:38). Peter repeats this message in Acts 10:43 in the story of the conversion of Cornelius. Paul brings the message of forgiveness at Antioch in Acts 13:38 and in his defense before Agrippa in Acts 26:18.

Options for Preaching

Jesus, the new covenant. In the account of the Last Supper in Matthew 26:26–29, Jesus proclaims that his blood is the new covenant, poured out for many for the forgiveness of sins (v. 28).

The barriers are broken. God's initiative in Christ breaks down all barriers between God and humanity and makes possible humanity's adoption as children of God (John 1:12–13).

Forgiving and forgiven. Forgiving one another is not only a prerequisite to receiving God's forgiveness, it is a mark of Christian community, a primary ingredient in solving human conflict (Eph. 5:32).

GOD

John Macquarrie

In Christianity, God may be defined as the one ultimate holy and personal reality, on which all else depends. The English word "God" has an equivalent in virtually every language of the world. But the word has been differently understood in different cultures. In some, there are many gods (polytheism), in others only one God is acknowledged (monotheism). This diversity makes it difficult to give any brief definition of "God." Where there are many gods, perhaps none is truly infinite, though all are supposed to be superhuman or supernatural. But generally in the history of religion the many gods tend to merge into a single universal deity. Where this happens and one god alone is recognized, such a god is held to be the source from which all finite beings have their origin, the ultimate reality as defined above.

Analysis

Basic attributes. If God is infinite, there is a unique difference between God and all finite beings. Thus the difficulty in defining God arises not just from the diverse ways of conceiving God but from the divine infinity, so all religions recognize an element of irreducible mystery in God. Thus God-language can never be precise or exhaustive. Everyday language applies literally only to finite beings within the world, so when words such as *wise* or *good* are used with reference to God, they are stretched beyond normal usage and employed analogically. Even to say "God exists" is not a simple literal statement, for "existing" usually means occurring within the spatiotemporal world, and God is not an item in that world. Again, although Christian, Jewish, and Muslim traditions generally use personal language about God, in some Asian religions impersonal language is used, and mystics in all traditions claim that personal language is not literally applicable to God.

God and the world. In some traditions, God is conceived as utterly transcendent of the world, unaffected by what goes on in it; in others, God is believed to be in varying degrees immanent in the world and therefore affected by it. In biblical religion, God's transcendence rather than immanence has been stressed, but not exclusively. In the Old Testament, God shares in the afflictions of the people and is involved in their history, while in the New Testament, through the incarnation of the Word, God actually enters the stream of human history, and the incipient doctrine of the Trinity teaches that God is permanently involved with the world.

God in theology and philosophy. The idea of God originates in religious experiences in which human beings believe that their lives are touched by a transcendent reality. Some experiences of this kind are so vivid and formative that they rank as "revelations." But as people have reflected on these experiences, the idea of God has become of interest to philosophy. Sometimes this interest has been critical, as in attempts to purge God-language of gross anthropomorphisms. Sometimes it has been constructive, as in attempts to construe arguments for the existence of God in the face of atheistic objections. Some writers have sharply contrasted the God of faith and revelation with the God of philosophical speculation. But a good case can be made that both theology and philosophy make valuable contributions to the question of God.

Biblical Instances

Old Testament. The Hebrew scriptures offer a noble and impressive picture of God. God is depicted in Genesis as the *Creator*, the source of all existent beings. No proof of God's existence is given. God is not another existent item in the world, but the precondition that anything whatever may exist. God is not another being, but rather "Letting-be." "God said, 'Let there be light'; and there was light" (Gen. 1:3). Creation culminates in the human couple, created in the "image" and "likeness" of God (Gen. 1:26). They are destined to be God's covenant partners, the special link between God and creation, though they reject the relation. The Abraham cycle of stories introduces further understandings of God. In electing Abraham and his descendants to a special vocation, God appears as the *Providence* that guides but does not coerce world history. In Exodus, God appears to Moses as the *Revealer* who makes known God's name as "I AM WHO I AM" (Ex. 3:14). This confirms God's position as ultimate Reality, while as the *Liberator* who leads the slaves out of Egypt and then as the *Lawgiver* who utters from Sinai the demand for righteousness, God is revealed as the great *Moral Power*, a picture that is reinforced by the teaching of the prophets and is the dominant theme in the Old Testament teaching about God. The story of Job teaches the *Mystery* of God, whose ways, as the Infinite, are not humanity's ways.

New Testament. It is the same God who is met in the New Testament, but Christians believe that with the coming of Jesus Christ a new and decisive insight was given into this God. Certainly in the Hebrew scriptures God was not only a lawgiver demanding righteousness, but a God of grace and mercy, and this point has been obscured by some Christian writers who have exaggerated Jewish legalism. But in the New Testament there is an undeniable shift in emphasis toward the grace, forgiveness, and love of God. This stems from Jesus' own teaching about God, in his parables, in the Sermon on the Mount, and above all in his own obedience to his vocation that brought him to the cross. Genesis teaches that all human beings were created to manifest the image and likeness of God, but that image was speedily marred by the Fall. Jesus Christ is the "new Adam," who fulfilled the destiny in which the first Adam failed and who is therefore, in Paul's language, "the image of the invisible God" (Col. 1:15). Very important, too, is the prologue to John's Gospel. The God who speaks has been uttering God's Word from the beginning, but that Word has become flesh in Jesus Christ, giving a living picture of God in concrete historical form. The Christian doctrine of God is summed up in the words, "God is love" (1 John 4:8).

Options for Preaching

Creation. The environmental dangers now threatening the future of the whole human race have given a renewed relevance to the doctrine of creation. But in presenting God as Creator, the preacher should maintain a proper balance between divine transcendence and divine immanence, to which attention has been drawn above. Where immanence is ignored and the creation is seen as simply the consequence of a divine *fiat*, the created order is secularized and "dedivinized" to the extent that it becomes merely material for human exploitation. But if God is immanent in the creation, putting God's own being into it perhaps as an artist puts himself or herself into the artwork, then creation has the dignity of a sacrament and calls for appreciation as well as exploitation. The human race is the highest reach of creation (at least, on this planet) but bears the image of God; humanity, in turn, reaches its highest point in Jesus Christ, the very image of the invisible God.

God as ultimate Reality. This is a world in which many enslaving idolatries oppress men and women. These can best be exposed by being set against the ultimacy of God, who liberates from their power. This is true of the idolatry of a book (fundamentalism), of technology, of material prosperity, of political or ecclesiastical tyrannies. Why was Jesus condemned? The details of the trial are not clear, but it seems obvious that the true reason was that the Jewish and Roman establishments alike saw that their claims to authority were undermined by this teacher's proclamation of the kingdom of God.

The crucified God. In spite of what has just been said, the power of God should never be so emphasized that it obscures the fact that in Christ, God came in weakness to stand with his creatures in their sufferings. This leads to the all-important proclamation of the love of God, but it is a love centered on the cross and therefore completely purified of the sentimentalism that has devalued the meaning of love as it is portrayed in much of today's culture.

The God of reason. In a world where many people have lost faith in God, the preacher, especially if he or she has had some training in philosophy, should be willing to preach on the *evidences* for God. Surely God is *for* reason, not against it.

GRACE

Stephen L. Stell

Grace is God's free and unmerited favor toward humanity. It may refer to God's personal attitude, God's actions, or their human effects. For Christians grace is revealed and communicated through the life, death, resurrection, and ongoing activity of Jesus Christ through the Holy Spirit.

Analysis

As the heart of God's being, grace is expressed in creation, in establishing a covenant community, and in the faithfulness undergirding that community.

God's gracious love poured out for humanity in Jesus Christ, poured out so supremely in God's forgiveness, evokes the response of faith. This trusting acceptance and personal commitment is itself a gift of God's grace, not overpowering, but transforming human will.

Such faith unites believers with Christ and thereby enables participation in God's grace. Union with Christ through the Holy Spirit naturally shapes believers into Christ's likeness. This re-creative grace of the Spirit transforms existence so that God's power and purposes become one's own. The church is nourished in this grace through Word and sacrament and empowered to extend God's grace to the world through active service.

Biblical Instances

In the Old Testament, various descriptions convey God's gracious character apart from the word "grace" (Deut. 7:7–8). God's grace is especially evident in actions and attitudes showing mercy and steadfast love (*hesed*). Such faithfulness generally surrounds the covenant, and also applies to humanity.

The undeserved favor of greater toward lesser (*hen*), often translated "grace" (Jer. 31:2–3), cannot be shown by humanity to God. This one-sidedness suggests that regeneration and obedience are finally God's gift (Jer. 31:31–34; Ezek. 36:26–27).

In the New Testament, grace is central. Jesus' inversion of first and last, his seeking to save the lost, and his parables concerning God's character (Matt. 20:1–16; Luke 14:16–24) emphasize divine grace. Paul develops grace and its defining context (Rom. 3:21–4:25), highlighting God's forgiveness of sinners through Christ (Rom. 5:8). This gift of salvation through faith (Eph. 2:8) creates a new justified and sanctified life of faithful action (1 Cor. 6:9–11; Col. 2:9–15; Titus 3:4–7).

Options for Preaching

The sufficiency of grace. Reliance upon God's grace does not lessen human effort and responsibility, but increases it (1 Cor.

15:10). All excuses for inaction are radically challenged by God's gracious power made perfect in weakness (2 Cor. 12:7–10). God not only provides grace sufficient for every personal need but also empowers human action addressing the needs of church and world in faithfulness to Christ.

From grace to grace. The grace of God poured out in Jesus Christ is the same grace transforming the lives of believers. This means that one learns about God's grace not only from biblical stories but also from faithful lives following Christ in the world. The church, in living from Christ and for Christ, becomes Christ's body participating in the further extension of God's grace to those in need (Acts 20:28–35).

GRIEF

David K. Switzer

Grief refers to that complex interaction of feelings, thinking patterns, and physiological responses to the loss by any means of any person, place, activity, or whatever with whom (or which) a person has identified, who (or which) has become a significant part of one's own self.

Analysis

The impact of grief is pain, distress, often anger and guilt, and uncertainty about how long one can bear such suffering. It also entails the disturbance of family and other relationships. As a threat to one's being, it is always a challenge to one's faith. Grief is absolutely universal, beginning with losses in infancy and continuing throughout one's life.

Biblical Instances

Old Testament. The many individual losses illustrate the universality and intensity of grief, the variety of losses, the similarities and differences in the way people grieve, and the way in which the people in the stories openly weep and speak of their pain. One cluster presents a series of such losses: 1 Sam. 15:35; 20:34, 41; 24:16; 25:1; 2 Sam. 12:15–23; 18:32–33.

The Lament psalms (such as 38; 39; 42; 71; 77; etc.) are powerful expressions of grieving and the various ingredients of grieving. The structure of these psalms provides a model for working through grief in the light of faith.

New Testament. "Blessed are those who mourn, for they shall be comforted" (Matt. 5:4). Though appealing, this verse must not be used to apply to mourning following a death. The *only* mourning this word (*pentheo*) refers to in the New Testament is that sad regret over one's own sin or the sin of one's community of faith (also Mark 9:15; Luke 6:25; 2 Cor. 12:21; James 4:9; Rev. 18:11). The word is used in each case to refer to the readiness or lack of readiness of Jesus' hearers to enter the kingdom of God. Readiness is the sincere mourning over one's sins.

Another verse, "that you may not grieve as others do who have no hope" (1 Thess. 4:13), refers to the grieving by Christians for those Christians who have died prior to the church's anticipated return of Christ. The statement has suggested to some that because Christians have hope of resurrection through Christ, it is improper for them to grieve or that grieving indicates a lack of faith. Rather, the meaning is to clarify that because of faith in Christ, grieving is set in a different context (the resurrection community) and has a different perspective (the resurrection hope). The person who has died is not to be grieved for. People *do* grieve at their own real and painful loss, as did Jesus, the very representative and conveyor of the hope of God's future for God's people.

Options for Preaching

The church as the community of the bereaved. The church has been referred to as the community of faith, the servant community, and so on. But it is also the grieving community. The losses Christians experience become a part of the continued life of the whole congregation and provide the opportunity for the reaffirmation of hope (see 1 Thess. 4:13).

The universality of grief. Scriptures in the Old Testament (as discussed above) point to grief's universality. The Lament psalms and their structures provide examples of the process of grief.

How may others help the grieving? A clue to the answer is found in Romans 12:15: "weep with those who weep." The whole of Romans 12 details examples of how members of the body of Christ are to relate to one another. Pat "answers" to a bereaved person have a negative impact. Rather, "weep with." Be empathetic, relate emotionally, share feelings.

GUIDANCE

James W. Crawford

Guidance refers to direction given one by another. For those who confess the biblical faith, the most significant guidance comes from the Spirit of God. Even through trouble, the faithful testify to God's guidance.

Analysis

Guidance by the Spirit of God is a component in the convictions of the faithful. Some people see direction for their lives given by their parents' priorities, their economic situation, their particular combination of genes. Others see in these "secular" circumstances the guidance of God.

Remarkable testimonies to God's guidance lie where men and women undergo severe trial. What some interpret as catastrophe, others understand as an opportunity to testify to God's goodness. What might paralyze some people, compelling them to deny God, others will understand as privilege to testify to the love and guidance of the Spirit.

Biblical Instances

Old Testament. Illustrations of God's guidance abound in the Old Testament. God appears to Abram in Ur and insists he leave for a promised land (Genesis 12). God guides Moses through his confrontations with Pharaoh (Exodus 5–14). God's guiding presence appears to Moses in the burning bush (Ex. 3:3) and leads the Hebrews across the desert (Ex. 13:17–27). Israel's story is uniquely one of God's guidance.

New Testament. God's guidance is no less evident in the New Testament. The Spirit guides Jesus through vocational tests in the desert, caring for him through crisis (Matt. 4:1–11). The Spirit undergirds and guides a ministry preaching the gospel to the poor, releasing captives, offering sight to the blind, proclaiming a new day of joy and freedom (Luke 4:18–21). Jesus' life is one guided by the Spirit.

Beyond the Gospels, the authors of the epistles tell of guidance by the Spirit for their troubled congregations, affirming time and again the new life they may be guided toward by the living God (see esp. Gal. 5:16–26, NEB).

Options for Preaching

Let the Spirit guide life. Paul is convinced the Spirit of Christ is a life-changing reality (Gal. 5:15–26). Life takes on new direction, new depth, new dimensions when God guides it. Love, joy, peace, patience, kindness, goodness, faithfulness, humility, and self-control reflect the character of life given guidance by the Spirit (Gal. 5:22).

Who guides people through tough times? The Spirit of God guides Jesus into the wilderness to wrestle with the dimensions of his vocation (Luke 4:1–13). He faces decisions regarding the integrity of his mission and the depth of his faith. The Spirit does not enable people to avoid tough decisions. The Spirit may lead the people of God to—and bear them through—tough times.

Guidance from the future. The people of the biblical faith gain guidance from God's future. Revelation 21 captures a picture of a glorious community where human life flourishes. John of Patmos is led by the spirit to a mountaintop and there he glimpses a "new Jerusalem" (Rev. 21:10). The Spirit is out there ahead of humanity, operating from God's recreated new future.

GUILT

Wayne E. Oates

Guilt is responsibility for an action or an event that offends, damages, or transgresses one's own sense of what is right or the well-being of another person. When a person feels directly responsible to God for this, the guilt is against God; it is sin. In a legal sense, guilt is the antonym of innocence, and one is innocent until proved in court of law to be guilty.

Analysis

One of the major distinctions in discussing guilt is whether or not the person *feels* guilty. The teachings and life-actions of Jesus, as described in the Gospels and the rest of the New Testament writings, provide criteria for informing and sensitizing the conscience of a person. The feeling of responsibility to God for one's behavior stimulates moral sensitivity. However, as is evident in 1 Timothy 4:2, a person's conscience can be seared. That person's *feeling* of guilt is thus anesthetized. As Paul says in Ephesians 4:18, people may be "darkened in their understanding, alienated from the life of God because of the ignorance in them, due to their hardness of heart; they have become callous and have given themselves up to licentiousness, greedy to practice every kind of uncleanness." Such apathy, or the incapacity to feel guilt, is certainly a factor in the homiletical treatment of guilt. Bringing people to an awareness of guilt is rarely done by harsh condemnation, but by purposeful persuasion and effective development of insight and personal conviction.

However, in contemporary thinking about moral responsibility, the word "guilt" is used prolifically to refer to having broken a law or to being convicted in court for breaking a law. Or, more often, it is used to refer to the *feelings* of guilt a person carries about in her or his spirit. These are rarely related to God. *Guilt,* then, is a term used to express feelings of self-condemnation or condemnation of another human being. *Sin* is used to speak of guilt for which a person feels directly responsible to God.

However, the modern burdensomeness of guilt is vividly portrayed in the teachings of both Jesus and Paul in their sensitivity to the weight of the Jewish law on the people. Jesus saw the masses of people as sheep without a shepherd, harassed and helpless under the crushing load of the legalism of his day. The same legalism in Christian circles today fills communicants with a load of guilt.

Biblical Instances

The experience of David when he sent Uriah the Hittite to certain death and then took unto himself Uriah's wife, Bathsheba, exemplifies high-handed sin. (See 2 Sam. 11:1–27.) But compare this with 2 Samuel 12:1–31 when in verse 12 David confesses his sin.

Jesus dealt with the issue of insensitivity to guilt with the metaphor of blindness. In John 9:39–40 he says, "For judgment I came into this world, that those who do not see may see, and that those who see may become blind." In response to this, some Pharisees said to him, "Are we also blind?" Jesus answered, "If you were blind, you would have no guilt; but now that you say, 'We see,' your guilt remains."

The word "guilt" in both the Old and New Testaments is synonymous with sin. Guilt is most often considered an accountability to God. Such guilt is sin. This is closely aligned with the Pauline conception of the law, "Now we know that whatever the law says it speaks to those who are under the law, so that every mouth may be stopped, and the whole world may be held accountable to God. For no human being will be justified in his sight by works of the law, since through the law comes knowledge of sin" (Rom. 3:19–20). The word for "guilty" or "held accountable" in this passage—*upodikos*—is used nowhere else in the New Testament.

Options for Preaching

The unnecessary loads of life (Isa. 61:103; Matt. 23:1–4; Matt. 11:28–30). These texts capture the essence of the comments above about the weight of the law upon people in Jesus' day and of the present day.

Understanding your own actions (Rom. 7:15–20). Here the weight of the law on Paul creates blindness of understanding to his contradictory thoughts and actions. The nameless burden of guilt lasts on in his life as a result of the deadening weight of the law.

Preparation for worship (Ps. 24:3–5). The ascent in the temple, the place of worship, calls for some heavy-duty self-searching. The prerequisites for full fellowship with God in worship are: (1) clean hands, (2) a pure heart, (3) freedom from all that is false, (4) freedom from deceitfulness.

HEAVEN

Cecil Murphey

Heaven expresses four concepts: an expanse over the earth, biblically called the firmament; God's creation and dwelling place; a substitute for the name of God; and, finally, the place humanity will dwell with God in the new heaven and earth at the end of time.

Analysis

The common Old Testament word means "the heights," while the New Testament word denotes "sky" or "air." Both refer to the atmosphere above the earth, making heaven "up" where clouds and tempests gather.

Heaven, identified as the dwelling place of God, is sometimes substituted for the name of God. Kingdom of heaven and kingdom of God are used interchangeably.

Sacred history looks toward Christ's return from heaven to gather God's elect. Because of sin, the old heaven and earth will then pass away. God has prepared a new heaven and earth as part of the divine plan.

Biblical Instances

The Old Testament uses heaven in a physical sense as an expanse over the earth (Gen. 1:7–8; Ps. 148:4). God possesses heaven (Gen. 14:19) and dwells there (Gen. 28:17; Ps. 80:14; Isa. 66:1).

In the New Testament, heaven is less geographic and more qualitative: the Holy Spirit comes from heaven at Jesus' baptism (Matt. 3:16–17); a sign from heaven (Mark 8:11) is a sign from God. It is the "better country" that God's people seek (Heb. 11:16); the abode of the Father (Matt. 6:9; 7:21), where the Christians receive rewards (Matt. 5:12), joy (Luke 15:7), and peace (Luke 19:38).

The new heavens (with new earth) refers to the perfected state of the created universe and the final dwelling place of the righteous (Isa. 66:22; 2 Peter 3:13; Rev. 21:1).

Options for Preaching

Names written in heaven (Luke 19:20; Heb. 12:23). This sermon could speak of the ultimate possession of the imperishable heritage (1 Peter 1:4–5) and assure believers of their relationship to God.

Something now, more later. Because heaven is the realm of God, God's people can now receive the blessings of citizenship (Phil. 3:20). In the future heaven will be a permanent dwelling (2 Cor. 5:1), an inheritance (1 Peter 2:4), where they will receive awards (Matt. 5:12) and treasures (Matt. 6:20).

Unknowable realm. Paul speaks of a rapture to the third heaven (2 Cor. 12:2–3) but does not describe the experience, which was beyond human language. Revelation uses symbolic language for this very reason (Rev. 21:1–22:7). While humans know little about heaven, they know it is beyond whatever they can describe or conceive.

The gathering. When the Son of man returns, he will gather the elect from the ends of the earth to the ends of heaven—a universal gathering (Matt. 24:30–31; Luke 13:29).

HOLY SPIRIT

Stephen L. Stell

The Holy Spirit is the third person of the Trinity, the Giver and Renewer and Lord of life. The Spirit is not only a powerful force, but a personal revelation of the triune God—God present with humanity. As the Spirit of the Father and the Son, this personal Spirit bears witness with the human spirit, joining Christians to God through their acceptance of God's gifts in creation and God's redemption in Jesus Christ through faith.

Analysis

The Holy Spirit has traditionally been understood both as the relation of love between the Father and the Son, and the divine relation uniting God and humanity. In this dual role, the gifts of God's inner triune love—poured out in creation and redemption—are graciously made available to humanity through the Holy Spirit.

Belief in the Holy Spirit thus always points beyond the Spirit alone to Jesus Christ and to the breadth of God's love for creation. Through acceptance as God's children, the Spirit engenders a life of love and trust, transforming the believer's identity through new relations with God, others, and the world.

This new life of faith, based on the forgiveness of sins and the community's continuing dependence on God's grace, is nourished by the gifts of the Spirit. Through these gifts, God builds up a diverse community and sends that community into the world with the good news of God's love and the promise of God's re-creative presence.

The nature and scope of these gifts is determined by the life that God calls, and therefore empowers, Christians to live. The same Spirit who inspired the prophets and apostles in word and deed likewise empowers Christians to speak and embody that Word in the world. The same Spirit who claims and nourishes believers in faith through the sacraments, calls Christians to be Christ's ministering hands to a broken world.

Biblical Instances

Old Testament. Although the word "Spirit" is employed in the Old Testament in diverse and unsystematic ways, Spirit often means the creative power and presence of God: in creation (Gen. 1:2; Job 33:4; Ps. 104:30); in Spirit-filled leadership restoring communal solidarity and action (1 Samuel 11; Judg. 3:10; 6:34; 11:29); in renewing a life of joyful obedience and purity of action (Ps. 51:10–12; Ezek. 3:24–27; 36:24–27).

In Isaiah (chs. 11; 42; 61), the one upon whom the Spirit rests creates community and exercises power by extending justice to the poor and helpless. While rejecting the standards of worldly power, such actions powerfully affect the world.

New Testament. This same creative work of the Spirit in Isaiah is attributed to Jesus (Matt. 12:18–50; Luke 4:16–44). The Spirit uniting Jesus with God enabled a self-sacrificial life of love given for those in need. Likewise, Jesus' gift of the Holy Spirit (John 14–17) is the basis of believers' union with Christ and their continuation of his work in the world.

In pouring out the Spirit upon all flesh (Acts 2), God's miraculous working through creation for redemption continues without ignoring human channels. The cultural barriers of language, race, sex, age, and social status are transformed into means of participating in God's purposes in the world.

The specific gifts of the Spirit (Gal. 5:16–26; Eph. 4:1–7; 1 Corinthians 12–13) are similarly directed toward building the community and extending the love of God through the community to the world. The entire Christian faith is thus energized and directed by the agency of the Holy Spirit.

Options for Preaching

The Holy Spirit and unholy humanity. The assorted, and sometimes sordid, characters upon whom the Spirit of God falls in the Old Testament (Judges; 1 Samuel) should remind believers that God graciously uses human imperfection. In the New Testament the Spirit aids human weaknesses (1 Cor. 2:1–4; 13:4; Rom. 8:26–27), even perfecting God's power therein (2 Cor. 12:7–10). The work of the Spirit does not demand utter holiness; rather Christians grow in holiness through the strengthening and sanctifying Spirit.

The Spirit and suffering. Life in the Spirit is sometimes portrayed as the happy and victorious life. In 2 Corinthians 11, Paul confronted the so-called "super apostles," giving his own credentials in 11:22–30 (see also 1 Cor. 4:8–13). While the Spirit testifies to believers' adoption as God's children and their inheritance as co-heirs with Christ (Rom. 8:14–17), this glory depends on sharing in Christ's suffering. Following Christ's self-sacrificial love in the Spirit does not promise the obliteration of suffering; it promises only that all will work for good and that nothing will overcome God's love (Rom. 8:28–39).

The wisdom of God. The Holy Spirit is the Spirit of wisdom (Eph. 1:17; 1 Cor. 2:4–16), but this wisdom is not the world's (Matt. 11:25–26; Luke 10:21; 1 Cor. 1:17–25; 3:19; 2 Cor. 1:12). Yet Christian faith is not thereby anti-intellectual or unaffected by worldly knowledge. Rather, as the Spirit unfolds the thoughts of God, the Christian's orientation is changed. The wisdom of God thus represents, not a series of theoretical truths, but a transformed life that judges and reinterprets all human wisdom.

HONESTY

Patricia Beattie Jung

Honesty is a characteristic attributed to people whose conduct is habitually marked by truthfulness, fairness, and steadfast devotion to their commitments. Honest people are straightforward, trustworthy, and reputed for their authenticity.

Analysis and Biblical Instances

All of the moral life can be encapsulated in the dictum: be honest. Perfect honesty will require a repentance and radical transformation so great that it is made possible only by the grace of God. Such is the full nature of the justice that springs from justification.

The Hebrew scriptures contain many injunctions against dishonesty. Business practices epitomize a person's character in this regard. For example, unfair pricing is repeatedly forbidden (Deut. 25:13–16); the acceptance of bribes is condemned (Isa. 33:15); and the failure to pay wages on a timely basis or at all is denounced (Lev. 19:13; Jer. 22:13). In addition, those with sufficient resources who charge the needy interest (Ex. 22:25–26) or who refuse altogether to grant charitable loans (Prov. 3:27–28) are condemned for their unfairness. Those who profit from any kind of commercial fraud or oppression are censured (Lev. 6:2–7; Job 24:2–4).

False praise (Ps. 62:4), lying about the recovery of lost goods (Lev. 6:3), concealing hatred (Prov. 10:18), and slander (Prov. 6:19) are rebuked. The nonpayment of debts (Ps. 37:21) and toleration of theft (Ps. 51:18) are judged abominations as well.

In contrast, honesty delights God. Many passages exhort rulers to govern with integrity of heart (1 Kings 9:4). Everyone is encouraged to hold fast to God's path (Prov. 4:25). Such a life is associated with authentic security and God's sustaining blessing (Isa. 33:15). It is linked with the "clean hands and pure heart" requisite for worship (Psalm 15).

When asked by their disciples what they must do, both Jesus and John the Baptist called for perfect honesty (Mark 10:17–22; Luke 3:10–14). In the New Testament the call to be honest is expanded to all times (Phil. 4:8) and to all people, even the Gentiles (1 Peter 2:12).

Options for Preaching

Honesty is a theme rich with possibilities for preaching.

People are inclined by sin to self-deception. They can bear to face the truth about themselves only when they trust God's forgiveness and experience it through one another.

People bear witness to God's Word when they call one another to honesty at work.

Church should not be a place where Christians "wash up, dress up, and shut up." Here is a place where believers really ought to practice being sincere with one another.

Authentic prayer requires that people be honest with God— honest about their indifference toward, fury with, and rage against, as well as love of, God.

Honesty is not only required but also enabled by God.

HOPE

Randall J. Hoedeman

Hope is best defined as an extension of faith. If faith is the process of *trusting* self, others, life itself, and ultimately God in the present moment, then hope is the extending of this trust *over time* and into the future. Pauline theology lists hope as one of the three great cornerstones of existence: "And now faith, hope, and love abide, these three" (1 Cor. 13:13, NRSV).

Analysis

Built into the very structure of existence, hope has emotional, volitional, behavioral, and cognitive components. Emotionally, hope moves in polar tension with anxiety. Just as faith stands out against the background of doubt, so hope must be experienced against the backdrop of anxiety. Ever vulnerable, hope knows of life's persistent conflict, confusion, and insecurity. Nevertheless, hope summons the will and the courage to step into the uncertain future. Thus, realistic hope inspires effective action, whereas unrealistic hope (manifest in either dark pessimism or bright optimism) eventually deadens the will to act.

Cognitively, hope discerns both reasonable limitations and imaginative possibilities. Reason sees the realities of the present situation clearly and in depth. Imagination impregnates these realities with new possibilities. A sick hope suffers either from the lack of reason (by which imagination takes flight into a fanciful future with no bridge connecting it to the actual present) or the lack of imagination (by which reason grinds to a mundane halt, idly sifting and maintaining the status quo).

Biblical Instances

Scripture gathers up the above characteristics of hope and points them to their ultimate source in the "God of hope" (Rom. 15:13). It bears witness to both the human experience and the divine grounding of hope.

Hope's human side. Hope is coextensive with human life (Eccl. 9:4) and salvation (Rom. 8:24). Hope bears the fruits of rejoicing (Rom. 12:12), patience (Rom. 8:25), peace (Rom. 15:13), boldness (2 Cor. 3:12), and purity (1 John 3:3), and thereby remedies a "cast down" soul (Ps. 43:5) and a "sick" heart (Prov. 13:12). At bottom, hope is a "sure and steadfast anchor of the soul" (Heb. 6:19), one that secures eternal comfort (2 Thess. 2:16) and holds fast to eternal life (Titus 1:2; 3:7).

Hope's divine side. Ultimately, a living, lasting hope pulsates with the very heartbeat of creation and redemption. Scripture uniformly identifies hope's divine heartbeat as the God of Israel (Pss. 78:5–7; 146:5) and, supremely, as God revealed in Christ, "the hope of glory" (Col. 1:27; Titus 2:13).

Options for Preaching

Hope versus anxiety. As noted above, several texts offer hope in God as a steadfast anchor in the midst of life's storm-tossed insecurity, discouragement, and despair (see Ps. 119:81; Rom. 5:3–5; Heb. 6:11, 18).

Hope that bridges present and future. Life is caught between the "already" and the "not yet" and, therefore, longs for a future good, for an "eschatology of hope" that patiently endures present suffering (Rom. 8:18–25). The gospel proclaims that such a "transitional hope" exists—namely, "Christ in you, the hope of glory" (Col. 1:27; cf. Rom. 15:4; 1 Peter 1:3, 13, 21).

Hope's unseen reality. Hope balances present realities and future possibilities. Judeo-Christian hope posits God as the unseen and decisive Reality that tips the balance in favor of a future so amazing that "no eye has seen, nor ear heard, nor the human heart conceived, what God has prepared" (1 Cor. 2:9, NRSV; cf. Rom. 8:24; Heb. 11:1).

HUMILITY

Basil Pennington

Humility is the virtue whereby humans know and accept the truth about themselves: their grandeur as men and women made in the image of God, their total dependency as all that they have and are is God's free gift, and their profound misery because they have failed in so many ways to live up to who they are and show their gratitude for God's gifts.

Analysis

Bernard of Clairvaux, the great medieval mystic theologian, states: "Humility is a virtue by which a person has a low opinion of himself because he knows himself well" (*The Steps of Humility and Pride*, I, 2). However, he insists, "Humility is not praiseworthy when it is not in accordance with the facts" (Epistle 201, n. 2). Humility without knowledge of the goodness of God leads to despair. With the knowledge of God's infinite goodness and mercy, humility leads one to plead for God's merciful forgiveness and to open oneself to receive it. In regard to one's neighbor, humility leads one to honor all and enter into compassion with them in their faults and failings, in their misery.

Biblical Instances

In the Hebrew Bible good examples of humility appear in Abraham, Joseph the son of Jacob, King David, and Job, among others.

The supreme example of humility is Jesus himself, who humbled himself, becoming obedient even unto death. Although he was divine, he did not disdain abiding in the Virgin's womb for nine months, being born in a stable, fleeing into exile as an oppressed person, and living as a displaced refugee and then later as a humble worker. When he was established as Lord and Master, he still came as one who came to serve and not be served; he even washed the feet of his disciples. In the end, having taken on the guilt of all humanity's sin, he freely accepted the death of a criminal and outcast, hanging naked on the cross.

Options for Preaching

Temperance. In preaching, one can develop theologically the theme of humility as an expression of the cardinal virtue of temperance, of tempering one's estimation of oneself, one's expressions of that, and one's relationships with others.

Jesus' example. Probably more fruitful than preaching about temperance is to set forth the example of Jesus and other biblical personages.

Mary's example. Mary is the great human example of humility, having participated as fully as possible in her Son's humiliation. She uttered the great hymn of the humble: "My soul magnifies the Lord, and my spirit rejoices in God my Savior, for he has regarded the low estate of his handmaiden. For behold, henceforth all generations will call me blessed; *for he who is mighty has done great things for me, and holy is his name*" (Luke 1:46–49, italics added).

IDOLATRY

James W. Crawford

Idolatry is the seeking of ultimate assurance, hope, and meaning for life in something other than the promises of the God made known though Israel's salvation history and the life, death, and resurrection of Jesus Christ.

Analysis

In a rapidly changing world, humankind seeks to discover something to give meaning. Men and women seek ultimate security amid threats of betrayal, the constraints of mortality, and the tragedy of existence. Amid this contingent existence they grasp a human construct—family, race, or nation, perhaps. In such constructs, humanity secures meaning. But these things tend to collapse and are no less transient than life itself.

Biblical Instances

Old Testament. The early encounter of the Hebrew immigrants with the inhabitants of Canaan is fraught with temptations to idolatry. Canaanite gods, linked to natural events and catastrophe, seduced the Israelites into trying to manipulate those gods, rather than serving the sovereign of nature and history (2 Kings 10). The prophets inveighed against the apostasy of people seeking meaning and life from human pursuits or natural processes, rather than from the transcendent "I am" who rules the universe (Isaiah 46).

New Testament. In his first letter to the church at Corinth, Paul warns the congregation against confusing humanly constructed religious doctrines with the truth of the cross (1 Cor. 1:10–24). Later, in the same letter, he cautions against mistaking spiritual gifts for true meaning in life. That could come only through love, he writes (1 Corinthians 13). And surely, Peter's imperative "We must obey God rather than any human authority" (Acts 5:29, NRSV) testifies to the New Testament's underlying confession, "Jesus Christ is Lord."

Options for Preaching

Searching for God in the wrong places. The First Commandment reads, "You shall have no other gods besides me" (Ex. 20:3). But humanity does have other gods. In these days people seek security in the cults of success; in incomes, titles, achievements; in degrees, credentials, and addresses. These gods—these sources of meaning—crumble. Ultimate meaning can be found in the God who liberates, heals, restores—the God of Israel.

True Christianity. Matthew 12:1–8 makes vivid the danger of placing ultimate confidence for salvation in the idol of religion's ritual practices. Jesus says going through the motions in church, only to be complacent afterward, is confusing a fraudulent god's requirements with the true service of the living God, that is, the care and feeding of humankind.

Yellow flag for patriotism. When Jesus instructs his disciples to render to Caesar what is Caesar's and to God what is God's (Matt. 22:21), he warns against mistaking the foreign and domestic policies of the nation for the will of God. No one dare confuse his or her nation, its polity, or its economic system with God's intentions for the human family. Such idolatry engenders national arrogance and frequently leads to destructive international conduct in God's name.

IMAGE OF GOD

James Leo Garrett, Jr.

Humankind in the image of God, also called *imago Dei*, is the biblical and theological concept that affirms a basic similarity or analogy between human beings and God. Christian thinkers have differed as to the precise nature of the image, suggesting bodily uprightness, dominion over nature, human reason, original righteousness, interpersonal relations, and various human capacities.

Analysis

Some patristic and scholastic theologians distinguished between "image" and "likeness" (Gen. 1:26–27). Whereas the "likeness" was equated with the lost relationship to God, the "image" was identified with reason and was said to be free from the effects of the Fall. The majority of present-day exegetes take "image" and "likeness" in Genesis 1:26–27 to be synonyms. Human dominion over nature has had its numerous advocates, but it can be seen as the corollary of the image rather than as its essence. The Protestant Reformers identified the image with original righteousness and posited its loss except for a relic or vestige. Any satisfactory answer must take into full account the different, but complementary, perspectives of Genesis and of Paul.

Biblical Instances

Among the Old Testament books, only in Genesis does one find specific mention of the image/likeness (Gen. 1:26–27; 5:1; 9:6), although Psalm 8 is often associated with the theme, and the Old Testament Apocrypha (Wisd. Sol. 2:23; Ecclus. 17:3) allude to it. In Genesis 1:26–27 mention is made of both "image" (*selem*) and "likeness" (*demut*).

Among the New Testament writers, only Paul specifically alludes to the image (*eikon*) (1 Cor. 11:7; 2 Cor. 3:18; Rom. 8:29; Col. 3:10) and only James to the likeness (*homoiosis*; 3:9). Whereas in Genesis nothing is said of the loss of the image by humans, and the image even serves as the basis for a command against murder (Gen. 9:6), Paul assumes the loss of the image and refers to a change into, conformity with, and renewal of the image.

Options for Preaching

Preaching possibilities include:

The uniqueness of the human in God's created order (Gen. 1:26–27).

Human beings as made for fellowship with God and as restless until coming into such fellowship (Ps. 42:1–2; Augustine, *Confessions*, 1.1).

Responsible dominion as stewardship over the nonhuman aspects of the created order (Ps. 8:6–8), including balance in nature and conservation of resources.

The divine origin of the male-female relationship in marriage (Gen. 1:27; Matt. 19:4–6).

The sacredness and value of human life and the sinfulness of destroying human life (Gen. 9:6).

The effects of sin upon humans in the image of God (Col. 3:5–10).

The renewal or restoration of the image in and through Jesus Christ (Col. 3:10; Rom. 8:29; 2 Cor. 3:18).

The awesome responsibility for the rightful use of human speech (James 3:9).

Human beings are not permanently satisfied with reductionist ideologies that deny the image.

Christlikeness as the goal of the Christian (Rom. 8:29).

INCARNATION

Richard B. Cunningham

Incarnation refers to the unique union of divinity and humanity in the one person Jesus Christ. It is the most universal model by which the church has attempted to describe God's unique presence in Jesus. Although "incarnation" is not a biblical word, the idea has profound roots in New Testament teachings. The word entered the church's language through the Latin translation of John 1:14 and is frequent from the fourth century onward.

Analysis

The idea of incarnation is widespread in the human family. It generally refers to a divine being taking on human or animal form. When utilized within Christian thought, incarnation is not just one among many other incarnations of a divine being. It is a one-of-a-kind union, the pivotal event upon which the redemption of the universe depends. It is a way of expressing Paul's idea that "God was in Christ, reconciling the world unto himself" (2 Cor. 5:19, KJV) or John's idea that the "Word became flesh and dwelt among us" (John 1:14). The incarnation is the central mystery of the Christian faith, which has stimulated profound reflection, debate, and controversy over the centuries. The normative Christology of the church has affirmed that Jesus Christ was very God and very man in one person. The incarnation is set within an eternal framework in which God through the Logos calls creation into existence and ultimately redeems it to himself.

Biblical Instances

In the fully developed Christology of the New Testament and the later church, incarnation includes such ideas as the preexistence of Christ (John 1:1–2), the creative activity of the eternal Logos (John 1:3; Col. 1:16–17), the laying aside of divine prerogatives in the Son becoming a human (Phil. 2:7), the virgin birth (Matt. 1:18–25; Luke 1:26–38), the sinlessness of Jesus (Heb. 4:15; 7:26), the full humanity of Jesus (1 John 1:1–2), the unique divine presence in Jesus (John 1:14; 10:30; Col. 1:19), the revelatory activity of Jesus (John 1:9; 14:9), the atoning death and resurrection (1 Cor. 15:3; 1 Tim. 2:5–6; Rom. 5:6–11), the ascension to the Father (Acts 1:6–11), the present reign of Christ in creation and history (Acts 2:32–36; 1 Cor. 15:27; Phil. 2:9–11), and the future coming of Christ to judge the world (2 Thess. 1:5–12; Rev. 22:12–20).

Reflections on the idea of incarnation are found throughout the New Testament. However, the classic New Testament thought for the incarnation is found in John and Paul, particularly John 1:1–14, Colossians 1:15–20, and Philippians 2:5–11. These are crucial passages for preaching the incarnation.

Options for Preaching

John 1:1–14. John's prologue utilizes the widely recognized first-century idea of the Logos, the word of speech or thought, to interpret the coming of Jesus into the world against the backdrop of eternity and creation.

He affirms the preexistence of the Son of God. "In the beginning was the Word, and the Word was with God, and the Word was God." Jesus Christ cannot be explained simply from within history, as one who is a revealer, miracle worker, prophet, or other familiar religious figure. He originates in eternity. Although born in time, he did not begin in time.

The Word is divine. Yet John differentiates the Son from the Father, so that the Word is *with* God and *is* God—an idea that ultimately forces the development of a doctrine of the Trinity.

The Logos or eternal Son is the agent through whom God creates the world and then makes himself known to the minds of all people. "All things were made through him, and without him was not anything made that was made" (1:3). The whole universe is tied to the creative activity of Christ. This eternal Logos does not enter the world for the first time in Jesus but is universally present throughout the world illuminating the minds of all people with the light of God's revelatory presence. The incarnate Jesus comes to people who have already experienced the Logos within their minds (1:9–11).

This Logos, the agent of creation and revelatory presence, becomes incarnate in Jesus of Nazareth. "The Word became flesh and dwelt among us, full of grace and truth" (1:14). The verb *became* provides no theory about how the union of the divine and human took place. The term underlines that the Logos really became flesh but was not reduced merely to flesh. John here asserts that the humanity of Jesus was not just an appearance, as docetic thought contended. There is a clear declaration that Jesus somehow embodies the truly human and the truly divine. The presence of the Logos in Jesus was unique, not just another instance of the eternal light's illuminating presence in every human being. So John can say, "We have beheld his glory, glory as of the only Son from the Father" (1:14).

Colossians 1:15–20. This is Paul's briefest yet most comprehensive statement of the person and work of Christ. His affirmation of incarnation is in his statement, "For in him all the fullness of God was pleased to dwell" (1:19, NRSV). Paul cites Christ's work in creation, redemption, and the church.

He begins with a declaration of the man Jesus' uniqueness as "the image of the invisible God, the first-born of all creation" (1:15). Paul is likely influenced here by Wisdom literature. Jesus bears the true image of God, what God had intended for Adam and all his descendants before sin marred the image. In that sense, he is the authentic human being through whom others are redeemed back into the image of God (Col. 3:10).

Paul affirms Christ's pre-incarnate status without providing an explanation: "He is before all things" (1:17). He did not originate with a human birth. Paul provides no Trinitarian formula of the relation of Christ to the Father.

As the eternal Son, he is the agent and goal of creation. Paul details the scope of Christ's creative work: "For in him all things were created, in heaven and on earth, visible and invisible, whether thrones or dominions or principalities or authorities—all things were created through him and for him" (1:16). For Paul, Christ is the interpretative principle that unlocks the mystery of the universe. He is also the continuing creative presence in the universe: "In him all things hold together" (1:17). Without the continuing creative activity of the eternal Son, the universe would collapse into nothingness.

The incarnate Christ is the redeemer. God chooses through Christ "to reconcile to himself all things, whether on earth or in heaven, making peace by the blood of his cross" (1:20). He is the beginning of a new humanity through his resurrection from the dead and is head of the church (1:18). As the agent of creation and redemption, God wills "that in everything he might be preeminent" (1:18).

Philippians 2:5–11. This is perhaps the greatest christological passage in the New Testament, possibly a hymn of the early church that Paul quotes. In encouraging humility among Christians, Paul points to the example of Christ as a humble suffering servant who is exalted.

In his pre-incarnate life, Christ was in the form of God. "Form" here means "the very substance or nature of God." It is a clear affirmation of Christ's divinity. Yet Christ "did not count equality with God a thing to be grasped" (2:6). He did not claim the glory that belongs to God or exercise all the rights or prerogatives that are God's alone.

The Son chose the path of condescension. He "emptied himself, taking the form of a servant" (2:7). Paul uses a form of the word *kenosis* here that is a source of a major approach to

Christology and of much debate within Christian theology. What does Christ empty himself of? The divine nature, metaphysical attributes, or moral attributes? Does Christ cease to be God? How can he be God during the incarnation without possessing the divine attributes? These questions go to the heart of the question of the incarnation and finally confront us with absolute paradox. Paul is not so much conerned with the "how" of the self-emptying but of the human status that the eternal Son chooses to enter—that of a servant.

The servant life is lived as a real man. Paul says that Christ was "born in the likeness of men" (2:7). He restates that he was "found in human form" (2:8). Paul affirms the full humanity of Jesus in opposition to all docetic theories that he merely appeared to assume human form but was actually totally divine. He alludes to Christ's earthly life and to what people who met him must have seen—a real human being, a carpenter of Nazareth.

As God in human form, Christ humbled himself as a servant and became obedient to God, even to death on a cross. This is the nadir of his condescension from his heavenly status. The earthly life of Jesus moves relentlessly to his death on a cross, the inevitable end of a servant life. The contrast between his heavenly origins and his earthly fate underlines his humility.

God has exalted Christ precisely because of his obedience to death and gives him a name, "Lord," that is above every name. He becomes the measuring rod for all people in the universe. Life's crucial decision is how one responds to Jesus Christ as Lord. Paul asserts that in the end time, every knee will bow and every tongue will confess—all those alive and dead—that "Jesus Christ is Lord, to the glory of God the Father" (2:11).

INSPIRATION

John P. Reed

Inspiration is the condition of being intellectually, emotionally, or spiritually stimulated by an enlivening force or agency. In art or poetry, the animating source of creative inspiration is called the "muse." Theologically, inspiration indicates that God has "breathed into" the thoughts and expressions of a human being God's own Spirit and Truth. In the event of divine inspiration, human cognition and feeling are profoundly and pervasively imbued by the Spirit of God.

Analysis

Implicit in the concept of inspiration is the notion that human beings possess the capacity to be inspired. Human life itself is depicted in scripture as a matter of inspiration (Gen. 2:7). It is through inspiration that God is revealed to humankind. That human beings are capable of being inspired is another way of speaking of their God-given spiritual capacity. This capacity is not, itself, the result of human achievement but is rather a receptivity to the divine in-breathing. Human beings possess in their createdness the spiritual lungs, yet it is always God who animates humanity. As Paul knew, the truest prayer is the one in which the Spirit does the praying (Rom. 8:26). The uniquely human thing is the capacity for self-transcendent participation in the Spirit, or "inspirability."

Without inspiration, humanity would suffocate for lack of the life-giving breath that comes from God. Divine inspiration means that human sighs and groanings too deep for words do not simply fade into the dark silence of a cold and empty space. In God's world, even the wheezing of the spiritually feeble can become prayer. Conversely, moribund minds and tubercular imaginations can be revived and filled with the mystery of the divine Word.

Biblical Instances

Joy and ecstasy. Scripture often links the human states of joy and ecstasy with the experience of inspiration. Perhaps the most impassioned and eloquent response to the news of the incarnation is Mary's joyful Magnificat, which begins "My soul magnifies the Lord, and my spirit rejoices in God my Savior" (Luke 1:46–55). The Holy Spirit also transported Zechariah to the heights of inspired proclamation (Luke 1:67–79). Paul lovingly reminds the Thessalonians that the gospel came to them not only in word but also in power and joy in the Holy Spirit, even in affliction (1 Thess. 1:5–6). And after shaking the dust off their feet following their preaching to an unresponsive audience in one town, Paul and Barnabus came to Iconium, where, despite the recent sting of rejection, they "were filled with joy and with the Holy Spirit" (Acts 13:52).

The church began in ecstasy with the outpouring of the Holy Spirit at Pentecost (Acts 2:1–13), fulfilling the promise of the prophet Joel (Joel 2:28–32). The apparent drunkenness of those in spiritual ecstasy on that day is reminiscent of the prophet Jeremiah's self-description: "I am like a drunken man, like a man overcome by wine, because of the LORD, and because of his holy words" (Jer. 23:9). The calling of several of the prophets included ecstatic visual and auditory experiences of inspiration (Isaiah 6; Amos 7–9; Jer. 1:5–19; Ezek. 2:1–2).

Confession. Confession of Christ as Lord is, itself, the work of the Holy Spirit (1 Cor. 12:3). The noblest examples of inspiration are those linked to trial and suffering, as was the case with Stephen in his brave confession of Christ (Acts 6:10–7:60). Jesus, in warning his followers of future persecution, had also both cautioned and reassured them with the promise of inspiration (Mark 13:11).

Options for Preaching

Inspired preaching that inspires faith. The story of Stephen in Acts suggests that, both in terms of content (disquieting and prophetic truths) and context (an unreceptive audience), inspired preaching may not always be pretty. For a modern audience accustomed to telegenic preaching, this story is a needed reminder of the relationship between inspiration, confession, and the kind of suffering that first sees and then participates in Christ. Such inspired preaching actually inspires its hearers, transforming them from audience into co-preachers, as was ultimately the case with Stephen's sermon.

On being in the mood for inspiration. The complex psychology of King Saul as depicted in 1 Samuel reveals the spiritual reasons for and consequences of the loss of inspiration (cf. 1 Sam. 16:14–23). Saul is thoroughly modern in his moodiness; he swings wildly between grandiosity and self-loathing. Like a neurotic novelist with "writer's block," his inner conflict produces opposite moods of disobedient arrogance and morbid despair, both of which close him off to inspiration (1 Sam. 28:15–25). Receptivity to the in-breathing of the Holy Spirit occurs in a mood of hopeful humility that trusts in God's future and that is neither self-degrading nor self-aggrandizing. (Contrast, for instance, Paul's attitude in Philippians 1 with that of the jealous, fear-ridden Saul).

Disciplined ecstasy. Throughout 1 Corinthians, Paul takes pains to show that authentic experiences of divine inspiration are those which are reasonable and edifying (1 Cor. 14:15–17). True inspiration does not lead to puffed-up claims nor to spiritual status consciousness (1 Cor. 12:14–26). The final proof of the authenticity of inspiration is that it produces love (1 Corinthians 13).

JESUS CHRIST

George W. Stroup

The most basic conviction of Christian faith is that Jesus of Nazareth, a first-century Jew, is the Christ, the Messiah, the one in whom all the promises of God to Israel come to fulfillment. In proclaiming Jesus to be the Christ, the church confesses that he is Emmanuel, "God with us," and that in him God's grace, love, mercy, and salvation are not a dream or an idea but a reality in human life and history.

Analysis

In confessing Jesus to be the Christ and that God raised him from the dead, the church proclaims its faith that Jesus is Lord over all those principalities and powers that threaten to separate creation from God. As the Christ, Jesus is lord of the church in every generation and will be lord when God's kingdom comes on earth. Because Jesus is a living lord, the church recognizes that faithfulness to him means that each new generation of Christians must answer the same question Jesus asked of his disciples at Caesarea Philippi—"who do you say that I am?" (Mark 8:29). Furthermore, precisely because Jesus Christ is a living lord, the church must listen to how previous generations of Christians have proclaimed him to the world but must not assume that its evangelical task is simply to repeat what previous Christians have said.

It took the church some four hundred years to agree on a formal definition of what it meant when it confessed Jesus to be the Christ. At Chalcedon in 451, the church declared that Jesus Christ is one person, truly God and truly human, "acknowledged in two natures without confusion, without change, without division, without separation." The debates that preceded Chalcedon were life-and-death matters for the church because it recognized that at stake in its confession that Jesus was the Christ was the church's experience and understanding of salvation.

In the modern age, the church has searched for new idioms to explain what it means when it confesses Jesus to be the Christ. The church has sought new forms of expression because it recognizes that the language of the fifth century is no longer easily intelligible to many twentieth-century Christians and that if it is to be an evangelical church it must find language that will enable all the world to hear the good news that Jesus is the Christ.

Biblical Instances

The writers of the New Testament use a rich variety of literary forms to identify Jesus as the Christ. The word "christ" is a title, a Greek translation for the Hebrew word for messiah. The use of the term "Christ" or "Messiah" demonstrates the church's belief that Jesus cannot be understood apart from the history of Israel. The genealogies in Matthew 1 and Luke 3 affirm not only Jesus' humanity but also that he cannot be separated from Israel.

Christ is only one title among many (e.g., Lord, Son of man, Son of God, Prophet, etc.) used in the New Testament to identify Jesus. In addition to the use of titles, the New Testament contains hymns, such as Philippians 2:6–11 and Colossians 1:15–20, and early creeds, such as Romans 1:3–4 and 1 Corinthians 15:3–7, which identify Jesus.

The most important material in the Bible, however, for understanding Jesus' identity are the Gospels. The Gospels are not theological arguments, at least not in the sense that Paul gives us theological arguments, so much as they are stories that describe what Jesus said and did and what happened to him. It is in the interaction between what Jesus said and did and the events that make up his life that we understand the claim that he is "the way, and the truth, and the life" (John 14:6) and what Paul meant when he wrote that "God was in Christ reconciling the world to himself" (2 Cor. 5:19, NEB).

Options for Preaching

Faithful and effective preaching of the good news that Jesus is the Christ, the chosen one of God, who brings humanity forgiveness and newness of life, might consider some of the following themes.

An ever-new question. The question of who Jesus is and what it means to confess him to be the Christ is never something that is settled once and for all but is new each day (Mark 8:27–33; Matt. 16:13–23; Luke 9:18–22).

The presence of Jesus. Because Jesus is a living Christ, Christians believe he is present in their lives and at work in their world (Matt. 28:16–20; John 17:20–26; Gal. 3:20).

Jesus' identity and salvation. According to the Bible, the question of Jesus' identity cannot be separated from the question of the meaning of salvation (Mark 1:21–28; 2 Cor. 5:16–21).

Jesus' identity and discipleship. Nor can the issue of who Jesus is be separated from the question and tasks of discipleship (Mark 8:31–38; Matt. 16:21–28; Luke 9:23–27).

The offense of the cross. Inasmuch as Jesus is the crucified Christ, Christians do not know him unless they can look beyond the familiarity of the symbol of the cross and see that it stands as a radical, even shocking, statement about the costly nature of God's love. If Christians fail to recognize that truth, then as Paul writes, "the word of the cross is folly" (1 Cor. 1:18–31).

The last shall be first. Jesus insists that his kingdom will be the reversal of what humans expect (Matt. 19:23–30; Luke 16:19–31), for "many that are first will be last, and the last first" (Matt. 19:30).

Jesus as parable. Jesus not only proclaims the kingdom by means of parable, but he is himself the parable of God (John 8:12–19; 10:30).

JEWISH-CHRISTIAN RELATIONS

Karl A. Plank

"Jewish-Christian relations" refers to the interaction between the kindred faiths of Judaism and Christianity. Historically, these communities have defined themselves in light of each other and pursued identities that witness both commonalities and estrangement. "Jewish-Christian relations" comprises the history and theological understandings of those identities as they have affected the life of each group relative to the other.

Analysis

Christianity originates as one of several renewal movements within the pluralistic context of Second Temple Judaism. As heir of the Jesus movement, it develops in Palestine as a Torah-conscious Jewish Christianity associated with the leadership of Peter and James; in the Diaspora, through the missionary activity of Paul and others, it grows as a Messiah-centered Judaism relating its faith to the ethnic situation of Jews and Gentiles alike. Following the catastrophic Jewish-Roman War (70 C.E.), pressure toward normative self-definition leads to an increasing tension and separation between the nascent Rabbinic communities—communities oriented primarily to the preservation of the Torah, written and oral—and the followers of Jesus as Messiah.

Christianity's growth within and increasing distinction from its prewar Jewish context places the issue of its relation to Judaism at the heart of the church's identity. At stake are the following questions: (a) In what ways is the church bound to be faithful to traditions of its past, especially those traditions of shared texts (the Hebrew Bible) and root images that unite Christianity and Judaism as the offspring of a common heritage? (b) What is the role of ethnic particularity in constituting the church as a covenant community? (c) In what ways does the church's authority respond to the pluralism of its environment or relate to outsiders?

Biblical Instances

Paul, the apostle. The relations between Jews and non-Jews provided an existential issue for Paul as he struggled to articulate his apostolic calling to the Gentiles and to interpret the covenantal convictions of his Judaism in light of the death and resurrection of Jesus Messiah. For Paul, the Christ event does not abrogate his faith as a Jew but provides a lens through which to see it anew: the community of God's people is not constituted ethnically nor legally, but in terms of a trusting fidelity to the God of Abraham and of the crucified Jesus who brings forth birth from barren wombs, life from death, and righteousness from ungodliness (Romans 4–6). Explicitly in his Romans letter, these convictions imply (a) the basic parity of the callings of Jew and Gentile within a covenant that brooks no ethnic nor ethical privilege (Romans 1–3), (b) the recognition of pluralism within the covenant community (Romans 9–11), and (c) a mutual dependence of Jew and Gentile upon the roles each plays for the other in one salvation history (Rom. 11:11–12, 25–26). If Paul's eschatological vision ultimately obviates the distinction between Jew and non-Jew (Gal. 3:28), his present reckoning affirms the integrity of each as a vantage point from which to hear and respond to God's call.

Jesus and the Gospels. The Gospels reflect a complex literary history requiring critical perspective. Written after the Jewish-Roman War, they presuppose a time of separation and growing antagonism between synagogue communities and followers of Jesus. In this context the evangelists, especially Matthew and

John, retroject into their stories the polemical situation of their own time, prejudicially stereotyping Jewish leaders (Matthew 23) and the Jews generally (John, passim). Vulnerable to this tendency, the passion narratives fostered tragic calumnies of Jewish deicide. Conflict likely attended the historical ministry of Jesus, particularly regarding his table-fellowship with "tax collectors and sinners." Still, such conflict is better seen as prophetic tension within a Jewish pluralism than as a warrant to estrange Jesus from his Jewish contemporaries.

Options for Preaching

The legacy of the Holocaust makes urgent a reconsideration of Jewish-Christian relations. In its shadow, Christian preaching provides the occasion for confessing the church's perpetuation of anti-Judaism. But the Christian preacher after Auschwitz may well have more to hear than to say; proclamation, in this case, should grow from a deep listening to God's word, not only in scripture but in the chronicle of shared history.

Historical criticism. Where proclamation interprets scripture, historical criticism has important implications. First, the history of early Christianity points to an understanding of Christian faith as an expression of Judaism that seeks to be faithful to texts and traditions yet held in common with the synagogue. This kinship calls into question any Christian triumphalism, be it in blatant forms of anti-Judaism or in the no less destructive efforts of conversion.

Anti-Jewish language in the New Testament. Historical study and moral sensitivity invite the Christian to relativize, if not repudiate, anti-Jewish language within the New Testament (e.g., Matthew 23), by pointing to its contingent shaping. Here theological responsibility may call for the criticism of scripture's oppressive language, that the New Testament's more fundamental claim of a common human covenant may be realized.

Liberating perspectives in the New Testament. The preacher may find within the New Testament itself liberating perspectives to challenge anti-Jewish convictions. For example, the consistent concern in Paul and the evangelists for including the Gentile (e.g., Galatians 2; Luke 2:29–32) or in the ministry of Jesus for giving hospitality to the stranger (e.g., Matt. 25:35–40) establishes a hermeneutic principle that asks the Christian to value the group or person who is outsider to the Christian's religious norm. If, in the context of early Christianity, that outsider appears as the "Gentile," from the vantage of the modern church the outsider from whom the Christian cannot separate is now the Jew. To receive that stranger in common covenant is to affirm the pluralism of the human community and to eschew all religious and ethnic bigotry.

JOY

R. Alan Culpepper

Joy is the experience of gladness, delight, pleasure, or bliss. It is often evoked by well-being, success, or good fortune. People experience joy at marriage, a birth, harvest, or times of celebration. People of faith, however, have a distinctive source of joy. They experience joy through their fellowship with God, even in circumstances that would not otherwise allow them to be joyful.

Analysis

Joy is the human response to the experience of God's love, God's grace, God's *shalom*. Those who recognize God as Creator can delight in nature, the fragile orb of life. All God's gifts bring joy to those who receive them: companionship in marriage, fulfilling work, children, music. Joy can be both an experience of unexpected gladness and the result of regular, planned, corporate worship.

Biblical Instances

Exclamations of joy erupt throughout the Bible. The Hebrews celebrated the joys of family life: marriage (Prov. 5:18; Isa. 62:5), sexual love (S. of Sol. 1:4), and the birth of children (Ps. 113:9). The harvest season brought joy (Deut. 26:1–11; Isa. 9:3). The Sabbath also was a time of joy, a day for rest and the family (Isa. 58:14; Deut. 5:12–15). Joyful celebrations marked the festivals of the ancient Israelites, especially Passover, the celebration of God's deliverance of the people of Israel; Weeks, the feast of first fruits, harvest, or Pentecost; and Booths, or Tabernacles, which celebrated alternately the harvest and the wilderness wandering. Dancing was an appropriate celebration of joy in worship (Ps. 149:3; 2 Sam. 6:14).

These feasts also pointed forward to the messianic banquet (Isa. 25:6–9).

Similarly, the birth of Jesus was announced as "good news of great joy for all the people" (Luke 2:10, NRSV). In the farewell discourse in John, Jesus promised his followers joy (John 15:11; 16:24; 17:13). The resurrection was announced with joy (Matt. 28:8; Luke 24:52), and joy is one of the fruits of the Spirit (Gal. 5:22). Joy turns losses into gains (James 1:2–8; Heb. 10:34; Rom. 8:18). Joy, therefore, fills the apostle Paul even in his imprisonment (Phil. 1:4, 18; 2:17; 4:10).

Options for Preaching

The biblical texts on joy offer the preacher an abundance of preaching themes.

Joy that sustains. Christians have wellsprings of joy that sustain them even in the midst of trials and sorrow (Ps. 30:5 and texts cited above).

Renewable joy. Joy can be renewed by celebrating God's goodness in worship.

Joy is OK. Hey, Puritan, it's all right to find joy in family, work, and recreation (Eccl. 5:18).

God delights in joy. Christians worship a God who delights in babies, weddings, and dancing.

JUSTICE/LIBERATION

J. Philip Wogaman

Justice, according to Aristotle, is rendering to each person his or her due. Justice is usually taken to include the notion of fairness in the distribution of social goods and duties and in the reward and punishment of good and bad behavior. Liberation is the action of securing freedom from some form of bondage.

Analysis

Both justice and liberation are essentially ethical concepts, and specific understandings of such terms vary with the ethical and theological traditions by which they are used. There are probably as many definitions of justice and liberation as there are philosophical, theological, and ethical traditions. Some are diametrically opposed. Thus, what is justice to a Marxist is injustice to a capitalist; what is liberation to a Marxist is enslavement to a capitalist; and vice versa. Such disagreements cannot be resolved by scholarly definition, for the problem is theological. One's understanding of justice and liberation hinge both on one's view of God and on the fundamental meaning of human life.

A crucial watershed in conceptions of justice is between compensatory and communitarian views. According to the first, justice is people receiving the rewards and punishments that they deserve: no more and no less. According to the second, justice is people receiving what they need to be accepted as participating community members. Both principles have abundant theological support. To the first, God is a righteous judge who punishes the wicked while rewarding the virtuous. To the second, God's intention is that all shall be included in the covenant community.

A similar theological watershed exists between conceptions of liberation that emphasize freedom from internal or spiritual forms of bondage, especially sin, and conceptions emphasizing freedom from external oppression.

Biblical Instances

Each of these conceptions has significant biblical rootage. The compensatory view of justice reflects the God of the Deuteronomic perspective and of the parable of the last judgment (Matthew 25). The communitarian perspective is expressed in the law of jubilee (Leviticus 25) and the parable of the vineyard (Matt. 20:1–16), the God whose sun rises and rain falls on the just and unjust alike (Matt. 5:45). Both approaches are biblical and not necessarily inconsistent. But it matters which has priority, for the one will be used to define the other. A moralistic God, meting out rewards and punishments, will be concerned about community only among the righteous while consigning the rest to damnation. A God whose love comes first will be concerned that each person have the material and institutional protections necessary to be a member of the community, with rewards and punishments serving as a means to that greater end. Paul's distinction between grace and law in Romans and Galatians speaks to this point. If justice is simply getting what one deserves, Paul despairs that any can be saved, for all have sinned and fallen short. But the grace by which one is saved is not an escape from the demands of justice if one understands justice in the second sense. For to be grasped by God's love is to come to understand oneself and one's relationship in a new way. Now one wants to join the effort to make it possible for all to be part of what God has intended in a new age of justice.

Such an understanding of justice also helps one understand liberation. Liberation, too, has its roots in God's love; internally, it is to be free from idolatries, fears, and self-centeredness. That is the clear message of Galatians, where Paul writes of forms of spiritual enslavement while proclaiming that "for freedom Christ has set us free" (5:1). Thus, liberation is not simply being released from external bondage; indeed, one can be freed externally while remaining enslaved within—a fate the Bible understands to be characteristic of the rich and powerful of this world. Nevertheless, Old Testament prophets, such as Amos, Hosea, Isaiah, and Micah, insist upon very worldly forms of liberation, as does the New Testament's Magnificat of Mary (Luke 1:46–55).

Options for Preaching

The deadly enemy of preaching on justice and liberation is moralism: Its God is unloving, its message disempowering, its invitation to despair or self-righteousness, building barriers between preacher and congregation. But when God's grace is taken seriously as the foundation for justice and liberation, the homiletical possibilities are endlessly attractive.

The First Commandment (Ex. 20:3) provides an excellent basis for analysis of how idolatries enslave the inner self while leading people to oppress one another for the sake of wealth, power, and prestige.

Paul's "the evil I do not want is what I do" has both internal and external implications—how, apart from grace, people are enslaved to sinful compulsion and how, in an unjust society, institutions structure people's lives in unjust directions. Serious spirituality therefore entails social action.

Ephesians 2 emphasizes the restoration of the wholeness of community through Christ and provides an excellent foundation for preaching on the communitarian conception of justice.

JUSTIFICATION

Richard L. Thulin

Justification is the doctrine stated systematically by Paul that sinners (the ungodly) are justified (forgiven, acquitted though guilty, made righteous) by grace through faith apart from works of the law. It is a central concept for expressing what God has done and still does in Christ. It asserts that salvation is totally the work of God. Salvation is offered as an unmerited gift, without conditions, and it is received by a faith that is itself a gift of grace.

Analysis

All Christian communities agree with what the doctrine of justification asserts, namely, that salvation is totally the work of God. They do not agree, however, on answers to fundamental questions raised by the doctrine itself: Is justification only one doctrine among many, or is it a principle that permeates every theological assertion? Is there any place for human cooperation in relation to God's justifying act? How can we describe adequately the effect that justification has on the believer?

At times, concentration on these crucial questions has diverted attention from other significant aspects of the doctrine. One of these is the eschatological perspective from within which justification is to be seen. That sinners are forgiven by grace through faith, that the ungodly are declared righteous apart from works of the law, is the sign and gift of the new age in Christ. Those who are justified participate in a new life, with new status and new obedience within a new context. Justification has social consequences. To limit the doctrine's reference to individual experiences of God's judgment and forgiveness would be misleading. Justification has a universal dimension. Because all people have sinned, all people are justified only by grace through faith. The new life in which the justified participate is a life in community. And that community is one in which there is no distinction between persons.

Biblical Instances

One of the classic Pauline texts on justification is Romans 3:21–26. An immediate eschatological note is struck in verse 21 with the words "but now." Paul has insisted that all people are under the power of sin and that no human being will be justified in God's sight by deeds prescribed by the law. But *now*, he announces, the situation has changed. In Christ, the faithful God has acted to save (God's righteousness). Now justification is given as a gift. God's favor cannot be earned by obedience, or by piety, or by any other work. It is a gift, and it can be received only by a faith that trusts God's mercy and is itself a gift.

An Old Testament passage such as Isaiah 51:4–8 provides both likeness and contrast to Paul's words in Romans 3:21–26. The likeness is found in Deutero-Isaiah's enlarged understanding of God's righteousness or justice. The righteous God enacts justice by punishing the wicked and vindicating the lawful. But God's righteousness is to be seen chiefly in God's redemptive acts (deliverance/salvation), which are extended to the whole world, even to the ungodly. Contrast is found in the fact that what Deutero-Isaiah saw only as a promise, Paul saw fulfilled in Jesus. It was in Jesus' death and resurrection that the righteous God accomplished a deliverance now available to all who have sinned and fallen short of the glory of God. God declared God's righteousness in the very act by which all people can be declared righteous.

Options for Preaching

Who's included? (Gal. 2:15–21). Paul insists that everyone in the Christian community has been included on the basis of justification by faith. There are no levels or degrees of membership and no special requirements legislated by some for others. To "live for God" is to live in solidarity with all other Christians.

Only God can save (1 Cor. 1:26–31). Even limited human wisdom proves itself to be the cause of unbridled pride. Whether intellectual or moral, it offers opportunity for self-praise before others and before God. It incites boasting and feelings of superiority. What it cannot do is save people from themselves. Only what God has done in Christ can do that. It is the cross that attacks human self-seeking at its root and shows it to be foolishness.

Just desserts (Matt. 20:1–16). In Jesus' parable, the laborers hired late in the day received more than they deserved. They worked only one hour, but they received the same pay as those who had worked since early morning. It was the vineyard owner's choice to be generous in this way. He enacted a justice that reflects the righteousness of God.

Piety versus faith (Luke 18:9–14). The Pharisee in Jesus' story was a pious man. He believed that his obedience to cultic rule and ritual was what made him acceptable to God. But it was the tax collector, who depended on nothing but God's mercy, who was declared acceptable.

KNOWLEDGE (OF GOD)

Dan R. Stiver

"Knowledge" means awareness or understanding with a certitude that sets knowledge apart from mere opinion. It also normally implies the possession of justified grounds or reasons for knowing. Knowledge is practical, "knowing how," as well as theoretical, "knowing about." Practical knowledge, furthermore, comprises expertise—for example, in a particular craft—and morality, the knowledge of right and wrong.

Analysis

Knowledge is as central in the Bible as it is in modern culture. The difference between the biblical world and the modern world is that the most highly prized knowledge in modernity—theoretical, scientific knowledge—makes a rare appearance, if at all, in scripture. Practical knowledge, or practical wisdom, particularly practical knowledge of how to "walk with God," is preeminent in scripture. Knowledge in modern society often has the connotations of being theoretical, detached, and abstract. Knowledge in the Bible is generally practical, engaged, and concrete—especially when it is a question of the knowledge of God.

Biblical Instances

Knowledge in general. The Wisdom books—Proverbs, Job, and Ecclesiastes—particularly emphasize practical ethical knowledge. Proverbs celebrates such knowledge, whereas Job and Ecclesiastes represent the perplexity and agony of straining at the limits of knowledge. The personal dimension associated with knowledge in general is especially brought out in the Hebrew euphemism for sexual intercourse, "knowing" another person (Gen. 4:1).

Knowledge of God. The primary type of knowledge emphasized in scripture, however, is knowledge of God. The psalmist counsels, "Be still, and know that I am God" (46:10). The great commandment in Mark 12:30 integrates knowledge with love: "You shall love the Lord your God with all . . . your mind." The practical and experiential dimensions of the knowledge of God are strikingly demonstrated in Paul's prayers in Philippians 3:10 and Ephesians 3:19. Knowledge of God is often a promise for the future (Ezek. 12:15–16; 1 Cor. 13:12; 1 John 3:2).

Options for Preaching

Three options for preaching represent contrasts between the modern world and the world of the Bible.

Integration versus fragmentation. The biblical conception of knowledge is opposed to the modern fragmentation of knowledge and of life. Ethical concern cannot be detached from "the pure search for knowledge." "Knowledge" and "wisdom" are closely related in scripture, not torn asunder as is frequent in modern life. In the Bible, the beginning of both wisdom and knowledge is "the fear of the LORD" (Prov. 1:7; 2:5–6; 9:10).

Credibility versus skepticism. The Bible's affirmation of the knowledge of God is opposed to modern skepticism about the knowability of God. Rather than assuming the irrationality of faith, the Bible assumes that knowledge of God is credible and highlights that knowledge.

Mystery versus objective certainty. The biblical affirmation of incomplete knowledge of God is in contrast to modernity's suspicion of mystery and craving for objective certainty. The modern penchant for exact, verifiable knowledge is often not at home with this experiential awareness of a mysterious spiritual reality.

LOVE

Randall J. Hoedeman

Love is an attitude of active concern for the life, growth, and general well-being of another. The source of this concern resides in an inner capacity rather than an outer object; consequently, genuine love can never be restricted to one "love-object." Instead, it is open-ended and enlivens all that it encounters—strangers and enemies included (see Matt. 5:43–48; 25:35). Love promotes the life and growth of others (and, thereby, oneself) not because of who *they* are, but because of what *it* is.

Analysis

The above definition emphasizes love's outgoing, self-giving, self-emptying nature (Greek: *agape*) in contrast to many of the popular meanings that speak (and sing) of love as a taking in, a possessing, a consuming, or an emptying of another for the sake of oneself. Such distorted meanings could better be named infatuation, greed, lust, or addiction. In contrast, love moves out of itself and toward others in compassion (feeling for and with another); responsibility (responding adequately to another's needs); respect (seeing and promoting the unique individuality of another); and knowledge (knowing at a deep level and, thereby, responding to another's core needs).

Biblical Instances

For preaching purposes, any discussion of love begins with biblical theology, which consistently places love as the cornerstone of existence (see Lev. 19:18; Deut. 6:4–9; Mark 12:29–30; John 13:34; and 1 Corinthians 13). Humanity is made, first and last, for the giving and receiving of love (1 John 4:7–8); therefore, love, as the "fulfilling of the law" (Rom. 13:8–10), sums up the source, the means, and the end of human existence.

Ultimately, this is so because of the One in whose "image" humanity is created. Groping its way to the edge of human existence—that dark and terrifying precipice—biblical theology leaps over and, to its surprise, discovers an abyss of love. Amazingly, it discovers that human being, contrary to appearances, is not careening wildly through an absurd and empty universe but is held securely in the loving arms of Holy Being (Rom. 8:31–39), of God, who is the very source and definition of love (1 John 4:7–8, 16, 19).

If the essence of love is active, self-giving concern for another (John 3:16; 15:12–13; 1 John 3:16), then God-revealed-in-Christ is its epitome. Christian faith makes the incredible claim that the fullest, most accurate expression of God's love has come in the form of Jesus Christ who "suffered under Pontius Pilate; was crucified dead and buried; he descended into hell" (the Apostles' Creed). If true, what depths of love rule the universe, as God empties the divine Self for humanity's sake and plunges headlong into body-breaking chaos and soul-swallowing void (Phil. 2:4–8). Consequently, when one's life-road cuts through hell, God's loving presence is already there waiting in this no-longer-God-forsaken vicinity. Jesus invokes a summary of the two great commandments: to love God thoroughly and love one's neighbor as one's self (Luke 10:27).

Options for Preaching

God's love song. The gospel of love all but defies description. In Old Testament Hebrew, a root word for God's loving essence is *rehem*—literally, "womb." God seems to delight in singing a love song from deep within—a divine lullaby to the "motherless child" in each person—written in the most basic and powerful of metaphors (cf. Rom. 8:15–17).

Love: the true point of divine-human contact. God's love calls each person into being (Eph. 1:4); frees and empowers people to be (1 John 4:16–17); counteracts a fearful, anxiety-ridden existence (1 John 4:18); and enables people to pass it on (1 John 4:19).

The abyss of love. Christian faith stands or falls with the affirmation that life is surrounded by a final, resilient, and indestructible reality it calls love (see any of the above-mentioned texts, especially Rom. 8:37–39). All Christian theologizing and sermonizing, therefore, must at heart be an exposition of this cosmic field of reality—of the good news that "Jesus loves me, this I know, for the Bible tells me so."

MARRIAGE

William H. Willimon

Marriage is the physical and spiritual union of a man and woman. Genesis contends that God created humanity as male and female and commanded them to "become one flesh" in order to "be fruitful and multiply" (Gen. 2:21–24; 1:28).

Analysis

By the time of Jesus, monogamy was definitely the norm for marriage in Israel (Mark 10:6–9), although the patriarchs practiced polygamy (Gen. 29:15–30). Childbearing was seen as the principal function of marriage, so much so that in Old Testament times a man could take a concubine in cases when his wife bore no children (Gen. 16:1–2). Prostitution was a grave sin and is a favorite biblical image for idolatry (Ex. 34:15; Hos. 9:1).

The church's rituals for marriage are a curious amalgam of pagan practices with Christian beliefs. Customs like carrying the bride over the threshold of the new home, throwing rice, and cutting the wedding cake all have their roots in pagan practices and fertility rites. The rites of matrimony in today's churches have their roots within Roman law, in which a contract was made by the bride and groom stating their willingness to promise to live together and to share their material goods.

The core of all marriage services consists of unconditional, exclusive, lifelong promises, uttered freely, in the presence of witnesses. While preparation by the church of couples for marriage may consist of a wide array of training in marital skills, the main preparation for marriage consists in all the large and small ways the church helps people to be faithful to their commitments and firm in their promises.

Biblical Instances

In Old Testament times marriage occurred at a young age and was arranged by the parents, or at least with parental consent. There was usually a betrothal period (Deut. 22:23). The central ritual of marriage in the Old Testament period appears to have been the bringing of the bride into the groom's house (Deut. 22:23), followed by great feasting and rejoicing (Jer. 16:9; Judg. 14:12). (Jesus often speaks of life in his new kingdom as similar to the joy of a wedding feast, as in Matt. 25:1–13.) Sometimes the groom was adorned in a crown (S. of Sol. 3:11) or a garland (Isa. 61:10). The bride wore fine clothes, jewels, and a veil (Gen. 29:23–25). Until fairly late in Israel's history, it is uncertain whether or not marriage contracts were used.

As with all of the Near East, a woman's place within marriage in ancient Israel was vulnerable and subservient to her husband. Marriage could be terminated by the husband giving the wife a written certificate, thus permitting the wife to remarry (Deut. 24:1–2). The rabbis debated sufficient grounds for divorce, although great power was given to the husband, and divorce could be granted for almost any reason. Adultery was prohibited (Ex. 20:14), and marital fidelity was praised as the supreme example of human love. Thus marital fidelity became a chief metaphor for describing God's faithful relationship with Israel (Hosea 3).

In the New Testament Jesus forbids divorce among his followers (Mark 10:2–9), a sign of the radical quality of his discipleship. Some speculate that he did so because of the vulnerability of women in the older customs of divorce. A single woman, particularly one who had been divorced by her husband, was obviously in a seriously disadvantaged position economically. Perhaps Jesus forbade divorce and remarriage after divorce as a sign of the radical fidelity demanded of his disciples.

In many ways the New Testament appears to be ambivalent

in regard to marriage. It is difficult to find within the New Testament a strong endorsement for marriage as the normal status for Christians. There are no extensive discussions on marriage in the New Testament and, when it is discussed (Eph. 5:21–33), it is discussed as a metaphor for Christ and the church. At other times marriage is used figuratively in connection with discussions of the nature of the kingdom of God (e.g., Matt. 24:1–13; Luke 14:16–24; Rev. 19:7, 9).

Marriage is considered to be an arrangement for the present rather than for the future age (see Mark 12:25; 1 Cor. 7:8). Paul (1 Cor. 7:26–31) urges early Christians in his churches to avoid marriage if at all possible. Paul's apparently negative views toward marriage were based on his expectation of the imminent end of the present age, not a negative view of marriage in general.

Options for Preaching

Marriage is a public matter. Just as Jesus began his ministry by attending a wedding (John 2:1–11), so marriage is a matter for public recognition and public proclamation of the gospel. In affirming the public, witnessed character of marriage through the church wedding, the church underscores the public nature of the marriage bond. Too much is at stake in the promises made by a man and woman to leave them to the purely personal and the utterly private. Many marriages have difficulty because they lack the communal, social support required for a man and woman to live together in the intimacy occasioned by marriage. Marriage requires the loving support, encouragement, and instruction of the whole community of faith if it is to endure the changes of time and individual personality.

Marriage is a promise. The promises made by a man and woman to one another in the church are seen as analogous to the lifelong, unconditional promise to love made by God to Israel and then to the church in Jesus Christ. God made a covenant with Israel (Genesis 15). Jesus is the evidence of God's faithfulness to his promises (1 Cor. 11:25). Through all circumstances, despite humanity's unfaithfulness, God remains faithful to his promises. The promise of marriage is a commitment to link one's life to another, no matter how the future shapes up. The church has long claimed that the fidelity experienced in marriage is analogous to the fidelity experienced in God's love for humanity in Christ (Eph. 5:21–32).

Marriage as Christian vocation. In the churches' theology of marriage, both singlehood and marriage are seen as valid forms of existence for Christians. The church must find creative ways to support all Christians—single and married—in living out their vocations as Christians. The best Christian rationale for marriage is that it is a means of living out baptism rather than a means of personal satisfaction or gratification of individual needs. Thus the English Puritans spoke of marriage as "a little church within the church." In marriage and family, Christians live out their discipleship in intimate and caring ways—as parents, spouses, and children. Faith is enacted in concrete, worldly, very human ways. The world witnesses that the love of Christ enables people to take responsibility to love one another in ways that are both faithful across the generations and also completely self-giving. Seen in this way, marriage is preparation for, training in, and support within discipleship.

MARY

Molly Marshall-Green

Mary, the mother of Jesus of Nazareth, has long occupied scholarly imaginations. Mentioned only briefly in the New Testament, Mary has received both veneration and marginalization in Christian tradition. Throughout the centuries, however, persons of faith have affirmed her significant role in God's redemptive action. For the Word to become flesh required the trusting receptivity of Mary.

Analysis

Mary's particular vocation has both challenged theological formulation (she was called "God-bearer" by the church fathers) and evoked great piety. A patriarchal ecclesiastical system has never been comfortable with a powerful feminine religious symbol. Roman Catholics have celebrated her perpetual virginity and called her "queen of heaven," effectively removing her from church sacramental and governing functions. Thinking of Mary as a real woman in a particular historical context has been scrupulously avoided—more often she has been characterized as a "second Eve," that is, one who could undo the mischief of her primordial mother. Protestants have given little attention to Mary; those who worked for reformation of the abuses of Catholicism often ridiculed her.

Biblical Instances

Yet Mary is central to the whole narrative of Jesus, although the New Testament contains surprisingly little about her, and the Gospels offer differing accounts of her significance. Matthew speaks primarily of Joseph's perplexity, the visit of the Magi, and the flight into Egypt. Mary is mentioned in Mark's Gospel only twice: once when Jesus seemed to take a certain distance from her (Mark 3:21) because she, like the clamoring crowd, seemed to believe he was possessed by Beelzebul, and again when some individuals were astounded at his wisdom and asked, "Is this not . . . the son of Mary?" (6:3). In the context, this exclamation hardly seems to be complimentary!

The first two chapters of Luke mention Mary in connection with the Annunciation (1:26–38), the Magnificat (1:46–55), the birth of Jesus (2:5–7), the presentation in the Temple (2:22–35), and the finding of the boy Jesus conversing with scholars in the Temple (2:41–52). Mary appears twice in John's Gospel: on the occasion of the wedding feast of Cana (John 2:3) and at the foot of the cross (John 19:25–27). The Acts of the Apostles mentions her among those gathered in the upper room prior to Pentecost (1:14). One scholar called it striking that not a single New Testament passage focuses on Mary directly.

Scripture does not idealize Mary. She is a poor and simple woman of Galilee; her life is immersed in the social, political, and religious situation of her people. She was a part of the *Anawim*, the faithful poor of the land; they were, in a very real sense, a part of the remnant of Israel that had no voice in the Sanhedrin and could only hope for the promised messiah.

Options for Preaching

Mary as model of discipleship. She, in humility and faith, trusted God. Mary willingly walks in the darkness of faith and is blessed for trusting (Luke 1:45). Her vocation was to offer herself fully to God's purposes. Her life gradually clarified what she had received by faith.

God's identification with the oppressed. Mary proclaims that "God's mercy is on those who fear the Lord from generation to generation" (Luke 1:50). Mary's powerful testimony is that God has chosen to come in flesh through one who admittedly was no more than a handmaid, a female slave. She is the symbol of freedom from the bondage of sexual and societal chains and a prophet of hope.

Humanity as God's partner in redemption. Through Mary one learns that God's power is seen in unlikely places and is shared with humanity. What could be more unlikely than the virgin's womb as the place of God's own enfleshment? God, in great condescending humility, has chosen to include humans in the redemption of humanity.

MINISTRY

C. Clifton Black

The word "ministry" is derived from the Latin root *ministerium*, which means "the service of a greater by a lesser." In the Bible, the religious significance of ministry unfolds from the term's usage in various secular contexts. "Humble service" is basic to the biblical concept of ministry.

Analysis

"Ministry" is used to translate related words with different emphases in the Old and New Testaments. In Hebrew, *'abodah* (Greek: *douleia* or *latreia*) can refer to menial servitude (Gen. 29:18) or to Israel's worship of almighty God (Josh. 22:27; cf. Heb. 9:1, 6). *Sheret* typically pertains to priestly ministrations in the Temple (2 Chron. 31:2); its Greek equivalent, *leitourgia*, describes Christians' offerings of service in the church (Acts 13:2; Phil. 2:17, 30). *Diakonia*, whose root meaning is "table-waiting" (Luke 17:8; Acts 6:1–2), becomes the most common term for ministry in the New Testament: the loving service rendered by one to another (Luke 22:26–27; 2 Cor. 8:1–6; 1 Peter 4:10–11).

In ancient Israel and the early church, certain persons exercised distinctive ministries, denoted by titles appropriated from religious or political arenas. The principal intermediary between God and the Jewish people was the priest, whose sacrifices, rites, and judgments were intended to maintain the holiness of Israel and its Temple (Ezek. 44:15–16; cf. Heb. 5:1). Possessed by the divine spirit, the prophet served as a channel of communication between God and Israel (1 Kings 17–2 Kings 10); centuries later, Christian prophets mediated inspired preaching within local congregations (1 Cor. 14:26–33; Rev. 1:9–11). Regarded as Christ's own plenipotentiary, the apostle was an itinerant, supervisory evangelist (1 Cor. 9:1–5). Teachers (1 Cor. 12:28) and pastors (Eph. 4:11) seem to have been more localized. In the Pastoral and Catholic epistles, the responsibilities of presbyters, bishops, and deacons appear more formally structured, if not officially demarcated (1 Tim. 3:1–13; 5:17–22; Titus 1:5–9; James 5:14–15; 1 Peter 5:1–5). Whatever their degree of spontaneity or regularization, such functions were conceived as representative of ministry offered by the whole people of God (Deut. 10:12–13; Rom. 12:1–2), a nation called to priestly service (Ex. 19:3–6; 1 Peter 2:9–10).

Biblical Instances

Old Testament. The source and possibility of Israel's ministry to Yahweh is Yahweh's providential love for Israel (Deut. 7:6–11; cf. Hos. 11:1–9). Essentially, Israel's ministry is complete devotion to Yahweh (Deut. 6:4–9), as shaped by Torah (Ps. 19:7–14). Holiness of life implies love of God and of neighbor; proper worship and ethical behavior are inextricably interwoven (Exodus 20–23; cf. Isa. 1:11–17). Israel's covenantal love extends beyond its own boundaries to resident aliens and all the nations (Ex. 19:3–6; Deut. 10:17–19; Isa. 2:2–4).

Jesus and the Gospels. Jesus proclaims the incursion of God's powerful compassion through a ministry of teaching, preaching, and healing, proffered to society's marginalized people (Mark 2:1–3:6 and par.; cf. John 4–5). Sharing in this mission are the Twelve, formed by Jesus and representative of a renewed Israel (Mark 3:13–19a and par.; Matt. 19:28; Luke 22:30; cf. John 15:16–17). The disciples' primary qualification is personal attachment to Jesus and commitment to his ministry of radical servanthood (Mark 10:43–45 and par.; John 13:1–20).

For the Evangelists, Christology and discipleship are correlative. As Jesus perfectly fulfills the law, so, too, is Matthew's church summoned to a higher righteousness (Matthew 5–7; cf. James 1:22–27). In Mark, discipleship is preeminently the taking up of one's cross, following the crucified Christ (Mark 8:31–9:1; cf. 1 Peter 2:18–25). Characteristic of the missionaries in Acts is their inspired, universalistic witness, commensurate with that of the Lukan Jesus (Acts 1:6–2:42; cf. Luke 4:16–30). Self-giving love, in remembrance of Christ, is the hallmark of ministry in Johannine perspective (John 21:15–24; 1 John 4:7–21).

Paul. Paul construed his apostleship as the establishment of the gospel, among the nations and in God's service: the proclamation of God's "word of the cross" at work among believers for salvation (Rom. 1:1–17; 15:15–16; 1 Cor. 1:18–2:5; 4:1–5; 2 Cor. 5:18–21; 1 Thess. 2:13). Nevertheless, ministry is the calling of the church as "Christ's body": a community graced with diverse gifts for different tasks, oriented toward mutual edification and faithful thanksgiving (Rom. 12:1–13; 15:1–6; 1 Cor. 12:4–31).

Options for Preaching

The Bible provides neither a "manual" for ministry nor precise equivalents for its modern forms. Assessed holistically, scripture does afford insight into the theological character and contours of ministry.

The normative pattern for authentic ministry has been revealed by God, both through Torah and through the self-giving service of Jesus Christ. The church's ministry to a broken world continues the living Christ's own healing and restoration (cf. Rom. 15:7–9a; Heb. 3:1; 13:20–21).

Although persons are set apart from the community for specific functions, ministry is the responsibility of all believers and is discharged in all settings, sacred and secular. Structured yet free, the human ministry mirrors that of God, who has promised to meet humanity in accustomed places (Ps. 27:4), yet whose Spirit "blows where it wills" (John 3:8).

Ministry is neither the believer's right nor possession but a gift from God, who graciously empowers its performance. Accordingly, the minister's highest priority is to serve God, not a given congregation (cf. Amos 7:10–17; Gal. 1:10). In cases of conflict, ministers and congregations alike might ponder the witness of Peter and the apostles: ultimately, "We must obey God rather than any human authority" (Acts 5:29, NRSV).

MIRACLES

Reginald H. Fuller

The popular view is that miracles are occurrences involving a breach in the laws of nature. The Bible, however, had no concept of such laws. Equally nonbiblical is the traditional view that miracles are proofs of some truth, for example, that the Bible is the word of God, or that Jesus is the divine Son of God. In the Bible, miracles are events so extraordinary as to draw attention to themselves, interpreted by faith as acts of God. One of the biblical words for miracle, especially in the Old Testament, is *sign.* Signs point away from themselves to something else, in this case the presence and activity of God. In the New Testament, miracles are often called *powers,* that is, acts of the power or Spirit of God.

Analysis

Two events recognized as acts of God in the Old Testament were the exodus (Ex. 14:21–29) and the return from exile in Babylon (Isa. 40:3–4). In the New Testament the basic miracle is the Christ event, the life, death, and resurrection of Jesus viewed as the saving act of God (e.g., Acts 2:22–24). In both Old Testament and New Testament the basic miracle is accompanied by lesser miracles. Thus the exodus is preceded by the plagues of Egypt (Exodus 7–11) and followed by miracles of sustenance (Ex. 16:13–35). In the New Testament the accompanying miracles are those performed by the earthly Jesus (e.g., Matt. 11:5/Luke 7:22 Q) and those accompanying the proclamation of the basic miracle by the apostolic witnesses (e.g., Acts 3:1–10). Sometimes miracles take the form of judgment or punishment, as with the Egyptian plagues or the deaths of Ananias and Sapphira (Acts 5:1–11). The miracles of Elijah (1 Kings 17:8–24) and Elisha (2 Kings 4–5) are related to the exodus as part of the prophetic struggle against the worship of foreign deities and to reassert the covenant of Sinai.

Biblical Instances

Old Testament Miracles. The ten plagues of Egypt are in the main explicable as natural phenomena, but whether they occurred historically as a continuous series cannot be confirmed. The important point is that the plagues are seen by faith as acts of God, as in the magicians' comment: "This is the finger of God!" (Ex. 8:19; cf. Luke 11:20).

The second major group of miracles, those of Elijah and Elisha, includes miracles of sustenance, or food miracles (1 Kings 4:24–44; 17:8–16), and resuscitations from the dead (1 Kings 17:17–24 and 2 Kings 4:18–37). Elisha also heals a leper (2 Kings 5). These miracles provide important models for the narration of Jesus' miracles in the New Testament.

Miracles in the New Testament. As a charismatic prophet, Jesus preached the good news of the inbreaking of God's kingly reign or salvation. This was the form the Christ event took during Jesus' earthly life. His preaching was accompanied by exorcisms (Matt. 12:28/Luke 11:20 Q) and healings (Matt. 11:5/Luke 7:22). They were "deed-events" of the coming of God's reign, just as his preaching, especially his parables, were "word-events" of its coming.

After Easter, Jesus' earthly miracles were shaped as "deed-events," no longer of the reign of God, but of the total Christ event. Thus they acquire a christological rather than a merely eschatological significance. This christological concern leads to the formation of new miracle stories, modeled on the miraculous deeds of Moses, Elijah, and Elisha (Mark 6:35–44, etc.; John 2:1–11; cf. 2 Kings 4:42–44). What basis these "nature miracles" had in the history of the earthly Jesus can only be conjectured. There are raisings from the dead (Jairus's daughter, Mark 5:21–23, 35–43; the widow of Nain's son, Luke 7:11–17; Lazarus, John 11:1–44; cf. 1 Kings 17:17–24; 2 Kings 4:18–37). The historical basis is again uncertain, except that Jesus himself, in an authentic saying noted above (Matt. 11:5 and par.), refers to such raisings. There are also water miracles modeled on the Moses tradition (Ex. 7:20–24; 14:26–29), including the stilling of the storm (Mark 4:35–41) and walking on the water (Mark 6:47–52). These stories were used to proclaim Jesus as God's anointed prophet-Messiah.

Over time, collections of miracles were made, such as those incorporated into Mark 4:35–5:43 or the seven signs in an earlier version of the Gospel of John. By themselves, these collections could be misleading, creating the impression that Jesus was simply a stupendous wonder-worker and overlooking the fact that the miracles were merely accompaniments to the great messianic miracle, Jesus' death and resurrection. Mark coped with this problem by using the miracle collections as a preface to the passion narrative and by the device of the messianic secret. Jesus must not be proclaimed as Messiah until after his death and resurrection (cf. Mark 3:12 with 8:30; 9:9).

Matthew, who designed his Gospel as a new Torah for the church as the new Israel, collected ten miracles in chapters 8 and 9, modeled on the ten plagues of Egypt. Luke introduces Jesus in his inaugural sermon at Nazareth (Luke 4:16–30) as an Elijah-Elisha–type prophet, and disperses miracle stories in his narrative to demonstrate his prophetic Christology (see esp. Luke 7:16).

John incorporated the seven signs of his source into a discourse Gospel, attaching a revelation discourse to several of the miracles. These discourses draw out the significance of the miracles as signs. They point not merely to the messiahship of Jesus, as in the Signs Gospel (see John 20:30–31, the original conclusion to the Signs Gospel), but to Jesus as the bringer of God's final self-revelation. Thus the Bethesda miracle (John 5) leads into a discourse depicting Jesus as the bringer of a revelation that results in either judgment or eternal life. The feeding of the multitude leads to a discourse on Jesus as the bread from heaven (John 6). The healing of the blind man at Siloam leads to a revelation of Jesus as the light of the world (John 9). The resuscitation of Lazarus leads to a discourse showing Jesus to be the resurrection and the life (John 11). Three signs (the Cana miracle, John 2; the healing of the royal official's son, John 4; the crossing of the lake, John 6) lack extended discourse. Perhaps, had the Gospel been completed, discourses would have been added to these signs.

Options for Preaching

As already noted, miracles should not be used today as proofs of Christ's divinity or assumed to be historical events involving a breach of natural law. Nor is it adequate to employ them as humanitarian examples, such as incentives to support hospitals or to care for those suffering from AIDS. Rather, the miracles of Jesus should be treated as prefigurations of the supreme messianic miracle, the Christ event itself. They are proclamations in miniature of the death and resurrection of Christ and their saving effect.

The walking on the water (Matt. 14:22–33, Common Lectionary reading Proper 14A). Matthew's insertion of the scene of Peter walking on the water shows that the evangelist intended the story to be treated as an allegory. The boat represents Matthew's storm-tossed church after its expulsion from the synagogue. The preacher should identify a crisis in the church today and proclaim the risen Christ coming to assure the community of his presence, overcoming their puny faith.

The paralytic (Mark 2:1–12, Common Lectionary reading Epiphany 7B). This story is an epiphany of the Son of man's authority to forgive sins. This was effected once for all through his death on the cross and is made available in Word and sacrament in the life of the church today. Like the paralytic, the sinner can get up and walk away forgiven.

The centurion's servant (Luke 7:1–10, Common Lectionary reading Proper 4C). One of Luke's major themes is the universality of the gospel, and this pericope is an important expression of that theme. How is it to be applied in a pluralistic world? The preacher has an opportunity to proclaim the working of Christ's Spirit to heal those who are "afar off" (adherents to other religions or none), as well as the Christian community.

The raising of Lazarus (John 11:1–6, 17–45, Common Lectionary reading Lent 5A). This reading comes two weeks after Easter, the traditional time for baptisms. It proclaims Jesus as the resurrection and the life. It reminds those who have already been baptized that they have died with Christ and must constantly rise to newness of life, a process incomplete until the last day.

MYSTERY

E. Glenn Hinson

A mystery is something kept secret or unknown. In religion the term may designate secret rites or rituals or cults emphasizing secrecy. In Christianity it refers to God's work in salvation and, by inference, has been applied to the sacraments of baptism or Eucharist. Theologically God is mystery, beyond human ability to comprehend.

Analysis

The Greek word *mysterion* designated cultic rites, especially those involving initiation. The "mysteries" assured devotees of salvation by participation in a cosmic redemption with the gods. Plato and other philosophers adopted ideas and terminology from the mystery cults. Both philosophical and religious ideas carried over into Christian mysticism that emerged from the confluence of Platonic and biblical thought.

The mystic's goal is union with or a vision of God. Eastern Christians conceived the mystical experience in more cognitive, Western in more affective, language and imagery. In Eastern theology God or the Godhead is utterly beyond knowing except in God's self-disclosure in the Trinity, surrounded by a kind of "cloud." In Western theology the cloud can be penetrated not by cognition but by affect, "a sharp dart of longing love" (*The Cloud of Unknowing*, an anonymous treatise on mysticism, ca. 1355).

Biblical Instances

The Old Testament supplies few instances of "mystery" with a positive religious nuance. In Daniel 2:28–29 and 4:9, however, it refers to divinely ordained future events. Jewish apocalyptic writings elaborated on the idea of disclosure of divine secrets.

Jewish apocalyptic thinking lies behind the New Testament. Jesus used parables not to increase understanding but rather to withhold knowledge and complete the hardening process (Mark 4:11 and par.). They reserve the "messianic secret" for an inner circle. In Paul's writings "mystery" designates God's revelation in Christ (1 Cor. 2:6–16). Christ is God's wisdom in a mystery (see 1 Cor. 2:7). Thence, mystery may refer to divine counsels concealed in Christ (1 Cor. 13:2) or the covenant between Christ and the church (Eph. 5:32). In Pauline usage, mystery thus has a close connection with revelation, not as revelation itself but as the object of revelation.

Options for Preaching

Several mystery texts suggest good sermon topics.

Parables emphasize the importance of "listening," that is, being sensitive to God's presence (Mark 4:10–12; Matt. 13:10–17; Luke 8:9–10). Contrariwise, they criticize humans' inattentiveness to God's nearness.

God's wisdom hidden in mystery (1 Cor. 2:7) offers intriguing possibilities for examining God's strange ways in history. Ephesians 3:9 might serve as a backup text on "God's mysterious plan for humankind." Both texts focus on Christ as God's unveiled secret in history.

The parallel relationships of Christ and church, and husband and wife, discussed in Ephesians 5:32, opens windows on the covenant bond that effects both church and marriage.

The heart of the mystery of the Christian religion is presented in capsule form in the hymn in 1 Timothy 3:16, a summary of salvation history.

NARRATIVE

H. Stephen Shoemaker

Narrative is a story-form means of communication involving plot, character, and narrator.

Analysis

Narrative is more than a deliverer of information. It conveys the meaning of things in the context of human relationships. It requires teller and told. Hunger for narrative may be as basic as for bread and love and may indeed supply the latter. Sacred narrative tells the story humanity most wants to hear: the history of God who knows humans and loves them, humans who are God's story; God is with them in terror and joy and will be with them to the end where all things will be well; Jesus Christ is God's favorite story, God making God's own self known in human flesh and telling humans that they are known by God.

The biblical canon is predominantly narrative in form and essentially narrative in character. The acknowledgment of this fact and of the profoundly narrative character of human life itself has led to a surging new interest in narrative theology, narrative ethics (i.e., of story-formed community), and narrative preaching. Narrative preaching seeks to make fuller use of narrative as the form of sermons.

The Bible is essentially narrative in character. Not only is narrative the main literary form of scripture, it is the heart of Hebrew scripture—Hebrew scripture can be pictured as three concentric circles, the center circle being the Torah, surrounded next by Prophets and then by Writings—and it is the overarching structure of the Christian scriptures, beginning with Creation (Genesis), moving to the moment of truth in Jesus (the Gospels), and ending with the culmination of things (Revelation). The great-story of scripture has these chapters: creation, fall, covenant, exodus, torah, nations prophecy, gospel, church, and apocalypse. Every smaller unit of scripture, nonnarrative as much as narrative, finds its place somewhere in the overarching story; for example, the Decalogue in the exodus experience, the songs of David in Israel's story, the parables in the story of Jesus, the epistles in the early church's story, and apocalyptic vision in the story of universal salvation.

Biblical Instances

Old Testament. Narrative in the Old Testament includes prehistory story proclamation (Genesis 1–11), historical narrative (from Abraham, c. 1800 B.C., to the Exile, c. 500 B.C.) and short story (Ruth, Jonah, Job).

New Testament. Narrative in the New Testament includes the genres of Gospel, parable, miracle story, historical narrative (Acts), and apocalypse (Revelation).

Options for Preaching

The form of the sermon follows the story-form of the text in narrative preaching. When the text is nonnarrative, the sermon may be narrative in character even if not in form if it places the text in the great-story of redemption.

Weaving the preacher's story and the hearer's story in and out of the biblical story creates the most effective narrative sermons.

Extrabiblical narrative (novels, short stories) may be used as a major metaphorical entry into a biblical text. Biography and autobiography may also be used as major sermon vehicles. In all of the above the extrabiblical story must *serve* the biblical story.

Long narrative sequences like the story of Abraham, Joseph, David, Ruth, Jesus, Peter, and Paul may be used as a kind of biographical preaching.

Short narrative passages—one episode in a gospel or in the life of a biblical character, a parable, or an episode in a historical narrative (Exodus or Acts), such as Pentecost in Acts 2—may become the focus of a sermon.

OBEDIENCE

Eugene L. Zoeller

Traditionally, obedience is a preeminent moral virtue or evangelical counsel by which a person submits in conduct and opinion to legitimate authority. Today, with the Western inheritance of the spirit of freedom and autonomy from the Enlightenment, obedience no longer appears to be a virtue but rather an inconvenience or a necessary evil. In precisely the way the nineteenth and twentieth centuries have come to experience a crisis in the manner in which authority is exercised, so these centuries have come to know its correlative, a crisis in obedience.

Analysis

This crisis in authority and the crisis in obedience are by no means limited to the social and political and educational sectors of life; they are being expressed, often in a painful way, in religious institutions. In contemporary practice, obedience has come to mean, both in society and among religious institutions, merely the willingness or need to collaborate for the achievement of certain goals or projects for the welfare of the community.

This represents a significant departure from the past. In some world religions, obedience becomes more necessary in the more sophisticated and higher stages of religious growth. It becomes one of the chief ways of submitting to the claims of the Holy by following absolutely the mind of the spiritual master. Obedience to cult and ritual, to precept and the guidance of another was the classic expression of the faith that humans are creatures always living in the presence of the Holy. Neo-Platonism, which became a powerful influence among many of the writers of Christianity, insisted that perfection could be achieved solely by abandoning one's freedom and will and submitting absolutely to the Holy and to all divinely established authority. Human alienation could be overcome only by hearing and recalling one's origins and destiny and by a radical acceptance of both in the act of obedience.

Biblical Instances

In the Hebrew scriptures, obedience is directly linked with hearing and, as in many other religions and languages of that area, the Hebrew word for it is derived from the verb "to hear." The prime relationship between God and all creation and the human race was first established by God's speaking a covenantal word in sovereign freedom. Obedience to God is expressed in hearing and heeding this manifold word of the Law and the Prophets, the commandments and the precepts of the Lord. Faithful hearing and heeding of the word will strengthen both the leader and the nation, and it alone will protect it from calamity and collapse. In fact, this obedient hearing of God's word is valued more than sacrifice. This covenant relationship, requiring careful hearing and obedience as a consequence, was by no means limited to Israel as a nation; it was to be reflected in the extended families and tribes within Israel. Hence the Fourth Word of the Decalogue captures an important place and insight in Israel's history, and moral conduct as obedience must be extended not only to the father but also to the mother.

If the Hebrew scriptures place great emphasis upon obedience, they also preserve a bitter memory of the failure of obedience. Genesis opens with the recitation of the collapse of God's original plan of order and harmony in the disobedience of

Adam and Eve (Gen. 3:1–14)—the great paradigm for the destruction of all relationships and for many of the personal and political failures in Israel's future history. The Letter of Paul to the Romans (Rom. 5:19) will build more directly and explicitly upon this text by contrasting the disobedience of Adam and Eve that has rendered all creation and all people wounded by sin, with the obedience of Jesus Christ, which offers to all creation and the human race redemption and new life.

In the Christian scriptures, especially the Synoptic Gospels, Jesus is described as the strong man who achieves his strength in his temptation (Matt. 4:1–11; Mark 8:33) and becomes absolutely faithful to God's mysterious plan for him. Having been tested in such obedience, Jesus himself will be obeyed by the demons and all powers hostile to God's creation (Mark 1:23–45; 55:12). Tested in every way, he does expound the law with new authority (Matt. 5:21–48), bids for the obedience of his followers, and urges all to imitate him and so submit their wills to God and the arriving reign of God (Mark 8:34–38).

The arrival of the reign of God, in the person of Jesus, of necessity requires obedience of the followers but never in a mere formal or legalistic sense. As the arrival of the kingdom announces a more personal and intimate relationship with creation and the human race, so obedience in this kingdom must also become more personal, intimate, and radical. The elder son in the parable of the prodigal son and his father illustrates graphically that Jesus was not always impressed with formal obedience (Luke 15:11–32). True obedience in the reign of God requires not only fidelity to God and to one another but also a heart open to the unexpected good news found in the arrival of God and of the neighbor.

In the life and the death of Jesus, obedience becomes the discovery and then the free submission to the "it must be" character of God's intent to save this world. In the letters of Paul, the Christian enters into this discovery and submission of Jesus by his or her personal surrender to God (Rom. 10:2, 16; 2 Cor. 7:15; 2 Thess. 1:8). So much is this the pattern of salvation in Jesus that Christians are identified as the people of faith and of obedience. Obedience never loses its christological emphasis in the Christian scriptures, for submission and obedience are given only to the one law that is Jesus Christ (1 Cor. 9:21).

While the major emphasis of the Christian scriptures is the radical obedience owed to God in the arrival of the kingdom, they also urge obedience to other people and other human institutions as well. Obedience is expected and reverenced within the family and among slaves and their masters, and it should be offered to all civil authorities. After the burning of Rome in A.D. 64, Christianity had the added task of showing conclusively that it was not a subversive group and that legitimate authority must be not only obeyed but prayed for (Rom. 13:1–7). In the struggle to strike a balance between obedience to divine and human authority, however, Christians remained faithful first and foremost to God. From this is born the famous limitation on obedience, expressed in the text of Acts 5:29 (NRSV), "We must obey God rather than any human authority."

Options for Preaching

Contemporary preaching must continue to be faithful to the biblical data and insight. It must stress that the human person is created and graced to hear God's word and, in such hearing, to achieve her or his communion with God. In this sense, obedience will no longer be one virtue among others, but the foundational virtue for all Christian living. It is precisely in such obedience to God's word that human freedom achieves its completion and fulfillment. So foundational is this aspect of obedience that in his treatise on moral virtues, Thomas Aquinas spoke of this not as obedience but as faith.

The contemporary difficulty regarding obedience to God is not to be found in this foundational structure of fidelity of the listener to God, but rather in the actual content of what God seems to demand. Today, it is the common wisdom of theological and biblical scholarship to recognize that God does not speak to people directly, not even in the Holy Scriptures, but God's word to humans is mediated in and through all existing human structures of thought, language, and social order. In certain cases, the problem of hearing God's word and knowing God's intent has become increasingly more difficult. The word of God, rather than dispensing with conscience, becomes the first word in a lifelong dialogue about God's claims on the human heart. In this dialogue, critical, biblical scholarship will have much to offer.

Preaching in the modern age that centers on the necessary but limited obedience within the family, society, and religious institutions has become much more difficult, not only because of the abuses in the exercise of authority, civil and religious but also because of the great imbalances of past preaching on obedience. Such crisis in the exercise of authority and in obedience to legitimate authority must be identified and frankly admitted. The very truth of the gospel permits the conclusion that no generation is able to see and speak of the virtues of Christian life in their proper proportions.

Education in obedience will never be an easy matter, and one would become quite suspicious if it should ever become such. Obedience is that graced, transcendent moment when the demands of God and the other person actually touch one's most precious personal self—one's freedom. If this freedom is viewed only as something that must be abandoned, education in obedience will not take place in a healthy, effective manner. But if obedience is seen and presented as freedom's adjustment and accommodation to what is present in all authentic self-realization and fulfillment, namely, the needs of the other and the demands of God, then this approach would return all thinking about obedience to the basic insights of the Bible and of the world religions, that freedom to hear and to heed God's word is the human destiny.

Even if the world is deeply troubled by the exercise of human authority and obedience to such authority, the homilist must not conclude that the world is more evil than in the past or that the world is thereby more resistant to putting its freedom and will at the service of others. The homilist must suppose that each generation brings to the moral virtues, and certainly to obedience, its own insights and presuppositions, many of which are quite legitimate. The task will be to guide the new generation between the extremes of uncritical self-surrender and mindless self-determination in the presence of God and of the other.

PARABLE

John R. Donahue

C. H. Dodd has offered the best description of a New Testament parable: "a metaphor or simile drawn from nature or common life, arresting the hearer by its vividness or strangeness and leaving the mind in sufficient doubt about its precise application to tease it into active thought" (*The Parables of the Kingdom*, 1961). "Parable," from the Greek *parabole* (comparison), in the Old Testament, normally translates the Hebrew *masal*, which encompasses various literary forms: proverbs (1 Sam. 10:12; Prov. 1:1, 6; 26:7–9), riddles (Judg. 14:10–18), taunt songs (Micah 2:4; Hab. 2:6), oracles (Num. 23:7, 18), metaphors and allegories (Isa. 5:1–7; Ezek. 17:3–24), and extended narratives (Psalm 78). The Gospels use *parabole* with the same wide range as *masal,* comprising proverbs (Luke 4:23), examples (Luke 12:16–21), similitudes (Luke 5:36–39), similes (Matt. 13:33), allegory (Matt. 25:1–13), as well as the more familiar narrative parables.

Analysis

Jesus taught in parables to proclaim the advent of the kingdom of God and to summon people to respond to God's offer of love and mercy. Jesus' parables employ images and situations familiar to his hearers, such as farming (Mark 4), domestic life (discipleship is like a lamp put on a lamp stand, Matt. 5:15), social life (weddings, Matt. 25:1–13, and funerals, Matt. 11:16–17). This realism of the parables means that Jesus places the point of contact between God and humans within the everyday world of human experience. While realistic, the parables are fresh and paradoxical. The novel twists in Jesus' stories make his hearers take notice. The harvest is not only bountiful but extravagant (Mark 4:8); wealthy hosts ordinarily do not react to the absence of invited guests by substituting the poor, blind, and lame (Luke 14:21). The parables also summon people to enter their world and to take a stand. Jesus' hearers are asked whether they, too, will complain with the grumbling workers over God's mercy shown to the undeserving (Matt. 20:1–16), or whether they will remain with the older brother outside the feast of reconciliation (Luke 15:11–32).

Biblical Instances

The "seed parables" in the New Testament contrast frequent failure to the hope of a bountiful harvest (Mark 4:3–8) and urge their hearers to contemplate the hidden growth of the kingdom, while remaining alert for the harvest time (Mark 4:26–29). From an insignificant beginning, like a mustard seed, God's kingdom becomes the greatest of shrubs (Mark 4:30–32). Jesus announces God's mercy for sinners and tells parables of a God who seeks sinners like a shepherd searching for a lost sheep or a woman for a lost coin (Luke 15:1–10). What he proclaims in parable, Jesus enacts in his ministry by eating with tax collectors and sinners (Mark 2:15–17) and by defending a sinful woman (Luke 7:36–50). Jesus' parables often shock his hearers. People are rewarded not according to their merits but from the generosity of the vineyard owner (Matt. 20:1–16). Even so devious a character as the "unjust steward" (Luke 16:1–8) can receive a master's praise, suggesting that God acts in a manner that shocks conventional virtue.

The Gospel writers not only transmit Jesus' parables but stamp them with their own theological perspective. Mark's parables contrast what is hidden to what will be revealed, just as Mark's Jesus both conceals and discloses his identity (Mark 4:21–25, 30–32; 8:31; 9:9–13). Distinct Matthean themes emerge in parable: God's searching love and merciful forgiveness (the lost sheep, 18:12–14, and the unmerciful servant, 18:23–35); the need for a life of discipleship that brings forth fruit (the wicked tenants, 21:33–44; cf. 7:15–23); the sheep and the goats, 25:31–46; cf. 23:23); warnings against both complacency and fear (the ten maidens and the talents, 25:1–30), even when faced with the threat of judgment (22:11–14; 24:45–51; 25:14–30). Luke's parables are shocking examples of that behavior which is to characterize Jesus' followers. They are to show mercy like the Samaritan (Luke 10:25–37) and are to invite the socially unacceptable to their banquets (the great supper, 14:12–24). Disciples are frequently warned about the danger of great wealth (the rich fool, 12:16–21; the rich man and Lazarus, 16:19–31). Marginal people and outsiders (e.g., the widow and the tax collector, Luke 18:1–14) teach the community to pray.

Options for Preaching

Context. Preachers should explain the background and images of the parables and pay careful attention to the Gospel context of each parable. In Luke 15:4–6, for example, Jesus tells the parable of the lost sheep to defend his ministry to marginal people (tax collectors), while in Matthew 18:12–14, the parable is directed more to community leaders to exhort them to seek out those who stray.

Allegory. Allegorical interpretation of parables should be avoided. It often uses the parable simply to illustrate a predetermined meaning. Allegory develops in the New Testament itself. The interpretation of the sower parable (Mark 4:13–20) can obscure the parable itself (4:1–9) as a story of the contrast between the repeated failures and the extravagant harvest, which embodies Jesus' own hope for the growth of the kingdom even in the face of rejection. The wicked tenants parable (Mark 12:1–2/Matt. 21:33–46/Luke 20:9–19) is a virtual allegory of the rejection of Jesus by Jewish leaders. It is also a parable of a God who continues to reach out to sinful humanity in the face of rejection.

Identifying with characters. People should be invited to enter the world of the parable and to identify with both the good and less attractive characters. They can rejoice with a widow who fights for her rights before a callous judge (Luke 18:1–7). They should also see themselves in the timid servant who hides his talent (Matt. 25:14–30) or the grumbling vineyard workers (Matt. 20:16). The first step in conversion is often the awareness of the fears and resentments that lurk deep in human hearts. The parables can unmask these basic dispositions.

The element of surprise. Preachers should capture the surprise and shock of the parables. In "the prodigal son" (Luke 15:11–32) it is shocking that a father in a traditional culture should "run" to the younger son or that he should "go out" to the rebellious older son. Also, the father accepts neither the younger son's desire to return as a servant nor the older son's claim that he lived as one. This is a parable about the surprising love of God, which breaks through servility. The shock of the good Samaritan parable (Luke 10:29–37) is that it is the hated outsider who teaches the true meaning of the great commandment to love God and neighbor. Preachers might ask today how the church can be challenged by the actions of those considered outsiders.

PATIENCE

E. Glenn Hinson

Patience is the will or ability to endure without complaint, or steadfastness in the performance of a task. It was a key virtue among the Greeks, especially in the sense of courageous endurance. Among Jews and Christians it has held a twofold nuance of "waiting on God" and "endurance" or "steadfastness" toward the world.

Analysis

The English word "patience" renders two Greek words in the New Testament: *hypomone* and *makrothymia*. The former picks up Old Testament themes of "waiting" on God and standing fast or persevering toward the world. The latter means literally "long suffering." God models an attitude of "long suffering" toward humankind; God's people should imitate God in coping with life's trials. During times of persecution and natural disaster, Christians have delivered many sermons or written many treatises on patience.

Biblical Instances

In the Old Testament, patience embodies the idea of "expectant hope" in God. God is Israel's hope in which individuals participate. Whoever forsakes God, "the hope of Israel," will suffer shame (Jer. 17:13). As the covenant God, God will not forsake those who trust in and wait upon God (Ps. 24:5). Unlike Greek thinking, Hebrew thought did not emphasize "human courage" but rather "waiting on God." Toward the world, however, this meant "enduring, standing fast" in the face of trials. Job became the outstanding example of pious endurance, as one who "waited" his whole life for God to intervene (Job 14:14; 17:13). The three youths in the fiery furnace of the Additions to Daniel appeared often in Jewish and Christian art as models of patience. Later writers looked increasingly for fulfillment of God's assurances beyond the present life.

New Testament writers used *hypomone* only twice (2 Thess. 3:5; Rev. 1:9) with reference to waiting on God. Characteristically they applied it to "steadfastness" or "perseverance" in the face of persecution or hardship. According to their eschatological scheme, "the one who endures to the end will be saved" (Mark 13:13, NRSV). The apostle Paul richly expounded on the connection with the hope rooted in Jesus' resurrection. People wait with patience for that which they cannot see (Rom. 8:25). The characteristic Christian attitude in the face of persecution or hardship is patience (Rom 12:12; 1 Cor. 13:7; 2 Cor. 12:12).

Options for Preaching

Two major biblical emphases supply ample material for sermons.

Waiting on God (so frequent in Job) is the first.

Steadfastness or endurance toward the world (2 Tim. 2:10–13; Heb. 10:32–39) is the second. The former should emphasize God's dependability (Ps. 24:5) despite human weakness, the latter how God supplies strength in our weakness (2 Cor. 12:9).

Subsidiary themes would include:

Affliction produces patience (Rom. 5:3), as Paul himself learned through what he suffered (2 Cor. 5:6–10).

A God of patience (Rom. 15:5) generates patience (Col. 1:11).

Models of patience: Job (James 5:11), Paul (2 Tim. 3:10), Jesus (Rev. 1:9), the three youths—Shadrach, Meshach, Abednego (Additions to Daniel 3:23–24).

PEACE
Glen Harold Stassen

The word "peace" is the Hebrew *shalom*. It expresses safety and security in relationship, wholeness and welfare in community, and health and justice in bodily, familial, economic, and political relationships. It is relational, not merely "peace of mind." It is realistic, not merely idealistic. It includes the reality of conflict and battle where injustices are confronted and movement toward deliverance is under way. New Testament authors use the Greek *eirene* to affirm basically the Hebrew meaning of *shalom*.

Analysis

Biblical proclamation does not so much seek to persuade hearers to be generally in favor of peace as to repent from ways that lead to destruction and take steps that lead to peace. It is realistic, naming idolatries and injustices that keep people and nations in bondage. It is concrete, naming steps of turning toward peace. Preaching cheap peace when there is no peace (Jer. 6:14; 8:11) does not give real hope, which comes in turning to God's ways of faithfulness, justice, and love of enemy in practical action.

Biblical Instances

Old Testament. The story of human sin comes in two acts: Adam and Eve, and Cain and Abel. When preaching ignores the second act, it misses the *shalom* dimension. Jesus sees Cain as describing the human situation (Matt. 5:22–26) and says to do right means to talk to your brother and make peace. See also the stories of Noah's rainbow and the tower of Babel. The prophets warn repeatedly of war's destruction as judgment. The way of peace is to turn to God and practice justice (Isaiah 31; 32:16–20).

New Testament. Jesus was born to fulfill the prophetic hope for peace (Luke 2:14). His humble entry into Jerusalem fulfilled the prophetic hope for a peaceful messiah. His teachings on peacemaking in the Sermons on the Mount and the Plain are realistic, practical deliverance from vicious cycles of war (see Walter Wink, *Violence and Nonviolence*; Pinchas Lapide, *Sermon on the Mount*; Roger Fisher, *Getting to Yes*; and David

Augsburger, *Caring Enough to Confront*). Paul's letter to the Romans is increasingly being seen as centering in the twin themes of grace and peace. Romans 12 reflects Luke 6, with practical peacemaking steps: talk and welcome one another, pray for and act in love toward enemies, take transforming initiatives, practice justice toward the poor, don't judge but forgive, and correct the beam in your own eye.

Options for Preaching

Jesus makes clear that peacemaking is participating in God's merciful role. Preach the passages above as good news, not a guilt trip—after realistically diagnosing the destructiveness of bondage to injustice and hostility so it's not false hope. There are infinite resources in the prophets.

Some topics:

Cain and Abel and what it means to be human (Genesis 4; Matt. 5:22–26).

Peacemaking worth dying for (Rom. 15:25–33; Acts 20:22–24; 21:17–26).

Practicing conflict resolution (Jacob and Esau, or Joseph greeting his brothers, or Mary and Martha—related to Matt. 5:21–26, 38–48).

Justice moves in and the offspring is peace (Isa. 32:14–18).

The followers of the beast make war; the followers of the lamb do his teachings (recurring theme in the book of Revelation).

Possibilities for series include:

The peacemaking steps in Romans 12, reflecting Matthew 5 and Luke 6.

The Letter of Paul to the Romans as grace and peace.

POLITICS

Theodore R. Weber

Politics refers to the struggle for power in any kind of organization, including family, church, and state, or to the authoritative ordering of the common life of a society according to its values, laws, and traditions.

Analysis

Politics as a theme in preaching is primarily the proclaiming of the divine ordering of the fallen world in the light of the reconciling work of Christ and the summoning of Christian believers to faith-informed participation in political society. In this ordering context, the preacher addresses issues of preservation of life, human rights, public order, and environment; of justifiable means in political action; of just distribution of goods, burdens, and responsibilities; of inclusive membership in political society; of the right order of obligation to God and human authorities. All preaching is implicitly political, for all preaching pertains to peace, justice, liberation, human community, the wholeness of creation. Yet preaching is an office of the church, not of the political community, and it is addressed first to the Christian community, not to the nation or "to whom it may concern." Preaching is not regulated by constitutional separation of church and state. It requires no political permission and tolerates no political limitation.

Biblical Instances

Old Testament. The Old Testament is the religious-political story of a people called into existence through God's covenanting love and given laws and leaders and a presence in history. God promises them peace and well-being (*shalom*), fights their battles, sends them into and recalls them from exile. Prophets of God address kings and people on covenantal justice and mercy (Micah 6:6–8; Zech. 7:8–14), warn against trusting in armies and alliances (Isaiah 31), and explore relationships of truth and justice to political stability (Isa. 59:9–15). In the controversy over Israel's kingship (1 Samuel 8), the sovereign authority of God is established over human authority.

New Testament. The New Testament tells the story of Jesus of Nazareth, perceived by Roman and Jewish establishments as a threat to their power and by fanatical religious nationalists as their promised messianic leader, crucified on the political charge that he aspired to become king of the Jews, abandoned by his followers as a failed messiah, and raised by God to victory over the seen and unseen powers of this world. This Jesus was subject to profound political temptation (Matt. 4:8–10), to dangerous testing of his obligations to God and Caesar (Matt. 22:15–22; Mark 12:13–17; Luke 20:20–28), and to pressure to political favoritism (Matt. 20:20–28). His disciples faced issues of political authority and obedience (Acts 5:27–42; Rom. 13:1–7, 10; 1 Tim. 2:1–2; 1 Peter 2:13–17), ethnic and religious rivalry, and state persecution (Revelation 13).

Options for Preaching

Favorite idolatries. Exodus 20:1–3, placed in contemporary settings, warns against idolatry in political forms, such as absolutizing of state or nation or their symbols (flag, patriotic songs), trusting for security in weapons of mass destruction, and placing leaders above criticism.

Cities of presence and hope. The God of Israel admonishes the exiles to "seek the welfare of the city" (Jer. 29:7) where they now live. Hebrews 13:14 reminds the readers that "here we have no lasting city." They should "seek the city which is to come."

Truth and the health of the city. Lying and deception in public life (Isa. 59:9–15) corrupt the foundations of public order, undermine trust, banish justice, and make every citizen a potential victim.

POVERTY

J. Philip Wogaman

Poverty is the state of a person who lacks a usual or socially acceptable amount of money or material possessions. The vast majority of humanity lives in poverty by the standards of middle-class Americans.

Analysis

There are strong Christian reasons for easing the plight of the poor. First, poverty causes physical deprivation and suffering. The Christian doctrine of creation affirms the goodness of physical existence in this tangible world. God's people are embodied. God's purposes for them in this world also have a physical dimension and can therefore be frustrated by human want. Is that not clear in the vacant eyes and emaciated bodies of Third-World children? It is not to say that human life is altogether physical; it is to grasp that there is a physical basis and precondition for deeper, covenantal fulfillment. Second, poverty impedes the realization of human community. People cannot readily be to one another what God intends them to be when great barriers of inequality separate rich and poor. In an affluent society persons can be relatively very poor even though their basic needs are met. Many poor people in the United

States are well off by Third-World standards. But they are still poor, relatively speaking, if they do not have the resources to participate normally in American society. The epistle of James obviously has that kind of relative poverty in mind when it speaks of showing partiality to the rich in church while dishonoring the poor (2:1–7).

Is there, then, a divine preference for the poor? Not if one means that God loves poor people more than others. But if one is concerned about community, as God intends it, then the problem of poverty must receive special emphasis because that is the point at which community is most vulnerable.

Biblical Instances

Some Christians quote Matthew 26:11 (also Mark 14:7), "For you always have the poor with you," to make the point that Christians need not be too exercised about the persistence of poverty. But most biblical sayings express God's deep concern for the poor—and God's judgment upon the complacency of those who could, but will not, help the poor. Even the Matthew-Mark verse is evidently a quotation from Deuteronomy, "For the poor will never cease out of the land," and that observation is immediately followed by the admonition "therefore I command you, You shall open wide your hand to your brother, to the needy and to the poor" (Deut. 15:11).

Concern for the poor permeates the writing of the great prophets. It is expressed with earthy practicality in Leviticus and Deuteronomy (where landowners are commanded to leave a portion of their crops for the landless to gather). Isaiah attributes the plight of the poor to oppression by the powerful: " 'What do you [elders and princes of the people] mean by crushing my people, by grinding the face of the poor?' says the Lord GOD of hosts" (3:15). Amos condemns those who "trample the head of the poor into the dust of the earth" (2:7). From a biblical standpoint it would seem to be better to be poor than rich! The Magnificat of Mary picks up the prophetic theme, linking it to the New Testament gospel: "He has put down the mighty from their thrones, and exalted those of low degree; he has filled the hungry with good things, and the rich he has sent empty away" (Luke 1:52–53). The parables of the rich man and Lazarus (Luke 16:19–31) and the last judgment (Matt. 25:31–46) make it clear that one's very salvation is tied up in one's sensitivity to the poor—and in doing something about it.

Options for Preaching

Ethical responsibilities of relatively affluent Christians include disciplining life-styles in order to share with others—through church programs and other kinds of aid, both domestically and internationally.

Perceptions of poverty need to be sharpened by firsthand experience with those in need.

Guilt at relative comfort needs to be recognized. Thanks for God's benefits can be expressed by hard work to alleviate the problems of inequality.

PRAYER

J. Estill Jones

Prayer is the action or the attitude in which a person or a group of people reach out beyond themselves to Deity. In the Christian sense, it is talking with God. It is not a monologue but a dialogue. The faith of the individual praying affirms that God can and will speak.

Prayer is spiritual communion. It may be absolute silence. Paul reminds the praying Christian that the Spirit interprets the deep longings to God, who is Spirit. Human spirits commune with God's Spirit, because "we do not know how to pray as we ought" (Rom. 8:26).

Prayer is praise and petition, silent contemplation and earnest expression.

Prayer is the basic religious exercise. Almost every religion practices some form of prayer, whether the prayer wheel of the East, the all-night meeting in the interest of a special petition, or the quiet meditation with unspoken requests. It may be public, led by articulate phrasing, or private, characterized by a deep heartthrob.

Prayer is an act of worship. The individual confronts God in prayer and responds with thanksgiving, confession, and petition.

Analysis

Good friends converse with one another. Such a relationship exists between God and God's children; prayer is a natural expression of a supernatural relationship. It is faith finding audible (to God) expression.

Prayer richly supplies a need. Trust thrives on prayer. A believer needs conversation with God; indeed, a believer needs God. Paul's counsel to the Thessalonians, "Pray without ceasing" (1 Thess. 5:17, KJV), expresses this need for continuing prayer.

Prayer helps to establish spiritual priorities. The objects of prayer are wide and varied; there are no limits. But as the person talks with God, he or she comes to realize that some causes are more important than others. To pray for God's will to be done is to reckon with a sovereignty more significant than the daily want list.

What is the effect of prayer? Again and again prayer is encouraged in the Old and the New Testaments. How does it affect God? Does it change God's mind, God's will? The answer depends on the individual's faith. For those who believe God is personal, concerned, loving, it is easy to pray in faith. For those who believe God's will is inscrutable and unchangeable, a mere prayer will have little effect. World leaders often offer prayer in times of crisis. The mention of prayer can become a fetish with little or no meaning of relationship.

Prayer certainly changes persons. A person can hardly pour out his or her soul to God, submitting to God's will, seeking direction, asking for help, without being changed. Perhaps she or he will find new support in love, a finely honed sense of guidance, or an affirmation of faith. Even a brief, heartbreathed prayer will have an effect. This is the faith of the church.

Does prayer indeed change "things"? A child prays earnestly for a pet or a toy, a youth prays about a relationship, a young adult prays for an ailing child, an older adult prays for direction: Are these legitimate prayers? Does God answer? Over and over the Bible assures believers that God hears and answers prayers . . . sometimes with a gentle no.

Prayer is easily misunderstood. God is not a heavenly servant responding to every expressed whim or desire. Nor is God necessarily impressed by long repetitive rhetoric. Jesus discouraged this. Prayer is not a part of a works-righteousness theology. Nor is it an end in itself; it is a means to an end. It is an attitude as well as an action.

Biblical Instances

Always God's people have been distinguished by sincere prayer. It is not always mature; it is not always wise—but it comes from the depth of being.

God's people prayed. One of the most memorable examples is 1 Samuel 1:9–18. So earnestly did Hannah pray for a son that the priest Eli thought she was drunk. But God heard her prayer and the son, Samuel, was born. The psalms are filled with prayers—of thanksgiving, of confession, for forgiveness, for guidance, for strength. Many are ascribed to David, whose spiritual pilgrimage is a vital part of the Old Testament. The fellowship of prayer bound David to obedience.

God's chosen leaders prayed. Abram prayed for an heir (Gen. 15:2–21). The response to the prayer is reported through the covenant that God and Abram cut and the actual birth of Isaac. The conception and birth of Ishmael appears as an interlude, as Abram's attempt to answer his own prayer. Isaac then became a prayer child. One of the significant prayer passages in the Old Testament may be read in the prophecy of Habakkuk. The prolonged conversation between the despairing, complaining prophet and the observing, caring God is a source of encouragement to frank conversation with God.

God's Son prayed. That Jesus prayed is the evidence of all the Gospels. He prayed when the crowds were threatening his mission (Mark 1:35). He prayed all night before choosing his apostles (Luke 6:12). And when the seventy returned from a successful mission, he offered a prayer of thanksgiving (Luke 10:21). He offered a prayer of thanksgiving when he broke the loaves for feeding the five thousand (John 6:11). Later he went alone to the mountains to pray: the multitudes were continuing to be a problem (Matt. 14:23). In the midst of controversy, "at that season," he entered into a period of personal prayer (Matt. 11:25–27). One of the choice prayers recorded was for the disciples and ourselves (John 17).

Jesus prayed in times of crisis and need. He continued as Son in close fellowship with his Father. He reached out to the reality beyond. He left his disciples a clear example of seeking and finding and doing God's will.

God's people still pray. The addition of the doxology to the Lord's Prayer at an early period indicates something of the prayer's popularity (Matt. 6:9–13). Jesus taught his disciples to pray (Luke 11:1–4), and they prayed before Pentecost (Acts 1:14). The subject of prayer continues to be treated through the New Testament. There are parables of prayer, examples of prayer, and exhortations to pray. Much of the first chapter of Ephesians (1:3–14) is a written prayer. Prayer is encouraged in 2 Thessalonians 3:1–5 and in 1 Thessalonians 5:17. A discussion of prayer in James 5:13–18 certainly reveals the author as a person of prayer.

Options for Preaching

Prayer: antidote for anxiety (Phil. 4:6–7). Anxiety is a real problem in current society. Paul pits anxiety against prayer and declares prayer the victor. Anxiety represents distraction from the main purpose; prayer focuses on the main purpose. Both petition and thanksgiving are therapeutic: the treatment results in peace. The peace of God, the *shalom* of Hebrew, will offer security to the person being pulled apart.

Prayer: an honest complaint (Hab. 1:2–4; 2:2–4). The prophet was a realist, a committed contemporary. He saw the evil in his world, unpunished. The modern Christian may well see his world through the same glasses. The prophet complained to God, a refreshing focus of earnest prayer. The modern Christian has the right to speak frankly with God. God answered the prophet's prayer, perhaps not as he had asked, but with a challenge to his faith. The modern Christian may be surprised at God's response, but his or her faith will be challenged.

Prayer: a challenge to faith (Mark 11:22–24). Prayer is an outreach of faith. Jesus repeatedly promised that God would answer prayers uttered in God's name. Always such prayers are expressions of faith. God is willing to move a mountain or a tree in response to such faith—but what faith! Follow the tenses carefully in the promise of verse 24: "Therefore I tell you, whatever you ask in prayer, believe that you have received it, and it will be yours." Freely translated that reads, "believe that you got them, and you shall have them." That is faith and hope all tied up together.

Prayer: a conditional petition (Matt. 6:12–15). The context of the model prayer underscores a condition for a petition. The petition is that of forgiveness, "forgive us our debts [trespasses]." The condition is added, "as we also have forgiven our debtors." The prayer suggests that forgiveness is impossible outside the experience of offering forgiveness. The petitioner does not understand his or her petition apart from having mercifully granted forgiveness to one who has offended . . . "for so the whole round earth is every way Bound by gold chains about the feet of God" (Alfred Lord Tennyson, *The Passing of Arthur*).

PROMISE

John D. W. Watts

For Christian faith "promise" is relevant to assurances God has given his people that are understood to be of continued application today. A promise is a declaration that God will do or refrain from doing something. It is understood to be binding, giving the person to whom it is given a right to expect or claim performance of the act promised.

Analysis and Biblical Instances

Although Hebrew has no equivalent word for "promise," modern translators have legitimately understood that when God speaks or swears of what he will do or not do, this may be understood as promise. New Testament Greek does have a word for it. The Bible throughout is permeated with the idea that God, through Jesus, assures God's people of what they can expect from God.

The promise to bless begins with Abraham (Gen. 12:2–3) and continues through the Bible.

The promise of God's presence, implicit for Abraham, is articulated to Moses (Ex. 3:12) and is confirmed by Jesus (Matt. 28:20b). The mirror image is the promise that believers will be with God and Christ (John 17:24).

God's promise to Abraham of a land for his seed (Gen. 12:7) is fundamental to assurances of future security for the people of God throughout scripture. God's promise to David of a throne and an heir (2 Sam. 7:12–16) forms the basis for New Testament understanding of messiah.

In the crisis period at the end of monarchy, prophetic promises assured incipient Judaism of God's intentions for them under the radically changed conditions of exile and dispersion.

In the crisis of Jesus' death and separation, his promises pointed the way to a continued life and faith for his followers (Matt. 28:20; John 14:12–14, 16).

Facing the crisis of each believer's mortality, God's promises provide confidence of his continued blessing and presence (John 14:19).

Options for Preaching

God's promises may be conditional. Promises are sometimes unconditioned and absolute, as in God's promise to Noah (Gen. 8:21–22). But more often they are implicitly or explicitly limited or conditioned. They imply application to those who obey or believe. Abraham is commanded and then promised. Covenant explicitly links obedience to God's blessing. The Great Commission commands and then promises.

Promises are subject to revision and reapplication within God's purposes. The promise of a land for Israel was radically revised by the exile, a change that the New Testament assumes and expands. The promise of God's presence with Israel is refined in relation to the church to apply through Christ and the Holy Spirit.

God's promises are restatements of his purposes and goals. They reflect his own being and character. They should never be applied woodenly, apart from a good understanding of both.

God's major promises. Major promised themes are things God gives: life, presence, blessing. Things not promised are well-being: wealth, health, security, which are conditioned upon keeping covenant with God (Deuteronomy 28).

PROVIDENCE

Phillip A. Cooley

Providence is the Christian belief that God who created the world continues to be involved within the created order and within human history in particular. General providence refers to God's preserving and sustaining activity in the overall structures of nature and history. Special providence suggests God's parental love toward, involvement with, and guidance of specific individuals and groups through particular events in time.

Analysis

For the preacher, providence bridges two crucial arenas of church life—theology and pastoral work. Any particular view of providence must be rooted in a theology of God's nature and relationship with the world. It presupposes, on the one hand, the creation of the world and the fall of humankind and, on the other hand, the purposes or intentions of God in the revelation, incarnation, and redemption of Jesus Christ and in the final consummation of history.

Yet the idea of providence is also shaped by some of the deepest and most searching questions of the human heart. Does God care? Where is God in the crises of life? What can a person expect from God when one prays? Does God have a purpose for the person's life? Can God's hand be seen guiding the events of life? How is God involved with human suffering? Are miracles still possible today?

Providence also bridges the gap between an individual spiritualized Christianity and a world-engaging Christian faith. The God who meets the individual in the heart is the same God who is Lord of nature and of history. The God of the sanctuary is the God of the marketplace. Therefore, the movements of God's Spirit can also be discerned in the larger social issues, justice issues, and liberation issues as viewed in the light of God's purposes revealed in Jesus Christ.

Providence, then, touches nearly every aspect of theology and church life. Hardly any sermon can be preached without presupposing some background perspective of providence, some undertaking of how God is related to the world and to humankind in particular. Though reinterpreted in many ways throughout the centuries, providence has historically enjoyed a prominent position in Christian theology.

However, the doctrine of providence has fallen on hard times in the twentieth century. Modern themes of secularism, humanism, scientific naturalism, human freedom and autonomy, monstrous evil, and historical contingency have made it difficult to conceptualize how God is involved within nature, history, and human life. Theologians and lay people alike have struggled with much confusion in this area.

Yet, now more than ever, the preacher must find ways to speak the name of God into a godless world. With sensitive imagination, the preacher can help the person in the pew see through eyes of faith the hand of God at work in individual lives and in the events of history. Faithful and clear preaching in this area can help people relate their lives to God in a larger context of meaning that can bring to them joy and fulfillment, courage and peace.

Biblical Instances

Witness to God's providential activity abounds in scripture. The Old Testament knew no abstract concept of providence, but spoke instead of the personal, almighty Lord at work guiding, blessing, punishing, and protecting God's people. Israel's understanding of providence grew out of its own experience of divine election. God took special interest in a slave-people and through a series of "mighty acts" led them to freedom, sustained them with manna in the wilderness, punished them for disobedience, and guided them into the Promised Land (Psalms 105; 106; 135; 136).

Gradually, the Old Testament viewed God's providence as embracing not only Israel, but all the nations of the world (Ps.

22:27–28) and the whole of creation as well (Psalm 104; Job 38–41). The theme of God creating, sustaining, and renewing creation is found especially in Genesis 1–2, Isaiah 40, and Psalms 8; 19:1–6; 148, while God as the Lord of history is underscored in the Deuteronomic view of history, the prophetic oracles (Amos 1–2, the judgment of nations), and Apocalyptic literature (Daniel).

Individuals, as well as nations, were the object of divine providence as seen in God's mighty acts toward the patriarchs (Abraham, Isaac, and Jacob), the choice of certain persons for special roles (Exodus 3; 1 Samuel 16; Isaiah 6; Jeremiah 1), and the individual focus of later prophetic traditions (Jer. 31:31–34).

The New Testament continues the theme of the "Lord of heaven and earth" governing and caring for the world, bringing forth Christ "in the fullness of time," and guiding history toward its ultimate consummation.

Jesus' ministry focused on the parental goodness of God, extending over all creatures large and small (Matt. 5:45; 6:26–34; 10:29–42). Jesus assured his disciples of God's responsiveness to prayer and knowledge of human needs so as to eliminate anxiety and lengthy praying (Matt. 6:7–13, 25–32; 7:7–11; Luke 11:5–30; 12:22–37).

Although there is no immunity to pain, God eliminates fear and grants peace in the face of painful circumstances (Luke 12:1–12; John 14:27; Phil. 4:4–7; 1 Peter 6:6–11) and even uses human suffering as a means of redemption, preeminently in the life of Christ, but also for the disciples (Matt. 10:24–25, 38–39; 16:24–25; Rom. 5:3–4).

God's power is demonstrated in the miracles and exorcisms of Jesus and most clearly in his resurrection. Themes of the return and victory of Christ over enemies, the consummation of history, and the apocalyptic vision of heaven point to God's ultimate victory as Lord of history. Little wonder the apostle Paul exclaimed that God works in everything for good to those who love the Lord and that nothing can separate the faithful from God's love (Rom. 8:38–39).

Options for Preaching

God's loving nature. Many individuals today have conceptions of God as remote, indifferent, or punishing. Preaching on providence can illuminate God's nature as the Creator God who redemptively loves and cares for humankind. The Bible claims that God supplies every human need: compassion in time of need (Mark 8:2), comfort in sorrow (Lam. 3:31–33; John 14), blessings for encouragement (Ezek. 34:26), strength in human weakness (Isa. 40:28–31; 2 Cor. 12:9), mercy to cover mistakes (2 Chron. 7:3–14), wisdom for the hour of decision (James 1:5), vision to inspire (Prov. 29:18), forgiveness for sin (1 John 1:9), and victory over tribulation (Rom. 8:18; Rev. 7:9–17) and death (1 Corinthians 15).

Help for human struggles. Furthermore, many people today struggle with enormous burdens without any awareness of God's help as revealed in scripture. Preaching on themes of providence brings divine resources and guidance to bear on nearly every situation of modern life—fear (1 John 4:18; 2 Tim. 1:7), grief (1 Thess. 4:13), anxiety (Matt. 6:25–34), loneliness (Matt. 28:20), suffering (Rom. 5:3; 1 Cor. 12:24–26), stress (Phil. 4:7, 11), discouragement (Ps. 147:6), and sin (Isa. 53:6). In fact, human worth itself is grounded in God's providential nature, in the fact that God takes special interest in humankind in general and in individuals in particular (Matt. 10:29–31).

Purpose and meaning in life. Much modern life is lived without a sense of direction, purpose, or meaning. As the Lord of history, God works within human life toward a divine purpose (Acts 24:10–21; Rom. 8:8) and a victorious goal (Phil. 2:9–11; 1 Cor. 15:25; Rev. 11:15). The discovery of God's purpose or will as revealed in Jesus Christ and a personal response of trust and obedience to God are the keys to human meaning and purpose (Matt. 12:50; Heb. 13:20–21; 1 John 2:17). The purpose of human life can be summarized in Jesus' call to discipleship.

Ecology and social justice. Preaching on providence can also move the church beyond individual issues to larger issues of ecology and social concern. Ecology has become a major concern today in the face of growing threats to the environment. The Bible affirms that God is the Creator and Owner of all the created order (Gen. 1:1; Ps. 50:10) and that humankind is the steward who is entrusted with and held accountable for the care of the earth's environment and resources. Furthermore, since the Bible portrays God as taking special interest in the poor, disenfranchised, and oppressed (Ezek. 18:5–9; Amos 4:1–3; Micah 2:1–13), issues of social justice (Amos 5:24) and liberation (Luke 4:18–19) become concerns for Christian service as well.

Faithful preaching on themes of providence serves to broaden the church's vision of God as Lord of heaven and earth, deepen faith in the God of the Bible who loves and cares for a weak and sinful human race, and strengthen commitment to a life of faithful service to the God who works redemptively and purposefully within human history.

RACISM

Preston N. Williams

Racism is a system of classification, often allegedly based upon biological science, that is employed to justify acts and systems of discrimination practiced upon an individual or group by supposedly superior people. Science's failure to validate these systems has led to their justification by custom, conventions, and religion.

Analysis

The Christian faith does not sanction racism, but Christian theological systems have approved it. Racism has also been practiced by Christian churches and people. In the United States, many denominations were divided on the basis of some Christians' belief in white supremacy. The white Dutch Reformed Church in South Africa long held that the Christian faith sanctioned apartheid, a vicious system of racial dominance and separation practiced by whites. In November 1990, these churches confessed their teaching and practices to be a sin.

Racism is a sin because it denies that all male and female human beings are created in God's image and that God does not sanction personal or social discrimination based upon race. The Christian God teaches that all people are created equal and are equally sacred. None has a privileged status or relationship to God based upon race.

Biblical Instances

The Old Testament teaches no doctrine of racial exclusion or superiority. Genesis 9:25–26, according to reputable biblical scholarship, does not teach racial differences. The particularism and exclusion found in Judaism is based upon a desire for religious, not racial, purity. The condemnations of interracial marriage found in Ezra (10:10–11) and Nehemiah (13:23–31) are balanced by the interracial marriages of Abraham, Joseph, and Moses and the interracial ancestry of David. The books of Ruth and Jonah also indicate that the Jewish concern was not with racial purity.

The New Testament's conception of membership in the Christian community (John 1:28) undercuts the basis of racism, as does Jesus' conception of neighbors (Luke 10:29–37) and the early church's understanding of the gospel as universal and to be proclaimed to all people (Matt. 24:14; 28:19). Paul's teachings confirm this view (Gal. 3:27–28). The Bible, then, provides no endorsement of racism.

Options for Preaching

One human family. Christians recognize diversity among human beings as a portion of God's good creation. All males and females are in God's image (Gen. 1:26–27). All human beings are crowned with glory and honor (Psalm 8).

Just and equal treatment. Human differences provoke a variety of responses and varying rewards and benefits. Christians are to seek justice in their relationship to different groups and individuals. Amos's call for justice among rich and poor (Amos 5:21–24) as well as his stress upon impartiality in the treatment of all people (races) and the nations (Amos 3:1–2) must be proclaimed as indispensable to the covenantal relationship to God.

The Christian's vocation. Christians must be reminded that the mission of their Lord is to proclaim liberty to the oppressed (Luke 4:18–19), and that his church is constituted of people from every corner of the earth (Acts 2:5–12). As members of the church, Christians are, like Paul, to speak the truth in love and to act to remove barriers among people (Col. 3:5–11; Gal. 3:27–29).

REIGN OF GOD

R. Alan Culpepper

The reign of God is the sovereignty or kingdom of God, God's exercise of royal power.

Analysis

While the term "reign of God" or "kingdom of God" does not occur in the Old Testament, the concept of God as ruling Lord is central to it. The reign of God has creative, revelatory, and redemptive aspects: God wrought creation and will bring it to redeemed perfection when all is subjected to God's will. The reign of God is therefore cosmic, corporate, and individual. God is both "Father" and "who art in heaven."

Because of the many facets of the Bible's references to the reign of God, a number of issues have fueled ongoing debates. Is the reign of God present or future? Is it a matter of social reform or individual faith? What is the relationship between the church and God's reign? On each of these issues the scriptures provide a rich diversity of perspectives while pointing to the sovereignty of God over all of life.

Biblical Instances

God is hailed as the ruler of Israel (Deut. 33:5; Isa. 43:15), the ruler of all nations (Amos 1:3–2:3), and the ruler of all the earth (Pss. 47:7; 94). The exodus was the paradigm of God's sovereignty. The prophets looked forward to the coming Day of the Lord, when God would establish justice and peace (Amos 5:18–24). The Day of the Lord would bring a new exodus (Isa. 51:9–11) and a new covenant (Jer. 31:31–34; Ezek. 37:26). The Day of the Lord would also represent God's coming to the covenant people (Mal. 3:1–2; Isa. 35:4). The Messiah, God's agent, would establish God's sovereignty both in Israel and among the nations (Isa. 9:2–7; 25:6–12; Ezek. 34:22–24).

The reign of God is the primary theme of the teachings of Jesus in the Synoptic Gospels. It is the theme of more sayings and parables than any other subject. The time of waiting was over; God was inaugurating the kingdom through Jesus (Mark 1:14–15). The references in Matthew to the "kingdom of heaven" are a circumlocution that avoids a direct reference to God, but the sayings are equivalent to the sayings about the kingdom of God in Mark and Luke. Jesus' mighty works illustrated the liberating and redemptive power of God's reign. His response to the question of John the Baptist—was he the "coming one" or should they look for another?—echoes Isaiah 35:5–6. What the prophets predicted was being dramatically fulfilled (Matt. 11:5; cf. Luke 4:18–21; Isaiah 61). Many of Jesus' parables illustrate the nature of the kingdom (Mark 4; Matthew 13). Jesus taught his disciples to pray for the kingdom (Matt. 6:10; Luke 11:2). The kingdom had come (Matt. 12:28; Luke 11:20) and was present among them (Luke 17:20–21), but its fulfillment lay in the future (Mark 9:1; 13:28–32; 14:25). At that time the Son of man will come to raise the dead and establish God's sovereignty over all the nations (Mark 14:62; Luke 17:22–37).

The reign of God is mentioned in the Gospel of John only in 3:3 and 3:5. Nevertheless, throughout the Gospel it is clear that Jesus is the divine agent of God's rule, who makes eternal life available to those who trust in him. God's reign is also a central topic of the preaching in Acts (8:12; 19:8). Paul declares that those who are "in Christ" are new creatures (2 Cor. 5:17). Those who are obedient to Christ will "inherit the kingdom" (1 Cor. 6:9; Gal. 5:21; 1 Cor. 15:42–54). The enthronement of Jesus is also a characteristic feature of the hymns of the New Testament (Phil. 2:6–11; Col. 1:15–20; 1 Tim. 3:16). The marriage of the risen Lord and his church will be celebrated (Rev. 19:9), believers will dwell in the new Jerusalem (Rev. 22:2, 10), and the Lamb will reign for ever and ever (Rev. 22:5).

Options for Preaching

Preaching on the reign of God can restore a sense of confidence to the church.

Christians are not to take the values of society as their own; they live under the sovereign authority of the Lord.

As God's covenant people, the work of the kingdom is the mission of Christians: restoring the broken; establishing peace and justice; proclaiming the gospel.

Christians can look to Jesus for guidance and authority, qualities of a ruler.

Because the Lord is ruler, Christians live for the praise of God's glory (Eph. 1:6, 12, 14).

The Lord's Prayer is the prayer of those who long for God's kingdom.

REPENTANCE

Wayne E. Ward

The English word "repentance" denotes the action or process of turning from sin and dedicating oneself to the moral improvement of one's life. It translates the Hebrew word *shuv* and the Greek word *metanoeo*, which literally mean "to turn around" or "reverse one's direction," in either physical or moral terms. Unfortunately, it was translated by Jerome in his Latin Vulgate (about A.D. 400) "do penance," introducing the idea of atoning for wrongdoing by undertaking some form of ritual self-punishment. In this translation it lost its primary biblical meaning of a radical reversal of one's life and conduct and a profound new commitment to do the will of God.

The Greek New Testament uses another term that is often translated "repentance" (*metamellomai*), but it has the quite different meaning, "to feel remorse." This feeling of remorse or regret may not involve any moral change. Judas, for example, experienced *metamellomai*, deep remorse, but went out and hanged himself (Matt. 27:3). Whereas Peter experienced real repentance (*metanoia*), turned away from his abandonment and denial of his Lord, and committed himself to faithful obedience throughout the rest of his life, even to his martyr's death (John 21:15–23).

Analysis

Repentance is always connected with faith. In fact, "repentance to God and . . . faith in our Lord Jesus Christ" (Acts 20:21) are two sides of the same reality. As such, it is a gift of God and impossible to attain without the working of the Holy Spirit. What is called for is not a massive human effort but a surrender to the Spirit of God, who alone can bring about the transformation that repentance involves.

Repentance requires radical moral change, the "fruits of repentance." These, also, cannot be separated from the act of "turning." Repentance is a repeated act of the believer's life; one repentance cannot suffice for a lifetime. Ongoing life requires renewal of repentance and reaffirmation of faith.

Biblical Instances

The call for repentance pervades both the Old and the New Testaments, and it demands a radical turning from sin and disobedience to faith in the living God. It is repeatedly used by the prophets to call Israel back to faithfulness in the covenant (Jer. 8:6; Ezek. 14:6; 18:30).

Even "the ends of the earth" shall "turn unto the Lord" (Ps. 22:27) in the vision of the psalmist, but the primary word of the prophets is a call to Israel to "return unto the LORD, and he will have mercy upon him" (Isa. 55:7, KJV); "return, thou backsliding Israel, saith the LORD" (Jer. 3:12, KJV); "Repent and turn away from your idols" (Ezek. 14:6).

John the Baptist picked up on this theme in his preaching, shocking the religious leaders by his demand that they repent

(Mark 1:4). Jesus sharpened the theme, relating repentance to the inbreaking reign of God and the radical moral change it required (Matt. 4:17). Early Christians made it the theme of their proclamation (Acts 2:38; 3:19).

Options for Preaching

The best options for preaching grow out of the meaning of the biblical term and its usage in the history of Israel and the church with themes such as these:

Relevance within the church. A sermon on repentance stresses its relevance for the people in the church, not just those "sinners" outside. This is its primary biblical thrust.

True meaning of repentance. This "teaching sermon" emphasizes the strong distinction between feelings of remorse and the decisive act of the will, producing the moral change that repentance requires.

A continuing need. A sermon on the continuing need of daily repentance corrects the overemphasis on "once upon a time" repentance.

The eschatological relevance. The emphasis of John the Baptist and Jesus upon the connection between repentance and the inbreaking reign of God opens up an eschatalogical theme for preaching. In the future-oriented theology of hope that dominates so much of the Christian world, the call to repentance can undergird the call for the liberation of the oppressed and exploited peoples of the world. Only by a radical repentance and redirection of the lives of God's people can this kind of liberation occur.

Grace. Emphasize the theme of "grace," because all the biblical calls for repentance assume that the repentant sinner will find that he or she is returning to a gracious God who "will abundantly pardon."

RESURRECTION

Gerald L. Borchert

Resurrection implies that following the death of a person there is a subsequent experience of bodily life. It is contrasted with the Greek concept of immortality of the soul, which implies that the body at death is shed and the soul alone continues. In the Bible resurrection refers to: (a) miraculous raisings or resuscitations, such as those performed by Elijah and Elisha (1 Kings 17:20–24; 2 Kings 4:32–37), Jesus (Mark 5:41–43; John 11:43–44), or Peter and Paul (Acts 9:40–41; 20:9–12); (b) Christ's resurrection and transformation accompanied by victory over death (1 Cor. 15:12–28); and (c) resurrection of dead persons in the hereafter (Rev. 20:5–6, 11–15).

Analysis

People hope to be assured that life will automatically have an ultimate happy ending to the state of mortality. But the biblical concept of resurrection does not imply either positive or automatic results for people. Resurrection is an act of God, and this idea developed slowly in Israel. Life and death at first were regarded primarily as physical realities. After death persons were said to enter Sheol, the shadowy place of hopelessness (2 Sam. 12:23; Job 7:9–10; Isa. 14:9–11). But gradually there developed a conscious hope with God (Ps. 139:8) and a questioning of whether Sheol was the end (Job 14:14; Ezekiel 37). By the time of Daniel 12:2, the possibility of some form of resurrection was considered.

In the intertestament period, the translations of Enoch and Elijah (Gen. 5:23–24; 2 Kings 2:1–12) were viewed as suggesting a future life (cf. Heb. 11:5; Jude 6). The Sadducees rejected such a personal hope (Sir. 18:28; also 10:11; 14:26) and viewed hope through one's offspring (Sir. 46:12). The Pharisees, however, developed a strong resurrection theology (2 Esdras 7; Baruch 50–51) while debating the future of the wicked, either a raising for judgment (Enoch 22; 67; 90) or no raising (Enoch 46; 51; 62). The resurrection body in these writings appears to be spiritual, but in 2 Maccabees it seems more physical (7:14–42). Qumran writings follow Pharisaic views on resurrection but focus primarily on the inauguration of the messianic era and the battle between light and darkness.

Biblical Instances

The resurrection of Jesus Christ is a foundational element of Christian theology. Without it there would be no church or Christian faith, and preaching would be meaningless (1 Cor. 15:13–14).

But its centrality does not mean the gospel stories of the resurrection of Jesus are trouble-free for interpreters. Many questions have been raised when the stories are compared—namely, the number of women and angels at the tomb, the words of the angel(s) concerning Galilee, the silence of the women, the places and order of Jesus' appearances, and the words that Jesus spoke.

Yet the resurrection of Jesus is a key affirmation in each of the Gospels. Even in Mark, where no appearance stories have been transmitted, the three crucial passion predictions (8:31; 9:31; 10:33–34) conclude with the announcement of the resurrection. Moreoever, in the focal transfiguration pericope the importance of proclamation and the so-called messianic secret are clearly set within a statement on the resurrection of Jesus (9:9). Matthew is similar: although Matthew expands on Mark, the organization at the beginning (1:23) and end (28:20) emphasizes a thesis of the resurrection, namely the constant presence of Emmanuel, "God with us," in the life of the follower.

The New Testament writers realized that Christ's resurrection was of strategic importance for life and destiny. They proclaimed it as the key to a living hope and meaningful inheritance (1 Peter 1:3–5; Eph. 1:16–20; 2:4–7), as the foundation for salvation and for appropriate living (2 Cor. 5:14–15; Rom. 6:1–11), and as the basis for a willingness to suffer patiently (Phil. 3:10; Rom. 8:17), realizing that God knows how to deal with frustration and sinfulness in the world (1 Thess. 1:9–10).

The task of contemporary proclaimers is to demonstrate again for this age that resurrection is not just the happy ending to a sad story but the hinge of the church's existence.

Options for Preaching

Just an idle tale, Luke 24:1–35. The Lukan questions provide the framework for challenging the disciples' doubt (24:11). The first question (24:5) confronted their status, the second (24:17) their evaluation of reality, the third (24:26) their understanding of scripture, and the fourth (24:32) the necessity of their reflecting on their discovery.

Resurrection or futility, 1 Cor. 15:1–28. After enunciating traditions concerning the appearances of Christ (15:3–11), Paul boldly asserted why the Corinthians had a poor record as Christians. Failing to apprehend resurrection power, their faith was empty (15:14), and they and their loved ones were in a pitiable state (15:19). But Christ had been raised (15:20) and resurrection is the foundation for hope (15:21–28).

The difference of one Sunday, John 20:19–29. Thomas missed an encounter with the risen Lord (20:24), together with the giving of peace (v. 19), the breath of the Spirit (v. 22), and the Lord's commission (v. 23), which led to skepticism and rationalistic conclusions (v. 25). But the next Sunday (v. 26) he was transformed and, following a searing encounter with the risen Lord, offered Christianity's amazing confession of Jesus as God (vs. 27–29).

REVELATION

Charles P. Price

The word "revelation" means disclosure or unveiling. In biblical literature it is used to describe the way in which God communicates with human beings. The fundamental account of ultimate reality is thus derived not from fallible human speculation but from God's own testimony historically given.

Analysis

Content of revelation. Until the eighteenth century, revelation was identified chiefly with scripture. This approach has the advantage of providing specific content, but with the adoption of critical methods in theology, the equation of scripture with direct divine words proved untenable. In the nineteenth century, a new theology understood revelation not as divine statements but as the imparting of God's own self. Scripture became the record of this revelation. This development has been most influential. It has required modification, however, since neither a person nor, analogically, God, can be self-revealed apart from some specific, hence propositional, content. Consequently some recent theologians have dealt with revelation as mediated by events recorded in scripture (event plus interpretation); others consider history as a whole to be revelatory, scripture providing the key; others see revelation in the engagement of believers with the divine Person through hearing the scripture. It would be widely said today that scripture participates in the revelation of which it is the record.

Recognition of revelation. Many recent theologians would hold that an event can be recognized as revelatory by its saving characteristics. There is no natural revelation, but every religion bears witness to some act of "unnatural" deliverance by which God's power is known. Yahweh defeated the pharaoh's army. Jesus overcame "the last enemy"—death. The ultimate saving act is the final revelation.

The Revealer. In every case, God takes the initiative. The "inward testimony" of the Spirit or Word of God reveals God to us.

Biblical Instances

The Old Testament articulates a close relationship among revelation, knowing God, and the Spirit of God. The Spirit of the Lord brings knowledge (e.g., Isa. 11:2); alternatively, knowledge comes by revelation (e.g., Dan. 2:21–22). By revelation, prophets are given the secret of the Lord (Amos 3:7). The agent of revelation to the prophets after Amos, of course, was the Word of God rather than the Spirit. These holy men distanced themselves from the ranting of those whom contemporaries called prophets. Hosea regarded those prophets as mad (Hos. 9:7). To insist that the Word reveals is to claim that knowledge of God is rational. To insist that the Spirit reveals is to claim that that knowledge is transrational, although it often falls to subrational folly. The work of the Spirit in prophetic utterance was recognized once again in Ezekiel and Joel.

In the New Testament, after Jesus' resurrection, the Spirit was poured out on "all flesh." Subsequently all believers can know God, not just prophets. Revelation is received by the faith of the whole community. Jesus himself is the Revealer of God (esp. Matt. 11:27). In him "the Word became flesh and dwelt among us" (John 1:14), and the power of the Spirit is evident in decisive moments in Jesus' life (cf. Luke 1:35; Mark 1:9–13; Luke 4:16–20). One notices the recognition of both Word and Spirit as revelatory agents.

The association between revelation and mystery remains significant. God does not reveal information discoverable in any other way. God reveals God's self by the revelation of the content of the divine mystery—the intended future judgment and redemption of the world in Christ (cf. Ephesians 3). Although Jesus is the full and final revelation of God (Col. 1:19), mystery abides. He *is* the mystery (Eph. 1:5–10). Humans know Jesus to be the saving revelation of God amid the sufferings they share with him, but these are not worth comparing with the glory that will be revealed (Rom. 8:18).

Options for Preaching

One can preach on a different facet of revelation in every season of the Christian year.

Christmas. One traditional reading, Titus 2:11–14, emphasizes the saving aspect of the appearing (revelation) of Christ in the flesh.

Epiphany. As the manifestation of Christ to the world, this is the major revelation season; one classic reading is Ephesians 3, where God's mystery for the redemption of the world is revealed by the Spirit. In Epiphany the preacher also might treat Jesus' words and deeds as revelatory of God's character.

Easter. Jesus was declared to be the Son of God by his victory over death (Rom. 1:4), a powerful Easter theme.

Pentecost. Since Jesus is recognized to be the divine Son through the testimony of the Spirit poured out upon the church, the subjective side of revelation deserves examination during Pentecost.

Further themes are:

The mighty acts of God. The preacher might focus attention on the mighty acts of God from the Red Sea to the cross as revealing to believers God's saving power objectively in history.

Inward experience. Texts such as Psalm 139, which express the personal knowledge of God made available by the Holy Spirit, allow the preacher the opportunity to explore revelation as inward experience of God.

RIGHTEOUSNESS OF GOD

Catherine Gunsalus González

The righteousness of God has two foci. First, it speaks of God's own righteousness, God's holiness that does not tolerate sin and injustice. Second, it speaks of the righteousness with which God clothes those who place their faith in God's promised mercy.

Analysis

To stress God's own holiness and righteousness without the gospel's word of grace is to bring humanity to judgment with no hope for redemption. To stress the righteousness God gives to humanity, without seeing God's own holiness, is to preach cheap grace that needs no repentance or amendment of life.

The Protestant Reformation can almost be summarized by the discussion of the meaning of the righteousness of God. For

Luther, the critical introduction to the issue was in Romans
1:17: "For in it [the gospel] the righteousness of God is revealed through faith for faith; as it is written, 'The one who is
righteous will live by faith' " (NRSV).

Biblical Instances

The Pauline epistles are the primary source for this doctrine,
most particularly Romans 3 and 4. However, once the doctrine
is clarified, it sheds a light on a much wider portion of scripture.

Because God is righteous, even the redeemed must become
righteous if they are to dwell in God's presence. That is the
meaning of sanctification. But since humanity is not righteous,
if God's righteousness did not extend to it, to cover its sinfulness graciously, humanity would have no way to enter into the
relationship with God. God's righteousness given to humanity
is justification. In 1 Corinthians 1:30, Paul writes that God has
made Christ Jesus humanity's righteousness.

This complex connection of God's righteousness that judges
humanity, and yet graciously redeems it, is particularly Pauline. However, the righteousness of God, in one sense or another, is a theme of the entirety of scripture. Prophetic passages
speak clearly of God's own righteousness and therefore condemn God's people who live in unrighteousness. The same
prophets also looked to God's love for the people and called for
repentance and trust in this righteous God who sought to make
the people righteous also. In Ezekiel, there is terrible judgment
upon Israel because of their unrighteousness, yet it is because
of God's holy name that they shall be restored, made clean,
and caused to be righteous (see esp. ch. 36).

Options for Preaching

Called to righteousness. God's people are called to walk in
the paths of righteousness, and yet it is God who leads them
there (Ps. 23:3).

Christ extends God's righteousness. The work of Christ fulfills the words of the prophets and extends the work of God's
righteousness far beyond the borders of Israel. God's righteousness, which people are called to live but cannot live without
God's own action in them, is known and understood in Israel.

Already righteous. The church understands that humans are
to grow in righteousness, and yet this does not contradict the

fact that, in Christ, God already deals with them as righteous, not counting their sins against them.

SACRIFICE

R. Alan Culpepper

The term "sacrifice" may refer to any offering to God that is wholly or partially consumed.

Analysis

In biblical times the worshiper brought an animal or vegetable offering to be burned, representing the worshiper's complete devotion to the deity. When the deity accepted the worshiper's sacrifice, deity and worshiper were joined in a covenant relationship. The worshiper offered a portion of the firstfruits in sacrifice as an expression of thanksgiving, or as an offering for sin, and the deity then looked with favor on the worshiper. In time, many different kinds of sacrifices were practiced. Christians look upon the death of Jesus as the ultimate, final, and sufficient sacrifice for sin. Sacrifice has subsequently served as a powerful metaphor for the service Christians offer to God.

Biblical Instances

Burnt offerings were first observed on family altars and local shrines. The burnt offering was offered for forgiveness for sin (Lev. 9:7; 14:20), for petitions (1 Sam. 13:12), or purification (Lev. 12:6; 16:24). A peace offering often followed a burnt offering as a symbolic meal with the deity (Lev. 7:28–34; 10:14–15). Other sacrifices included the votive offerings (Lev. 7:16–17), sin offerings (Lev. 4:1–5:13), and guilt offerings (Lev. 5:14–6:7). None of the offerings, however, atoned for deliberate sin, sin committed "with a high hand." The notion of sacrifice also seems to be present in Isaiah's description of the servant (Isa. 52:13–53:12).

In the New Testament, the concept of sacrifice informs many references to the death of Christ on the cross (Phil. 2:8; 1 Peter 1:18–19; Rom. 5:9). Jesus is described as "the Lamb of God, who takes away the sin of the world" (John 1:29, 36), the ransom for many (Mark 10:45). In Hebrews 9, especially, the death of Christ is described as the once-for-all sacrifice, superior to the sacrifice offered on the Day of Atonement. Jesus is both the sacrifice and the high priest (Heb. 9:11–14). In a derived sense, the death of Christ is described as an expiation (Rom. 3:25; 1 John 2:2; 4:10). Suffering and servanthood are therefore the acceptable response of followers of Christ (Mark 8:34; Rom. 12:1).

Options for Preaching

Sacrifice is a central biblical theme, but one often neglected in preaching. With that in mind, a preacher trying to reclaim the subject should take care to explain the concept and its evolution.

Preaching can approach sacrifice from several angles intended to provoke thought:

Role of sacrifice. What constitutes acceptable worship, and what role can sacrifice play in it?

Cheap grace? Has the modern sanitized, bloodless practice of religion led Christians to assume that grace is cheap? The story of Abraham and Isaac (Gen. 22:1–19) would surely indicate that it is not.

A suitable offering. God gave the world God's Son; what can humans give in return?

SALVATION

Wayne E. Ward

Salvation is deliverance from destruction, danger, or difficulty. In Christian theology the term "salvation" has focused primarily upon deliverance from the power and effects of sin, the securing of forgiveness and fellowship with God, and the guarantee of eternal presence with the Lord in the life beyond.

Analysis

The term "salvation" had a broad meaning in biblical history, including salvation from famine or sickness, deliverance from slavery in Egypt, or escape from the destruction of war. The eschatological meaning of the blessed future destiny of the righteous person was a later development from the basic meaning of the term.

The wide usage of the term "salvation" in biblical history and the long development of its meaning throughout Christian history generate several important theological concerns:

First, salvation has always involved the total needs of human beings and is not restricted to a concern about their eternal destiny. It has been all too common for some Christians to stress "concern for souls" over social concerns for the physical needs of human beings. This distortion has brought criticism of a "social gospel" that seems to be primarily concerned with human pain and suffering. The liberation theologies that are so influential in the world today are exactly in line with the historic meaning of "salvation" in both Old and New Testaments.

This does not mean that salvation has no reference to the eternal destiny of the individual person. Rather, it means that this spiritual destiny is included in a much broader understanding of salvation as a transformation of life, here and now, and a fulfillment of that life in eternal fellowship with God.

Another theological emphasis in the biblical history of the term is its corporate nature. The hyper-individualism of Western culture has tended to distort this understanding of the term. Salvation involves a change in all relationships and in one's entire life-style. It is not a private affair, and it should be especially significant in family relationships, in one's vocation, and in all of society. In fact, the term "salvation" is used more of Israel as a people than it is of individuals wherever it is found in the Old Testament (Ex. 14:30; Judg. 6:14, 15; 1 Sam. 9:16; 2 Sam. 3:18). Similarly, it refers to the church as the sphere of salvation in the New Testament (Matt. 1:21; 27:42; John 12:47; 2 Tim. 1:9; Titus 3:5).

One of the most serious distortions of the doctrine of salvation in the history of Christian theology has been its preoccupation with a *single event* that secures eternal salvation for the believer. The language of salvation in the Bible has never concentrated on a single transaction by which this destiny is assured. In fact, the language of salvation is present (continuing) and future more than it is past tense throughout the entire Bible.

When salvation is seen as a continuing journey with the Lord, it places the emphasis upon the ongoing relationship rather than a transactional arrangement about one's eternal destiny. It also moves away from a static or positional view of salvation to a dynamic growth in grace for the believer. While assurance belongs to the biblical experience of salvation, that assurance is based upon the faithful relationship of the believer to the Lord, not simply upon a past transaction. It is a journey of faith all the way, yet even that faith is "a gift of God, not of works, lest anyone should boast" (Eph. 2:8–9).

This view of salvation also includes the dimension of service. The calling of God is not limited to the arrangement of one's eternal destiny; it is a call to serve. Salvation and service are two sides of the same reality in biblical thought. There is no salvation that does not involve service. The suggestion that one might accept God's call to salvation but not the call to service is a contradiction. One can experience salvation only by its expression in obedience to the call of God.

Biblical Instances

The three tenses of salvation are abundantly illustrated in scripture:

The beginning of salvation is seen in Luke 7:50, "Your faith has saved you" and in Luke 19:9, "Today salvation has come to this house." The evidence that salvation had come to the house of Zacchaeus that day was seen in his radical change of attitude toward the people and his desire to make restitution for any wrong he had committed. In Ephesians 2:8, "by grace you have been saved," the emphasis upon a past event is also pulled into the present by the use of the perfect tense, which means that an event in the past (salvation) is exerting a continuing influence upon one's life in the present moment.

The continuing present experience of salvation is seen in Philippians 2:12–18, "Keep on working out your own salvation" (author's translation). This certainly does not mean "Keep on trying to get yourself saved" but rather "Keep on working out in your life the service and relationships that express the true meaning of salvation." Paul often refers to those "who are being saved" (1 Cor. 1:18; 2 Cor. 2:15), showing his perception of salvation as an ongoing process.

Salvation is also future in biblical perspective: "Now is our salvation nearer than when we [first] believed" (Rom. 13:11, KJV); "Who by God's power are being kept through faith unto a salvation which is ready to be revealed in the last time" (1 Peter 1:5, author's translation).

Options for Preaching

The biblical examples cited and the discussion of common misunderstandings of the term "salvation" suggest several options for preaching:

Salvation and service. The relationship between salvation and service is illuminated by taking the call of Abraham (Gen.

12:1) or Jesus' call of the disciples (Mark 1:16–20; Matt. 4:18–22; Luke 5:1–11; John 1:35–42) and showing that the emphasis is upon their journey with the Lord and their faithful service to him. It is impossible to find a single point at which they were "saved." In fact, the journey often involved misunderstanding, disobedience, and backsliding, as well as growth in the relationship. Salvation is bound up with obedient service and cannot be separated from it. Even the contrasting experience of Paul on the Damascus Road, decisive as was his conversion, confirms this understanding of salvation. Throughout his letters, Paul stresses the journey, insists that he has not yet attained the goal, and looks forward to the future culmination of salvation (Phil. 3:12–14; Rom. 13:11–14).

A wider perspective. One of the greatest needs in preaching is the correction of the narrow view of salvation as relating only to the final destiny of the believer. Two different emphases will clarify this common confusion:

First, the many examples of salvation as deliverance from slavery, as escape from war's destruction, as healing from illness, or as escape from great danger could be used to broaden and enrich the meaning of the term. These can be shown as foundational to the later spiritual meanings that attach to the term.

Second, the development of the three tenses of salvation will correct the exclusive emphasis upon a past event or transaction and show the continuing relationship of the believer to God and the ultimate fulfillment in the heavenly home (Eph. 2:8–9; Phil. 2:12–13; 1 Peter 1:4–5).

Grace and faith. Finally, a strong emphasis upon the divine initiative in salvation, God's grace, together with the human response, faith, will show the meaning of salvation in its biblical wholeness. From one point of view, as Calvin insisted, it is the gracious gift of the sovereign God from beginning to end. Yet, it is never forced upon the human will; it must be accepted as God's gift, even though the faith to accept it is made possible by the working of God's Spirit.

SCRIPTURES

O. C. Edwards, Jr.

Scriptures (from the Latin, "writings") are a collection of documents considered by a religious community to have a special status, such as containing revelation, being inspired, being authoritative for matters of belief or morals, and deserving to be read at assemblies for worship. For Jews the scriptures are the Hebrew Bible; for Christians, the Hebrew Bible together with the New Testament.

Analysis

The Bible provides little guidance to a Christian understanding of Holy Scripture, since few places in the New Testament suggest that there can be Christian writings on a level of inspiration equal to that of the Hebrew Bible. The least ambiguous is 2 Peter 3:16, where the letters of Paul are contrasted to "the other scriptures." Only the book of Revelation claims to be inspired (1:1–3). The first list of Christian books proposed as a canon was offered by the heretic Marcion in the middle of the second century; it consisted of highly edited versions of Luke and the Pauline epistles. By A.D. 200 the fourfold Gospel was accepted with Paul's letters. The first list containing exactly our twenty-seven books was in a festal letter Athanasius issued in A.D. 367.

A list of books regarded as scripture does not automatically answer the question of how the authority of those books is applied to theological questions. The use scripture makes of scripture is by no means uniform. For example, the story of Abraham's two sons has different emphases and even meanings through its use in the various literary strands of the Pentateuch and in Paul (Genesis 16; 21; Galatians 4). By the time of Jesus, the Pharisees treated scripture as a ceremonial and moral code, while the community at Qumran regarded it as a veiled prediction of its own life. Much of the New Testament provides a christological interpretation to the Old (e.g., Luke 24:27, 44–47), an interpretation that may not have been in the minds of the original writers. Thus agreement over which books were authoritative did not guarantee agreement over how they were to be interpreted.

Biblical Instances

While the inflected forms of the Hebrew word for "write" (*katav*) are not the only vocabulary in the Bible referring to a concept of Holy Scripture, they are important from early on, as in a command from God that something be written down (e.g., Ex. 24:4). The first document treated as scriptural is the portion of Deuteronomy found in the Temple around 621 B.C.

that Josiah and the people covenanted to observe (2 Kings 23:1–3). Next the entire Torah, which had been completed during the exile, was accepted when Ezra read it to the people (Nehemiah 8). Although the oracles of the prophets are described as "the word of God" and were authoritative from the beginning, the first written indication of their having canonical status on par with the Torah is in the preface to Ecclesiasticus (c. 132 B.C.). Luke has the risen Lord place the Psalms (from the third section of the Hebrew canon, the Writings) on a par with the Law and the Prophets (24:44), but the full list of Writings comes from the rabbis at Jabneh (A.D. 90–100). In the New Testament, scriptural citations are often introduced by some formula such as "as it is written" (*gegraptai*). The noun form *graphai* ("writings") also appears. Except for 2 Peter 3:14, however, these always refer to the Hebrew scriptures. Second Timothy 3:16–17 (NRSV) suggests "all scripture is inspired by God and is useful for . . . correction . . . so that everyone who belongs to God may be . . . equipped for every good work."

Options for Preaching

Preaching from the Bible about biblical authority is difficult because the Bible has very little to say about distinctively Christian scriptures. It seems legitimate to transfer to the New Testament the authoritative claims that are made in it for the Old Testament, but honesty requires being explicit about this extension. One's doctrine of biblical authority would have a lot to do with what one said, since beliefs of Christians range from accepting plenary verbal inspiration to according the Bible only an exemplary or symbolic value.

One way of getting around these difficulties would be to preach on the theme of what the Bible has meant to Christian people through the ages.

Nehemiah 8:9 could be a text for such a sermon: "For all the people wept when they heard the words of the law."

Psalm 119 can be regarded as a rhapsody on a faithful person's love for God's word, as in verse 105 (NRSV): "Your word is a lamp to my feet and a light to my path."

Romans 15:4 (NRSV) could be a New Testament text on the role of scripture: "For whatever was written in former days was written for our instruction, so that by steadfastness and by encouragement of the scriptures we might have hope."

Those preaching from these texts should not treat them as proof texts to be snatched out of context but should rather show their real belief in scriptures by respecting what these words meant in their original application.

SECULARISM

Charles P. Price

Secularism is first an attitude and then a doctrine that regards the world as self-sufficient. Science is eventually to explain all natural phenomena without recourse to God, and moral behavior is to be determined by the well-being of human life in the present, without appeal to future rewards and punishments. This world is all there is.

Analysis

Although the word "secularism" appeared for the first time in the mid-nineteenth century (cf. OED ad loc.), the idea was taking shape throughout the eighteenth. It was a consequence of deism, the religious philosophy that taught that a watchmaker God had created the world and then retired to let it run on its own mechanisms, rarely interfering in its affairs. Such an idle God is easily dismissed.

As the necessity of God in the natural order seemed to be removed by the progress of science in the eighteenth century, God was made unnecessary for explaining historical events by nineteenth-century philosophies of history, especially those of Hegel and Marx, and unnecessary to account for psychic phenomena by the psychological explorations of Freud and his successors. Until recently, conventional theology fought a losing battle (Dietrich Bonhoeffer described conventional theologians as vainly trying to hold onto a "God in the gaps"). Much modern Western thought has been uncompromisingly secularist.

Biblical Instances

The Bible has no patience with secularism. To be sure, it is not acquainted with modern scientific attitudes, but biblical writers regarded attempts to eliminate God as the controlling factor in world affairs as foolish (Pss. 14:1; 53:1). Wisdom literature of the Old Testament consistently presents God as the source of all wisdom and knowledge (see Prov. 9:10; Jer. 10:12). The Spirit of God bestows ability on the craftsmen of the tabernacle (Ex. 31:3) and wisdom on Davidic kings

(1 Kings 3:12; Isa. 11:2). Paul develops a dialectic between divine and human wisdom (1 Cor. 1:18–2:16). Human wisdom (secularism!) is made foolish by God, for humanity cannot know God through its wisdom. The folly of the cross is God's wisdom for the world's redemption.

Options for Preaching

Limitations of human inquiry. One important emphasis in preaching about secularism is to recognize its basic biblical truth—that human inquiry alone cannot discover a holy, living, loving God (1 Cor. 1:21).

God's initiatives. A complementary approach to the first option begins with God's initiatives, which reveal to believers both the world and themselves in a fresh way. Resultant knowledge, even when human acquired, is God-given (1 Kings 4:29–34).

The heavens declare the glory. The preacher might also take as a starting point the declaration of the psalmist (Psalm 19) that "the heavens declare the glory of God," establish the fact that this God is the God known by Red Sea deliverance and Christian salvation, and then affirm that secular knowledge imparts truth about this God, for then, as the seventeenth-century astronomer Johannes Kepler remarked, "we do but think God's thoughts after him."

SEXUALITY

Earl E. Shelp

"Sexuality" is a general term encompassing and incorporating a range of phenomena and concepts relating to being gendered (male and female) persons in the world. Contemporary understandings of sexuality include more than genitals and genital conduct. Body, gender, sex role, sex identity, masculinity, femininity, physiological activity, emotional states, behaviors, and practices are some of the interpersonal and intrapersonal components of a comprehensive definition of sexuality. Since the term "sexuality" has such diverse general and specific connotations and referents, care and precision are indicated in any discussion in order to minimize confusion and to maximize understanding; for example, the biblical distinction between body and flesh.

Analysis

Preachers have two basic tasks in sermons touching upon sexuality. The first task is to appreciate the strength and weaknesses of the faith traditions. Scripture contains countless references to sexual concepts and conduct. Which texts to draw upon for sermons is part of the challenge preachers face. Fairly distinguishing between description, illustration, and precept will require careful consideration of the biblical record in order to avoid distortion and misrepresentation. It is equally important to determine whether a simple passage or groups of texts convey an enduring theological insight or principle, or an ancient cultural, personal, or other bias. It should be noted that the potential for bias exists apart from the text in the person who interprets it. The at times intense debate about the correct interpretation of Gen. 19:1–29 illustrates the difficulty in reaching consensus about the meaning and relevance of a text. Proper regard for exegetical, hermeneutical, and theological matters should help form an appreciation of the value of scripture and its diverse references to sexuality. This sort of understanding also could inform an evaluation of subsequent biblical commentary and theological reflection.

The second task is to appreciate expanding empirical and scientific knowledge of human sexuality. Some issues and practices that provoke questions and concerns today were simply unknown to biblical authors. Accordingly in these instances, nothing specific is to be found in scripture. Yet the biological, behavioral, and social sciences are very aware of birth control and transsexualism, for example. Secular research can inform thinking about these and other matters. The limitations of secular resources, as with scripture, ought to be recognized. Individually and collectively they provide an understanding of nature at a particular time and from a particular perspective. Dissent and debate among the secular disciplines can be as common and confusing as that among and within religious disciplines. It may be tempting to rely solely on the latter for sermon preparation. Doing so, however, may risk criticism for being ignorant of evolving understandings of the complexity and diversity of sexuality. In short, integrating the findings and observations of relevant secular disciplines with the resources of the faith traditions may be required in order for the truth of each to inform the content of sermons.

By giving proper attention to both tasks and by holding the two in tension, preachers will be better equipped to prepare sermons that help people understand, from a Christian perspective, what it means to be sexual. In addition, preachers and congregations may be enabled to acknowledge and appreciate the pervasiveness of sexuality and the diversity of sexual self-perception and expression.

Biblical Instances

References to sexuality appear nearly throughout scripture, from concrete references to genital activity to metaphorical references to sexual relationships (for example, the metaphor of marriage). Discerning the original and enduring messages of these diverse texts that reflect and address religious, cultural, and social concerns is a basic prerequisite for sermon preparation. Otherwise, a distorted understanding of sexuality may result.

Old Testament. Sexuality is a basic and good condition of human existence, created by God, and subject to the divine will. It is one aspect of human life, for which, in itself, there should be no shame. It is understood within the concept of human fullness and social relationships (Gen. 2:18). It a gift from God that draws people together and joins them in fulfilling relationships (Gen. 2:24).

This is not to say that sexuality is seen in its positive light in every instance. A number of examples show that sexuality, like any other human quality, can be misused (see esp. Gen. 19:4–8; 38:12–30).

Patriarchalism pervades the Old Testament. This social institution contrasts with passages that portray women as equal (Gen. 1:26; 2:17; 3:16–19) and honored in relationships (e.g., Song of Solomon; Ruth; Esther; 1 Samuel 1; 2 Kings 4). The social and economic influences of these and other representations of sexuality, and in particular sex roles or practices, must be regarded in order to appreciate the progressive development of a view that sexuality is meant to serve human relationships, not subjugate them. The potential for union between persons is analogous to the covenantal union between Israel and Yahweh (Hosea 2; Isa. 54:4–17; 62:4–12; Jer. 2:2).

New Testament. As in the Old Testament, references to sexuality in the New Testament tend to be occasioned by particular questions and concerns regarding particular circumstances. It simply is not possible in either testament to discern a systematic or comprehensive sexual ethic. The first Christians addressed issues in light of their faith and "scientific" knowledge. This methodology has been employed throughout Christian history. Changing beliefs and scientific information inevitably mix to inform understandings and norms of sexuality and sexual morality.

The Gospel witness presents Jesus as understanding the intent of the law to be the welfare or wholeness of people (John 15:11; Matt. 23:23). He affirmed women (Luke 8:2–56), regarding men and women equally subject to the double law of love (Mark 12:30–31). He affirmed fidelity (Mark 10:2–12; Matt. 5:31–32; 19:3–9; Luke 16:18). His mission is described with the image of a wedding feast and the joy and fulfillment associated with it (Matt. 25:1–13; Mark 2:19; Matt. 22:1–14).

Paul thought that sex is good (1 Cor. 7:5) but the world was passing away (1 Cor. 7:26–27, 31). He responded to teachings and practices that threatened the faith and discipline of early Christians (especially Corinthians). Passion and desire took on negative connotations due to secular influence (1 Thess. 4:5). "Flesh" referred to that which is weak, corruptible, mortal (Rom. 8:6; Gal. 5:19). In Paul's use, flesh is not synonymous with the body, which warrants no rejection or denial of pleasure, including sexual pleasure. Paul's teaching on marriage varies from place to place, while holding to its goodness (1 Corinthians 7). Paul and other authors honored married life (with its implicit sexual features), using marriage as a symbol of the union of Christ and the church (Eph. 5:22–23). The devotion and mutuality inherent to this symbolism are the norms. All else is commentary.

Options for Preaching

Sermons are invitations to growth (spiritual and personal) and pastoral care on a congregational level. In neither the Old nor the New Testament is a specific sexual morality a major concern. Instead, a central message of each is the primacy of faith and obedience. In and through text, people are invited to be open to God and God's will. Sermons on sexuality should be characterized equally as open and inviting, recognizing that people tend to be sensitive, and often confused, about sexuality. Intrapersonal and interpersonal growth should be the goals of sermons on sexuality.

Sex without shame. Sexuality serves the creation and maintenance of human relationships. Sexual urges reveal the incompleteness of humans in isolation from others. In relationship with another, a person is opened to discoveries about self and others: what is similar and different between people; what fulfills, satisfies, and completes, and what does not. The body is crucial to this process, since it is the means by which the self is revealed and the world is experienced. The body is good (Gen. 1:31) and an instrument of God (John 1:14), and its sexual nature is no reason for shame (Gen. 2:18–25).

Sexual equality. Patriarchalism in scripture should be seen in relation to the progressively egalitarian view of males and females. Both male and female are created by God (Gen. 1:27), blessed (Gen. 1:28), and pronounced good (Gen. 1:31). Both are equal in Christ and called by God to faith and obedience (Gal. 3:28–29). The love command (Mark 12:28–34) applies to both, as does the Golden Rule (Matt. 7:12). The personhood of women demands respect; hence Jesus' proscription of divorce was given as a means to protect women from exploitation (Mark 10:2–12; Matt. 19:3–9; Luke 16:18). Social, cultural, and personal attitudes of either male or female superiority must be measured against this biblical standard of equality and mutual respect.

The body erotic. The Song of Solomon demonstrates that the ancient Hebrews could value the psychophysical relations of man and woman. The pleasurable and exciting characteristics of desire, passion, and sexuality in its many dimensions are celebrated. The book offers several messages regarding sexuality. One is that it is permissible to find delight in sexuality. Another is that the goodness and value of sexuality, including heterosexual intercourse, is not linked to procreation. The canonical text, with its open and frank discussion of the erotic, sanctions it for responsible discussions and discovery among the faithful.

SIN

Molly Marshall-Green

Sin is the deliberate transgression of the known will of God. It has a distinctly theological definition because it is fundamentally related to God's intention for humanity, set forth in scripture, and to the human moral conscience. The Bible regards sin as a personal affront to God.

Sin can be characterized as a comprehensive and personal disorder. All persons sin, according to scripture, and sin is as much a state of rebellion against God and one's true identity as a bearer of God's image as it is a series of specific wrongful acts against others. Not only do all persons experience this contradiction but they each manifest some awareness of being a sinful being needing forgiveness.

Analysis

Though extrabiblical sources have not specifically called this human dilemma sin, they have attempted to unravel the problem of the human being who wills to do good but is not able to do it. The liberal perspectives on humankind in nineteenth-century philosophical and theological writings, flavored with evolutionary optimism, nearly eclipsed a doctrine of sin.

The writings of many traditional religions offer additional insight. Although early anthropological studies put forth romantic notions of humans, emphasizing a natural "innocence," the religious literature of widely disparate cultures reflects a common concern to assuage guilt and placate or avert "the holy," usually conceived in a distant, punitive manner. Shrines, rituals, forms of sacrifice, and holy days all suggest that religious expressions grow out of a universal human need for cleansing.

Social analysis has often sought to remove individual responsibility for the world's ills, speaking instead of "systemic evil." Avoiding the category of sin, these analyses have suggested that social structures such as unjust governments or economic systems are the source of harmful actions toward humans.

Psychological studies of human conscience also wrestle with the empirical reality of the failure of all humans to live in consistent harmony with others and the betrayal of their sense of right and wrong. While certain theories, such as the Freudian, relegate the notion of human guilt arising out of a divine claim on humanity to the status of a neurotic projection, many try to make sense of the spiritual dimension of this human phenomenon.

Yet these nonbiblical descriptions lack sufficient depth, for they presume the efficacy of human moral effort and view sin in impersonal terms. The Bible offers the clearest insights into the origin and effects of human sin.

Biblical Instances

In the Bible, God continually moves to restore broken relationships with humanity. Nevertheless, while the Bible everywhere assumes the presence of sin, it refuses to consider that reality the normative experience for humans. It remains a betrayal, a contradiction of the human's essential being, created in God's own image.

Genesis 3 is the *locus classicus* concerning the origin of sin. This narrative depicts the temptation and consequent disobedience of Adam and Eve. The Yahwist writer clearly portrays that the action of humanity's forbears had catastrophic consequences.

What was "lost and ruined by the Fall," as Joseph Hart's hymn text puts it? Clearly, the primeval pair did not lose their humanity; subsequent texts in Genesis still speak of humans bearing the image of God (5:2; 9:6); indeed, culpability and a new accountability seem to go together. Yet, the beautiful harmony of the edenic existence was disrupted and intense struggle and conflict ensued.

In addition to Genesis 3, the stories of the "Watchers" (Gen. 6:1–8), the flood (6:9–9:29), and the tower of Babel (11:1–9) further explicate the characteristic rebellion of created beings, both heavenly and earthly. Many of the psalms (e.g., 14; 28; 51) probe the human penchant for wickedness that defiles God's way. That God desires "truth in the inmost being" (51:6) suggests the human ability to deceive. The prophetic tradition of Israel also offers penetrating analyses of the sinfulness of the human. External acts of piety account for nothing, the prophets proclaim (cf. Isaiah 58), if one remains internally impure, without compassion or mercy.

The apostle Paul offers a more systematic treatment. He sketches an Adam-Christ typology to assist Christian understanding of the bondage caused by sin (Rom. 5:12–21; 1 Cor. 15:21–22).

First, he affirms the conjunction of sin and death, interpreted primarily in a spiritual sense, that is, being separated from God.

Second, he declares the corporate solidarity of humanity in Adam and Christ. He is not suggesting a doctrine of original sin, the biological transference of a depraved nature (as Augustine taught) of the inheritance of guilt because of the transgression of Adam, but our human likeness to or sinful imitation of Adam and potential incorporation into and likeness to Christ. The gracious action of Christ effects acquittal and life.

Third, Paul notes the universal power of sin. First John echoes this reality: "If we say we have no sin, we deceive ourselves" (1:8). The book of Hebrews accents the exception of Christ as one who has in every respect "been tempted as we are, yet without sin" (4:15).

Fourth, each bears individual responsibility for his or her sin, even though one is born into a situation that inclines one to problems. Corporate expressions of sin, such as the attempted genocide of the Jews under Nazi Germany or the economic greed of many Western nations, resist correction and make complicit many persons who unwittingly participate.

The Bible views sin as a fundamental relational disorder; the creature is defying the Creator's good purpose: fellowship between God and the human and among people. It expresses itself in unbelief, in pride, and in sensuality. First John 2:15–16 sums up these dimensions of sin as lack of love for God, the lust of the flesh and the eyes, and the pride of life.

Biblical metaphors for sin include ungodliness (Ps. 119:163; Rom. 1:18), idolatry (Ex. 20:3–4; Rom. 1:25), and estrangement from God and others (Job 19:13; Eph. 4:18). It is regarded as a power (Rom. 5:21) that enslaves humanity and distorts all of the created order. It is more than simply making a mistake; rather, it is the refusal to live with the limitations accorded to finite beings.

Both the Old and New Testaments outline that there is no self-salvation; only God can restore humans to their true identity and make possible eternal life. Two encompassing movements in God's salvific history with humanity are chronicled in scripture: the giving of the Law and the giving of the Son. By providing the covenant and extensive sacrificial system as expressions of God's faithfulness, despite humanity's infidelity, God demonstrated unwavering commitment to redemption. Under the Law, God's gracious disclosure of how to live, the reality of the sins of the people were ever before them and they were without a means to "perfect the conscience of the worshiper" (Heb. 9:9). Repeated sacrifices reminded them of the temporal nature of this remedy for sin.

Christ mediates the new covenant, a new and living way to justify persons before righteous God. In Christ, "the righteousness of God has been manifested apart from law" (Rom. 3:21) and sinners are "justified by his grace as a gift, through the redemption which is in Christ Jesus" (3:24). Thus, God in Christ makes possible reconciliation and freedom from attempting to justify oneself before God. The power of sin is broken, for there is "no condemnation for those who are in Christ Jesus" (Rom. 8:1).

While the Christian will undoubtedly continue to sin, the "law of sin and death" from which he or she could not escape has been overcome in the atoning death of Christ. And the promise of the Christian life is that the indwelling presence of the Holy Spirit transforms and conforms the believer into the likeness of Christ.

Options for Preaching

The power to dehumanize. Sin compromises a person's well-being. Estranged from God, self, and others by sin, one lives with self-recrimination or false blaming of others. One flees from interpersonal relations because of fear of discovery; one's humanity is diminished by the power of sin.

Release from guilt. Scripture accents God's desire to deal with human guilt and to change human beings from "enemies of God" into reconciled friends (2 Cor. 5:18) through the cross of Christ. Not only does God provide this pivotal act of grace, but one is encouraged to confess one's sin on a continual basis (1 John 1:9) so that one may continue to feel justified before God.

The groaning creation. Human sinning affects all of the created order (Gen. 3:14–19; Rom. 8:20–39). Humans should not be blamed for all the world's natural disasters, but greed, jealousy, and lack of proper "dominion" further disturb the interdependence of creation. Biblical redemption involves more than humanity; the groaning creation will join in the liberation of the sons and daughters of God (Rom. 8:21).

Imitating Christ. The Christian is called to "put on" the way of Christ (Col. 3:12) so that his or her life reflects the purity and relational harmony intended by God. John's Gospel recounts Jesus' command to his followers (John 13:14) to do as he had done. Such obedient imitation overcomes evil with good, that people might no longer "live for themselves" but for the one who died and was raised for sinful humans.

SOVEREIGNTY OF GOD

Timothy George

The sovereignty of God refers to the extension of the divine rule or purpose over every realm of existence. Based on scripture, Christian theology views the will of God as the supreme ground of all that is. God stands above both the universe that God made and human history, which God entered redemptively in Jesus Christ. The sovereignty of God expressed the unlimited, unconditioned freedom out of which God has chosen to accomplish that which was purposed in creation and redemption.

Analysis

The sovereignty of God is related to three moments in the economy of divine activity: creation, redemption, and consummation.

Creation. "I believe in God the Father Almighty, Maker of heaven and earth." This early Christian confession posits the reality of a creaturely world that exists in absolute dependence on its Maker. God created the world from nothing as an act of freedom. God spoke the world into being and sustains it by providential care (Heb. 1:3, 10–12). God upholds the creaturely freedom of that which has been made; thus, the sovereignty of God should not be equated with fatalistic determinism.

Redemption. In the history of salvation God has rescued fallen humans from sin and damnation. Through the chosen people of Israel (Ps. 147:19–20) and preeminently in Jesus Christ, God's way of salvation has been made known. The doctrine of predestination refers to God's gracious calling of elect persons to faith and repentance. This teaching, though variously understood, has not generally been taken to preclude either personal moral responsibility or the missionary mandate to proclaim the gospel to all persons.

Consummation. The biblical view of last things assumes that God will bring to completion what was begun in creation and redemption (Phil. 1:6). The fact of evil in this present world often obscures the pattern of God's sovereign purpose, but Christian hope looks forward to a "new heaven and a new earth" where justice and peace are reconciled.

Biblical Instances

Old Testament. God's sovereignty is often portrayed in terms of God's relationship with nature. This is a recurrent theme in the Psalms, which declare God's power over earthquakes (46:1–3), thunderstorms (97), high mountains (65:6; 114:4), vast seas (93), the heavenly bodies, and all living creatures (148). By contrast, false gods are vain and impotent: idols cannot act or speak, "but our God is in heaven; He does whatever pleases Him" (Ps. 115:3, NIV).

God's sovereignty is also seen in the choice of Israel as a special people and the covenant relationship God enjoyed with them (Ps. 147:19–20). God's election of Israel derived not from their ability or goodness, but solely from God's gratuitous mercy and divine purpose (Deut. 7:7–9; Mal. 1:1–5). While Israel stands in a unique relationship to God, other nations and peoples are not exempted from the sway of divine sovereignty. For example, God "rules over the nations" (Ps. 22:28), establishes and dethrones princes (Dan. 2:37–39; 4:25), and sends prophets to warn of coming judgment (Jonah 1:17); God hardens the heart of one ruler (Ex. 10:27) and softens that of another (Isa. 45:1–5).

New Testament. The Synoptic Gospels relate the sovereignty of God to the coming of the kingdom that Jesus proclaimed. Jesus taught his disciples to pray, "your kingdom come, your will be done, on earth as it is in heaven" (Matt. 6:10, NRSV). The nature miracles of Jesus, his healings and exorcisms, and, above all, his pronouncement of unconditional forgiveness (Mark 2:1–12; Luke 15:11–32) constituted a claim to authority that could be regarded only as that of the Sovereign Lord. In later New Testament writings Jesus' own fate, his death and resurrection, are interpreted as the outworking of God's eternal purpose of redemption (John 12:23–28; 17:1–5; Acts 2:23–24; Rev. 13:8).

In Pauline theology the church's mission is closely related to fulfillment of God's sovereign plan. Despite the suffering and persecution that mark the church in the present age, God's people look forward to the day of resurrection and triumph over the forces of oppression and evil (1 Thess. 4:13–18; Eph. 3:20–21).

Options for Preaching

The God who acts. Psalm 77 is a lament from one, overwhelmed by life's tragedies, who has begun to question the very love and promises of God. The turning point comes when the psalmist determines to "remember the deeds of the Lord" (v. 11). When one considers who God is and what God has done, one finds assurance of God's nearness even in the midst of distress.

God meant it for good. The story of Joseph concludes with a forgiving confession to his brothers: their betrayal and foul play against him God had intended for good! What Joseph's brothers meant as harm God used as a means to save the family from starvation (Gen. 50:15–21). God's sovereignty works in people's lives to overcome the limitations and suffering of human existence. See also Paul's classic summary, Romans 8:28.

Chosen for service. The doctrine of predestination is set forth clearly in Eph. 1:3–14. God's people were chosen "before" the foundation of the world, "in" Christ Jesus, "in order that" they might be holy and blameless. God's choice was based not on human worthiness, but rather on "the pleasure and will" of God alone. This election, however, is not a static condition but rather a summons to commitment and service.

STEWARDSHIP

Richard B. Cunningham

Stewardship is the individual's management of all life's resources, the gifts of God in creation and redemption, in responsible freedom, according to the will of God as revealed in Jesus Christ. Stewardship principles apply to the individual's management of personal resources as well as to those of various social groupings, such as family, church, and state. In every case, one will finally be accountable to God.

Analysis

The basic principles of stewardship are best found in two parables of Jesus with explicit stewardship vocabulary—the parable of the wise and foolish servants (Luke 12:42–48) and the parable of the unrighteous steward (Luke 16:1–13). These involve the basic ideas of the master of an estate who places his property under the care of a servant during his absence. The servant is to manage the estate in responsible freedom and is accountable for good or bad stewardship upon the master's unannounced return.

In the New Testament, this accountability is applied to such things as one's physical, mental, and spiritual health; the use of time, abilities, and wealth; one's vocation and calling as a Christian; and one's involvement in various spheres of social life. In every case, stewardship requires responsible management and proportionate giving to the work of God and the needs of fellow human beings.

Biblical Instances

Preaching would best reflect the broader meaning of stewardship as the framework within which preaching about money or giving should occur. Examples of these broader themes are in the following texts: God as owner of creation (Ps. 24:1–2), time (Eph. 5:15–17), the physical body (1 Cor. 6:19–20), the mind (Luke 10:27; Rom. 12:2), conduct (Eph. 2:10; 4:1), conversation (Matt. 12:36), influence (Matt. 5:16), abilities (1 Cor. 12:4–7), relationships (Luke 10:27), family (1 Tim. 5:8), and material things (Matt. 6:19–21).

Jesus' teachings about financial stewardship focus primarily upon one's relationship to material things, particularly the obstacle wealth creates for entering the kingdom, and the imperative to give alms to the poor as an expression of life in the kingdom. The epistles focus on general stewardship and provide helpful principles for financial giving.

Options for Preaching

Some important preaching themes on the relationship to material things are found in the following texts:

Trusting God for basic physical needs (Matt. 6:25–34).

The proper acquisition of wealth (2 Thess. 3:10–12; James 5:1–6).

The proper use of wealth (1 Tim. 6:6–8, 17–19).

The danger of wealth (Mark 10:25; 8:36; Matt. 6:24).

The limitations of wealth (1 Tim. 6:7).

The most important New Testament passages on giving are 2 Corinthians 8 and 9 and 1 Corinthians 16:1–4. Second Corinthians 9:13 provides a comprehensive statement of the purpose of giving. The following are some other important sermon themes on giving:

Giving as a response. Give as a response to God's grace (2 Cor. 8:7), to Christ's example (2 Cor. 8:9), and to human need (2 Cor. 8:14).

Giving as thanksgiving, sacrifice, proof of love, symbol. Give to God as an expression of thanksgiving (2 Cor. 9:12), as a form of sacrifice to God (Phil. 4:18), as a proof of love (2 Cor. 8:24), and as a symbol of one's total commitment of life and resources (Ex. 22:29–30).

How to give. Give the self first (2 Cor. 8:5), voluntarily (2 Cor. 8:3; 9:5), proportionately (2 Cor. 8:12), generously (2 Cor. 8:2; 9:11), sacrificially (Luke 21:1–4), spontaneously (Matt. 6:2–4), and systematically (1 Cor. 16:2).

SUFFERING

Wayne E. Oates

Suffering is the bearing or undergoing of pain, distress, or tribulation. Literally, suffering means to be pressed or put under pressure. Symbolically it means oppression, to be persecuted or to be stressed unduly. The contemporary literature on stress describes suffering in behavioral-science terms. The term implies a condition that calls for patience and endurance of painful or oppressive conditions that do not have an end in sight for the sufferer. To the contrary, suffering has an unremitting, ceaseless quality to it.

Analysis

Suffering and the nature of God. Since the time of the early church fathers the question as to whether God suffers has haunted the minds of theologians. Does God suffer? God fully participated in the crucifixion, death, and resurrection of Jesus Christ. God is involved in fellowship with persons in pain. This rejects abstract theodicies that portray God as impassively nonparticipant in human suffering. Even the cry of absence of Jesus on the Cross, "My God, my God, why hast thou forsaken me?" expresses God's suffering with humankind when suffering is so acute that it shuts out the awareness of God's presence.

The suffering of God in human suffering is described by Elie Wiesel in *Night*: "Where is God?" asks a witness to an execution in a Nazi concentration camp. He was answered by another witness standing nearby. Pointing to the prisoner being hanged, he said: "There God is, hanging on that gallows!"

Cataclysmic suffering. The whole New Testament was written against a backdrop of cataclysmic suffering, the persecution of Christians. The New Testament speaks of Christians being oppressed by principalities, powers, the world rulers of the present darkness, the spiritual hosts of wickedness in heavenly places.

Suffering of severe, chronic pain. This suffering presents the Christian with the meaninglessness and absurdity of existence. He or she is tempted to end the pain with suicide. Short of suicide, he or she is tempted to idolize the pain and permit the suffering to be the main preoccupation of life. Often, the pain becomes a means for the sufferer to dominate the lives of other people around him or her.

The secret of patience and endurance is the capacity of the human spirit in fellowship with God to transcend the pain with a passionate commitment to ministering to other people.

Biblical Instances

The primary example of suffering in the Bible is the suffering of Jesus in the garden of Gethsemane, the trials and scourgings that went before his crucifixion, and the tension-filled sayings on the cross. The preacher does well in addressing the sufferings of Christ to consider two all-inclusive sermons found in the scriptures themselves on the crucifixion and resurrection of Jesus: Peter's sermon at Pentecost in Acts 2:22–35, and Paul's sermon at Antioch in Acts 13:16–41.

The case of Job and his suffering takes the preacher into the critical issue of why just and upright people suffer. Satan appears as a sort of prosecuting attorney to build a case against Job. Satan disappears from the drama in Job 2:7. He is replaced by Job's wife and his counselors. Job is tempted, tested, admonished, and cajoled by them. He insists that he will maintain his integrity before the Lord. This story challenges the conventional wisdom of that day and this—that only the unrighteous suffer. One homiletically intriguing section is in Job 42:10–17. He has all his fortunes restored twofold! Does it really happen that way often?

Another record of human suffering is found in Numbers 11:4–25. Moses was filled with anger, bedraggled and exhausted, as he struggled to please and lead the children of Israel. To *please* and to *lead* at one and the same time is the quiet suffering of every leader of people. Moses became so discouraged and depressed with the overwhelming responsibility that he wanted to die. He asked the Lord to kill him! Numbers 11:15 states his wish clearly. The Lord heard his prayer and provided him with seventy elders of Israel to take some of the spirit that was upon Moses as the Lord put it upon each of them. The Lord said: "they shall bear the burden of the people with you, that you may not bear it yourself alone." The loneliness of leadership was healed by the community of sharing power and responsibility.

A final example of suffering is that of Paul and his thorn in the flesh, found in 2 Cor. 12:1–10. He found meaning in the suffering in that it kept him from self-elevation, pride, and elation. The Lord did not, apparently, answer Paul's prayers in the way Paul wanted but assured him of God's grace in bearing his weakness.

Options for Preaching

A major meaning of suffering (2 Cor. 1:3–7). This sermon should address the human dilemma of the meaninglessness of the suffering of a person. The persistent cry of the sufferer is, Why, O Lord? This text provides a substantive and practical approach to what otherwise can be an abstract attempt to "justify the ways of God and people."

The text has the following ideas for a sermon structure: First, the *kind* of God is explicitly stated. This is not a vengeful God who causes people to suffer. This God is "the Father of mercies and God of all comfort." Second, God comforts people in all their affliction. This God does not discriminate between the afflictions people have brought on themselves and those for which they have no responsibility. The comfort extends to *all* their afflictions. Third, the *purpose* of God's comfort is that the comforted person may become a comfort to other people in their affliction. This is a core meaning of suffering. Fourth, people are *equipped* to minister to others by means of the comfort with which God has comforted them.

Maturity through suffering (Rom. 5:1–5). This text makes an audacious statement: "we rejoice in our sufferings." This is a beginning statement, but it summarizes the end result of a process of growth through suffering. Suffering produces a kind of knowledge that moves sufferers from the milk of the world to the strong meat of the gospel mentioned in Hebrews 5:11–14. The process of growth toward rejoicing in suffering is fourfold: First, suffering produces endurance. Second, endurance produces character. Third, character produces hope. Fourth, hope heals the sufferer of disappointment. All this growth is nurtured by the pouring of God's love—the chief agent of maturation—into the sufferer's heart through the Holy Spirit.

The divine alternative to suicide (Num. 11:14–15). The suicidal person is often a person, like Moses, who has an "Atlas complex," that is, he or she carries the whole world on his or her shoulders. This particular kind of suicidal person usually is not in conversation with God because he or she feels compelled to do all of God's work for God. Such a person may even unconsciously think he or she is a god. This text can be rightly divided into (1) Moses' dilemma and prayer to God to kill him; (2) God's response to Moses' plea; (3) Moses' learning to share responsibility and power with others, the secret of effective leadership.

SUICIDE

James T. Clemons

Suicide is defined in several ways, depending on the purpose of the definer. The common notion that it means "to kill oneself," as the Latin etymology implies, is inadequate to cover all the essential aspects of suicide. One's definition determines which biblical evidence to consider and how one makes ethical decisions. The following discussion assumes this broad definition: *the deliberate choice and successful effort to end one's life, regardless of the motives, circumstances, or methods used.* An attempted suicide is an act in which the effort to end one's life has been made but has not been successful.

Analysis

Traditional religious attitudes against suicide and a prevailing social stigma make preaching on the subject particularly difficult. At the same time, recent studies in sociology, psychology, and medicine, along with increased media attention and action by national and state governments, challenge church and synagogue to reevaluate their positions and response.

Positive results of recent research include new biblical and theological resources, official statements from religious groups, and an expressed openness among congregations to deal with the issue. Thus, preachers need have no lingering reluctance to bring all their resources of faith and homiletical skills to bear on a topic of deep and widespread concern.

The task requires two types of sermons: those for funerals of suicides and those for other services of worship. The former will rightly focus on pastoral care and the needs of the bereaved. Only the latter will allow sufficient exploration of the broader dimensions of suicide. The resources and themes listed below can be of value in preparing a sermon for either occasion.

Biblical Instances

Specific accounts of suicide are noted six times in the Hebrew Bible and once in the New Testament. The account of Abimelech's death (Judg. 9:50–54) is concerned with perpetuating male superiority, not condemning the manner in which he died. Samson's prayers to God for vengeance and the strength to bring death to his tormentors as well as himself (Judg. 16:28–31) is an example of altruistic self-chosen death (see also Heb. 11:32). Neither Saul nor his armor-bearer is ever condemned; rather, David laments his death and honors those who showed respect for Saul's body (1 Sam. 31:1–13; 2 Sam. 1:1–27; 2:4b–7; 21:10–14; 1 Chron. 10:1–14). Ahithophel (2 Sam. 17:1–23), Zimri (1 Kings 16:15–20), and Judas (Matt. 27:3–5; see also Acts 1:5–19) were not particularly favored by the biblical writers, but they were not accused because they chose suicide. The Philippian jailer's attempted suicide (Acts 1:15–18) was prevented by Paul's intervening cry, but Paul's reasons for intervening are not specified. By the above definition, Jonah (Jonah 1:7–12) also attempted suicide but was prevented from doing so because God had a specific reason for him to live.

Biblical writers were concerned not with the morality of suicide but only with recording the event. Reading either a condemnation or condonation of suicide into these texts requires a previously held conviction that is forced upon the text. The texts that have been most influential in shaping attitudes toward suicide do not refer specifically to a self-chosen death but have had an already existing attitude read into them.

Texts used to condemn suicide are numerous and include: specific commandments (e.g., Ex. 20:13; Deut. 5:17; 30:19); notable examples of those who in difficult circumstances refused to choose death, among them Job (2:7–10) and Paul (Phil. 4:11); and the assumption that only God may take away human life (e.g., Deut. 32:39; Ps. 104:29).

Texts used to condone or forgive suicide are fewer but are used in much the same way, that is, by reading into them a favorable attitude toward the act. Prominent types of condoning arguments include, but are not limited to: God's unfailing love (Matt. 12:31; Mark 3:28–30; Luke 12:10; Rom. 8:1–2; 8:38–39), a rejection of the present world (1 John 2:15; John 12:25 and par.), calls to martyrdom (Dan. 3:17–18; John 15:13–14), examples of suicidal behavior and self-sacrifice (Jonah 4:3; 1 John 3:16).

Texts used to condemn or to condone suicide require careful exegesis as to their immediate context. Often that is sufficient to show that originally suicide was not being addressed by the biblical writers. The question then arises, when and under what circumstances did the negative attitudes arise in the history of the church? A brief summary of the church's changing positions will provide a helpful perspective and will negate the erroneous but prevailing notion that there has always been only a negative position against suicide. In turn, a historical survey can further encourage religious groups to examine their entrenched notions, which often hinder needed social response.

Options for Preaching

Biblical themes. Explaining what the Bible says and does not say about suicide is basic to all other dimensions of the issue.

Sacrificing oneself for others or for a worthy cause is admired in many biblical stories. Samson, Jonah, Jesus, and Paul offer sermonic possibilities. Less worthy motives include disgrace or dishonor. Zimri, Abimelech, Ahithophel, Judas, and the Philippian jailer chose death in the face of disgrace or dishonor. Of special relevance to today's aging society and the advances of medical technology are Saul and his armor-bearer, who faced intense physical and mental suffering in the present and fear of torture and torment in the future. In such soul-wrenching situations, preachers must evaluate each text carefully and select those which best suit the goal of the sermon. For a different group, namely young people, they would do well to point out that suicide is a permanent solution to what is often only a temporary problem.

Ethical themes. Suicide is a topic fraught with ethical issues that demand homiletical attention. The preacher can help troubled individuals, concerned congregations, and confused communities to make informed, compassionate decisions. Each listener or reader needs to know the basic warning signals of persons at high risk, proper methods of intervention, and how to hold medical and law enforcement personnel, legislators, and the media accountable. By presenting the roles that the Bible and tradition play in decision making, and by presenting clearly the urgent issues that arise from this tragic human experience, the preacher puts faith at the forefront of the ongoing ethical struggle. This can include encouraging the removal of conditions that contribute to feelings of helplessness and hopelessness in their communities, urging suicide prevention programs in schools and their own religious groups, and creating a more loving atmosphere that leaves no room for oppressive stigma. Those who study suicide insist that removing the stigma of it is one of the most important ways to prevent it.

Theological themes. Most ethical discussions revolve around two theological foci. The older focus sees God as the giver of life and the one who alone can take life away, a point often assumed in Hebrew scriptures. Efforts to prolong life are justified because life, God's gift, is in itself good, and so it should be preserved whenever possible. At least since the Renaissance, however, the emphasis has been on the notion that regardless of the source of one's life, the choice of when, where, and how one dies is strictly up to the person. Some see that choice as a God-given right. Religions usually allow for the latter option, at least indirectly, by affirming that their followers should be ready to give their lives, one way or another, for their faith.

Pastoral themes. The assurance of God's unfailing love, even for those who take their own lives; the deceased's altruistic intent of "making things go better" for others; and the fact that the survivors don't know what thoughts were present at the last minute are appropriate themes for sermons at the funerals of suicides and also for sermons on the broader issues related to the subject. At the same time, preachers must be extremely cautious not to glamorize suicidal deaths, especially those of youth. To do so might unintentionally prompt a copycat reaction. In seeking to be pastoral, they must be very clear on basic ethical guidelines. The text must not be distorted to foster a preconceived position, and personal illustrations must not violate the strict canon of confidentiality. A caring, sensitive sermon can in itself model a caring response for those who hear and read it.

Social themes. A tragedy so complex and widespread and so fraught with ethical problems demands a response from religious communities in the midst of the social context. Social issues are directly related to religious life, and sermons remain one of the most effective means of communicating the ways in which one impinges upon the other. In addition to the ethical issues cited above, experts on suicide frequently raise questions about the accessibility of handguns, the inadequacy and inequity of proper medical and psychological care, and the need for more funding for research and education. Society's oppressiveness against women must be addressed in the light of one glaring statistic: three to four times as many women attempt suicide as do men. To be effective in addressing these crucial areas, religious communities must look to their preachers for genuine biblical understanding, adequate information, sound reasoning, and compassionate admonition.

TEMPERANCE

Wayne E. Oates

Temperance is the practice of restraining oneself in provocation, passion, or desire. The word is a variation of the verb "to temper," as in the tempering of steel or a person's character. Sometimes the word is used colloquially to mean abstinence from alcohol use. However, the word means habitual moderation in any kind of behavior or thought.

Analysis

The word "temperance" as defined above is rarely used to-day. The word has developed a connotation that means total abstinence, specifically from alcohol use. This change in basic meaning is because of the temperance movement, which led to the Eighteenth Amendment to the Constitution forbidding the manufacture, sale, or use of alcohol. Any homiletical use of the word must take this into consideration. The biblical meaning of temperance is much richer than abstinence from alcohol.

Theologically, temperance means self-discipline according to the teachings of scripture. For example, temperance in response to wrongs done one by others is prescribed in Jesus' teachings in Matthew 18:15–35. The temperate person should try to get the person who has offended "to listen." Similarly, the apostle Paul admonishes a more temperate handling of grievances against an offending person than going to a court of law for judgment by the unrighteous (1 Cor. 6:1–6).

Biblical Instances

"Temperance" is an Elizabethan word used in the King James Bible. In biblical lexicons it is translated "self-control." In the Old Testament, Proverbs 25:28 says, "A man without self-control is like a city broken into and left without walls." Proverbs 16:32 gives a more positive side: "He who is slow to anger is better than the mighty, and he who rules his spirit than he who takes a city." The virtue of self-control or temperance is referred to only in the Wisdom literature.

The New Testament presents a larger picture. Paul identifies self-control as one of the fruits of the Spirit. Self-control is brought about in "those who belong to Christ Jesus [who] have crucified the flesh with its passions and desires" (Gal. 5:23–24).

Titus 2:2 exhorts older men to be "temperate, serious, sensible, sound in faith, in love, and in steadfastness." In another sense self-control means being of good mental health, as in 2 Timothy 1:7.

Options for Preaching

Temperance and the way of the cross (Gal. 5:23–24). The popular use of the word "temperance" can be explained and set aside so that people may understand the rich meaning of self-control as taking the cross as a way of life. Note also Galatians 2:20 and Romans 6:1–4.

The gift of self-control (2 Tim. 1:7). Self-control is not lifting oneself by one's bootstraps. It is a by-product or a side effect of (1) daily choosing the way of the cross as a way of life, (2) lifting one's fears and anxieties to God in prayer, and (3) freely receiving the gifts of power, love, and self-control.

TEMPTATION

Wayne E. Oates

Temptation is enticement, allurement, or attraction, especially to evil or wrongdoing. Further, it is the process of testing or proving the strength, endurance, or character of a person or persons. Temptation is also a severe or painful trial, tribulation. In the Old and New Testaments, temptation also means the testing of people by God, as in the case of Abraham in Genesis 22:1–24, or the testing of God by people, as in the case of the children of Israel in Exodus 17:2.

Analysis

Temptation is a neglected theme in modern preaching and in modern thought, for that matter. The realm of fantasy, desire, enticement, and allurement is coalesced in popular religious thinking with the conception of sin. In fact, many think that to be tempted *is* to sin. This is a popular heresy, because the New Testament particularly makes clear distinctions between temptation and sin. Jesus was tempted in all ways as ordinary people are, yet he was without sin. Therefore, to consider temptation and sin as synonymous strikes at the very core of the redeeming grace of Jesus Christ.

One of the sources of this misunderstanding is the misinterpretation of Jesus' teachings in Matthew 5:21–31, in which he probes the motives for murder in the depths of anger in the human heart and the genesis of adultery in the lustful looking of people upon one another. Martin Luther insists that one cannot afford to make an equation of temptation and sin here. He says it is one thing for one to allow birds to fly over one's head and quite another to invite them to build a nest in one's hair! Then, too, to *equate* passing impulses of rage with actually murdering a person overlooks the fact that the person is unharmed by the rage but is a corpse with the murder. The whole realm of pastoral psychology has reopened the labyrinthine ways of the mind and enriched the homiletical approach to the meaning and healing of temptation.

Biblical Instances

The difference between temptation and sin is vividly portrayed in the temptation and sin of Eve and Adam in Genesis 3 and in the temptation of Jesus in the wilderness. In both accounts the source of temptation is from an outside agent: the serpent in Genesis 3 and the devil in Matthew 4 and Luke. In Genesis 22:1–24 Abraham is tested or tempted by God.

However, James 1:13–15 states: "Let no one say when he is tempted, 'I am tempted by God'; for God cannot be tempted by evil and he himself tempts no one; but each person is tempted when he is lured and enticed by his own desire. Then desire when it has conceived gives birth to sin; and sin when it is full-grown brings forth death." Also, Paul in Romans 1:25 says that "they exchanged the truth about God for a lie and worshiped . . . the creature rather than the Creator." Thus he describes a voluntary choice of self-deception and idolatry.

Options for Preaching

Providence and temptation (Gen. 22:1–24; 1 Cor. 10:13). God put Abraham to the test. On the way up the mountain Abraham answered Isaac's question by saying that God would provide an animal to sacrifice. After God did so, Abraham named the place Jehovah-jireh, meaning "the Lord provides." In 1 Corinthians 10:13, the theme of providence again appears. God will provide a way of escape so God's people can endure the temptation.

The internal forum of temptation (James 1:13–15). This text locates the source of temptation within the internal forum of a person's own choices and decision making. It describes the process of the growth of temptation from the luring and enticement of one's own desire. It describes the full-grownness of temptation into sin and death. Hence temptation is a matter of life and death.

The father of lies (John 8:44). In this text Jesus describes the devil as the father of lies. Temptation calls for self-deception. Paul in Romans 1:25 speaks of people as having exchanged the truth of God for a lie. A sermon on this topic must deal with the unreality of the devil, whom the apostle Paul calls "the god of this world," the deceiver at the heart of the many idolatries that enchant. When one puts anything or anyone less than God in the place of God, one becomes an idolater. The idol exercises demonic, possessing power over the idolizer. This is the way the father of lies works.

THE TEN COMMANDMENTS

William R. Cannon

The Ten Commandments are ten specific laws given by God through Moses to the Hebrew people. Since Christianity accepts the Old Testament along with the New Testament as scripture, the commandments are the code of conduct for Christians as well as Jews. They are found in Exodus 20:1–17 and Deuteronomy 5:6–22. The first four define our behavior toward God: the prohibition of (1) polytheism, (2) idolatry, (3) blasphemy, and (4) work on the Sabbath. The other six define our behavior toward one another: (5) devotion to parents, and the prohibition of (6) murder, (7) adultery, (8) theft, (9) bearing false witness, and (10) covetousness.

Analysis

Though the commandments are the same in both accounts, the reasons for observing them in every instance are not. For example, the sanction for the Fourth Commandment in Deuteronomy is that it is for a humane purpose, namely, to provide rest for servants as well as masters. The Hebrews are reminded that they once were servants in Egypt. The reason given for this commandment in Exodus is theological: God rested from creation on the seventh day.

The form of expression varies throughout the two accounts, indicating, no doubt, different authors, but this does not alter in any way the laws themselves or call in question the time, place, and circumstance of their deliverance. They purport to come directly from God (Deut. 5:22), who gave them to Moses on Mount Sinai (Ex. 31:18) in the wilderness between the Red Sea and Canaan during the second millennium B.C.

What God disclosed to Moses for the chosen people, God instilled into the nature of other peoples, so that conscience itself testifies to the validity of these laws (Rom. 2:14–15). Therefore, the Ten Commandments form a bridge between natural and revealed religion.

Biblical Instances

Old Testament. The Old Testament abounds in instances of how the violation of these laws brings disaster, while the keeping of them assures the blessings of God. The book of Judges from start to finish portrays this: when the Israelites disobeyed God, God deserted them and their enemies prevailed; when they kept the commandments, God gave them victory (Judg. 2:20–23; 3:7–11; 10:6–11; ch. 33). God rejected King Saul for his disobedience (1 Sam. 15:26) and rewarded David for his obedience (2 Sam. 22:21–25). National apostasy led to the captivity of both Israel (2 Kings 17:1–18) and Judah (2 Kings 25:1–12), while turning back to God and keeping the commandments brought forgiveness and restoration (Neh. 1:8–9).

New Testament. Jesus emphasizes the necessity of observing the Ten Commandments in his interrogation of the rich young ruler (Matt. 19:18–19; Mark 10:19–20; Luke 18:20–21). He summarizes the Decalogue by affirming, "You shall love . . . God . . . with all your heart, . . . soul, . . . strength, and . . . mind; and your neighbor as yourself" (Luke 10:27). "On these two commandments depend all the law and the prophets" (Matt. 22:40).

With Paul the law shows what sin is but lacks the power to overcome sin (Rom. 7:7–23). Sin is overcome only by grace through faith in Jesus Christ (Romans 5). Thus the law is kept, not as an obligation, but as a privilege (Romans 6 and 8). The law is the schoolmaster who brings the pupil to Christ (Gal. 3:24).

Options for Preaching

Law and gospel (Matt. 5:17–19). Law means requirement and obligation, while gospel is good news of salvation in Jesus Christ. Paul finds the law impotent, even deadly (1 Cor. 15:56; Gal. 3:11–13, 22–23). And so it is, unless salvation assures its observance, almost without notice, as second nature, by the believer. Jesus does not destroy the law but confirms it. His grace empowers his followers to obey its precepts (2 Cor. 12:9).

The nature of law. The law is a mirror of the character of God. The Old Testament asserts that the Ten Commandments were written by the finger of God, as if God himself chiseled the words on two tables of stone (Ex. 31:18). The New Testament teaches that the moral law is inflexible. How a person behaves, the character one forms, bad or good, determines one's destiny (Gal. 6:7–8).

The goal of the law. Moral perfection is the goal of the law. Jesus admonishes his followers to seek to be perfect, even as God is perfect (Matt. 5:48). He says the sure sign they love God is that they keep the commandments (John 14:15). Grace assures this through faith in God (Eph. 2:8).

THEODICY

Wayne E. Ward

The literal meaning of "theodicy" is "to justify God." It is the defense of God's goodness and omnipotence in the face of evil. It expresses the classic struggle of devout believers in God who find it difficult to reconcile their belief in an all-powerful, all-loving Creator God with the reality of evil and tragedy of epic proportions in such a world as this.

Analysis

The theological and philosophical answers to this dilemma usually take the form of limiting God's power, or even asking whether God is not always loving. Since there has been no resolution of the problem that finds universal acceptance, most believers leave the mystery to the answer of eternity: "We'll understand it better, by and by!" Many believers also see the self-limitation of God in creation and the freedom given to human beings as the doorway through which evil and sin have come into the world.

Many other sensitive and thoughtful persons have been compelled to give up belief in God because they are unable to reconcile belief in God with the pervasive evil in the world. Some others redefine their understanding of "God" in terms of matter, natural law, or impersonal forces in the universe and reject the biblical picture of a loving and omnipotent personal God altogether.

Biblical Instances

It is striking that the Bible never viewed this problem as an abstract theological problem. Rather, the psalmist cried out in dismay at the prosperity of the wicked (Pss. 73:3; 94:3–7). The Wisdom writer told the story of Job, and through the arguments of the "friends" of Job showed the bankruptcy of their explanations of evil and suffering (Job 4:1–5:27; 8:1–22; 11:1–20). Early Christians believed the ultimate answer lies in the theme of the suffering Servant of Isaiah (Isa. 42:1–4; 49:1–6; 50:4–11; 52:13–53:12), which culminated in the cross of Christ. This theme portrays the redemptive character of righteous suffering, and, most important, claims that God personally entered into human sin and tragedy in order to redeem it.

Some interpreters consider this theme of divine suffering to be the central message of the New Testament. Early Christians directly cited the suffering Servant role of Jesus (Acts 3:13; 4:25, 27, 30). Jesus himself directly quoted from the fourth Servant Song of Isaiah (Isa. 53:12) in Mark 10:45, identifying himself as the suffering Servant who would "give his life as a ransom for many." This is the ultimate Christian theodicy: God, out of infinite love, bears the pain and suffering of the world in God's own infinite Being, vicariously redeeming it through the divine suffering of Christ.

Options for Preaching

Surely the biblical teaching about the goodness of God, even in the full awareness of the evil in this world, suggests the right direction for preaching:

Steadfast belief. Instead of speculative arguments, which have dominated the classic debates on theodicy, the biblical proclamation emphasizes steadfast belief in the goodness of God, even when faith is tested by suffering. The book of Job suggests that telling the experience of people who have believed in God in spite of all their suffering may be the most effective way to deal with this issue in the pulpit.

The cross. The ultimate expression of the love of God in the face of evil is in the cross of Christ. This supreme example of the suffering love of God, coupled with the self-limitation upon God's power, offers the only hope for the redemption of the world.

Taking up the cross. Christ calls his followers to take up their cross by a deliberate choice, seizing the opportunity to bear whatever life may bring, in unwavering testimony to the grace of God, which is "made perfect in weakness" (2 Cor. 12:9).

TRADITION

Karen E. Smith

The word "tradition" has been defined as a belief or custom handed down from ancestors to posterity. Within the church, tradition is sometimes used to mean all the practices or teachings of Christianity that, through the centuries, have been kept and handed over, either orally or in documents, by the faithful within the church. Tradition sometimes refers to a particular Christian doctrine generally, or in one denomination or group specifically, such as the tradition of believer's baptism or infant baptism. A custom or belief that may not necessarily be historically verifiable but has been widely accepted, such as the belief that the apostle Paul was martyred in Rome, may also be described as a tradition.

Analysis

The most common ecclesiastical usage of the word "tradition" is that it is the teaching or practice of the church, which has been held to, albeit in varying degrees, by the church for centuries; though conditioned by the scriptures, and often believed to have been taken from the same "divine source," tradition is considered distinct from the words of scripture. The words of the Apostles' Creed, for instance, are not found in the New Testament canon, but are believed to have developed alongside it within the early church.

Since the Reformation era, Protestants and Roman Catholics have discussed the significance of tradition within the church. At the Council of Trent (1545–1563), Roman Catholics stated that scripture and tradition were to be received as having equal authority. Protestants have opposed any attempt to elevate tradition and insisted on the sole sufficiency of scripture. At the Second Vatican Council (1962–65) Roman Catholics attempted to clarify their understanding that scripture and tradition were not to be viewed as distinct, but "flow from the same divine wellspring, merge into a unity and tend to the same end."

By contrast, Christians within the Orthodox church insist that scripture exists within tradition. While admitting that not everything received from the past is of equal value, they maintain that the Bible, the Nicene Creed, and the doctrinal definitions of the first seven ecumenical councils of the church have a special authority and cannot be revised or altered.

Biblical Instances

While opinions differ on the relationship of tradition to scripture, it is commonly agreed that the biblical story itself attests to the importance of tradition. Old Testament narratives reflect the value of tradition by repeating stories of God's faithfulness for generations (Deut. 6:1–25; Ps. 145:4; Psalm 105). God's glorious deeds should be remembered and repeated to coming generations (Psalm 78).

Gospel stories reflect Jesus' knowledge of traditions handed over by Old Testament prophets and contained in the law (Luke 4:4, 8, 12). Yet Mosaic law and the traditions of the elders, as the New Testament points out, are completed in the teaching of Jesus. Likewise, the apostle Paul proclaimed that the gospel breaks through the restrictive bonds of tradition as it was known (Gal. 3:23–25; 6:2; Romans 10:4).

Anyone seeking to interpret scripture should note that the New Testament, too, represents part of Christian tradition (John 21:24–25). First collected orally by early believers and preserved over the years, the New Testament canon itself points to the need to affirm tradition within the church (John 20:30–31; 1 Cor. 11:2; 2 Thess. 3:6; 2:15; 2 Tim. 2:2).

Options for Preaching

Sermons on the theme of tradition should uphold the value of historical teaching as a way of reminding the church of its apostolic heritage. At the same time, they should not fail to point out that the gospel is never bound or limited by tradition and may even provoke new interpretations in the contemporary context.

Tradition as an act of remembering. Special occasions for remembering God's love and deliverance, such as the Passover feast, are established as traditions among the Hebrew people. In the New Testament, remembering God's love is one dimension of the celebration of the Lord's Supper (Luke 22:15–20).

Tradition and the ministry of love. Throughout the Gospel accounts, Jesus was confronted by people who wanted to know why his disciples did not keep the tradition of the elders. While recognizing tradition and the teachings of the law, Jesus pointed out that observation of tradition was not to take the place of a ministry of love (Matt. 5:17; 15:2–9).

Tradition that binds together. In spite of varied traditions within denominations or groups, a common faith in Christ is shared by all Christians. In Acts the unity of early Christians is depicted in some of their shared traditions (Acts 2:43–47). The apostle Paul reminded the church at Corinth that they were to maintain the traditions he had delivered to them, and he claimed he had received the tradition of the Lord's Supper from the Lord (1 Cor. 11:23–26).

TRINITY

Daniel L. Migliore

According to classical Christian doctrine, the living God is Father, Son, and Holy Spirit, "one in substance, distinct in three persons." This doctrine upholds the unity of God while affirming that Jesus Christ and the Holy Spirit are, like God the Father, fully divine. The three persons of the Trinity are eternally united in a perfect communion of self-giving love in which humanity is graciously invited to share.

Analysis

Scripture and Christian experience alike testify that God was truly present in Christ (2 Cor. 5:19) and continues to work transformingly by the Holy Spirit (2 Cor. 3:6, 17–18). Since salvation has come from God through Christ by the Holy Spirit, Christians know God not as a solitary deity but as a Trinity of love. Both in eternity and in relation to humanity, God lives in loving community as Father, Son, and Holy Spirit. In the history of the church's reflection on this mystery, two primary analogies have been employed: the psychological analogy favored by Augustine, which begins with the oneness of God and likens the mystery of the Trinity to the triad of memory, understanding, and will in the human mind; and the social analogy favored by the Cappadocians, which begins with the threeness of God and compares the Trinity to a community of three persons.

Biblical Instances

The Bible does not contain an explicit doctrine of the Trinity. Nevertheless, the raw materials for this doctrine are present in the gospel story which tells of the Father who out of great love gave up his only Son for the world (John 3:16), the Son who freely gave his life for human salvation (Gal. 2:20), and the Holy Spirit who pours God's love into human hearts (Rom. 5:5). A Trinitarian pattern of divine agency is implied in many New Testament passages, including Jesus' baptism (Mark 1:9–11); Paul's description of life in Christ (Rom. 5:1–5); the apostolic benediction (2 Cor. 13:14); and the Great Commission (Matt. 28:19).

Options for Preaching

The doctrine of the Trinity offers numerous themes for preaching:

God's love freely shared. God's own eternal life-in-love is freely shared with the world through the grace of the Lord Jesus Christ, the love of God, and the fellowship of the Holy Spirit (2 Cor. 13:14).

The church's mission. The mission of the church to all nations is a participation in the missionary activity of the triune God (Matt. 28:19).

Created for friendship. Human beings are created in the image of the triune God and thus are made not for existence in isolation but for friendship and partnership with others (Gen. 1:27).

A model of solidarity. The mutual love of the triune persons provides a model of life in solidarity with others (John 17:21).

Acknowledging the mystery. The prayer of the church is directed *to* the Father *through* the Son *in* the Holy Spirit and thus acknowledges the mystery of the Trinity (John 14:16).

Family mirrors God. The structure of the family mirrors God's own life in community.

A paradigm for community. The Trinity offers a paradigm for Christian imagination in its search for forms of human community that transcend both destructive individualism and depersonalizing collectivism.

TRUTH

Stephen L. Stell

Truth commonly refers to an accepted standard of what is right, real, or factual. It can also indicate one's conformity or fidelity to such a standard. Truth in a deeper sense may denote ultimate reality or the meaning and coherence of reality.

Analysis

The fullest expression of true reality for the Christian is not to be identified with theoretical formulations but with God. Thus truth has a personal dimension in its divine source, which subsequently affects its human expression, reception, and response.

Jesus Christ, as the embodiment of God in history, expresses divine truth for humanity and confronts humanity with its claims. Today this personal truth of Christ encounters people through concrete human lives and communities shaped by God's true word and empowered by the Spirit of truth. Being thus led by the Spirit into the truth of Jesus Christ and his gospel, believers can know this truth, follow it, obey it, act upon it, abide in it, and live from it. Such lived truth accordingly displays both cognitive and existential meanings.

Biblical Instances

Old Testament. Truth sometimes refers to accurate speech or facts (Deut. 13:14; 2 Chron. 18:15). Yet truth expressed by human beings is often recognized by actions demonstrating truthfulness (1 Kings 17:23–24). Thus speaking truly is associated with such characteristics as justice and righteousness (Isa. 59:14–15; Jer. 9:5).

Such existential truthfulness is intrinsic to the Hebrew word that is more often translated "faithfulness." Accordingly, God's people are led in the way of truth (Pss. 25:5; 43:3; 86:11), not as something external, but as part of one's being (Ps. 51:6).

New Testament. The truthfulness of God in the Old Testament is confirmed in Jesus Christ (Rom. 15:8). Truth is so integral to Jesus' character (Matt. 22:16; John 1:14, 17) that truth is identified with him (John 14:6; Eph. 4:21). Likewise the "Spirit of truth" bears witness to Christ (John 14:17; 15:26; 1 John 5:7) and leads believers into all truth (John 16:13), sanctifying them in God's true word (John 17:17–19).

This truth of the gospel accordingly transforms believers' lives: granting freedom (John 8:31–32), claiming obedience (Gal. 5:7; 1 John 2:4), and offering knowledge, sanctification, and salvation (2 Thess. 2:13; 1 Tim. 2:4; 1 Peter 1:22).

Options for Preaching

Being led into truth. Difficulties in understanding and accepting Christianity are often related to one's conception of truth. While one can learn about Christianity, Christian truth extends beyond theoretical reflection. One does not fully understand Christian faith and then follow it; rather in following, one grows in understanding. Walking, abiding, speaking, following, obeying are images that demand the active pursuit of Christian truth.

Truth and consequences. The marketplace has transformed truth into a commodity to be packaged and sold. The image of truth is important, but its substance is rarely emphasized. Yet one's choice of truth entails consequences. Acknowledging the truth of the gospel commits one to a certain life (1 John 1:6, 8; 2:4; 2 Cor. 4:2; 13:8; James 1:18–27), and rejecting divine truth likewise has its effects (Isa. 59:14–15; Rom. 1:18–32).

VIOLENCE/WAR

Allan M. Parrent

Violence generally refers to the overt use of physical coercion. Some distinguish between violence, the unjust or unwarranted use of physical coercion, and force, its justifiable or lawful use. Others distinguish among systemic, counter, and repressive violence. War refers to conflicts carried out by force of arms between or among nations or other organized groups. In war, as well as in domestic situations, coercion may be used in justifiable or unjustifiable ways.

Analysis

Can a disciple of the Prince of Peace engage in violence? Conversely, can a disciple of the One who commanded humans to love their neighbors ignore the needs of those persecuted or subjected to aggression? Within societies there are laws governing the legitimate and illegitimate uses of force or violence. Among nations there are few such laws, and none that can be effectively enforced. For the majority of Christians, the classical justifiable war tradition is an attempt to provide moral guidelines for determining when the use of force is morally justified and what the moral limits and restraints are on its use.

Most Christians accept the fact that one of the morally legitimate roles of government is to maintain a rightly ordered and sufficiently just political community. This may necessitate the use of coercive force. The high rate of crime in U.S. society testifies to the need for such a function. Most Christians also recognize that there may be circumstances in which, with certain limits, the use of coercive force may be necessary internationally. This perspective is generally based on a Christian understanding of sin in a fallen world and the conviction that the obligation to love the neighbor includes protecting the weak and overcoming oppression.

Biblical Instances

Old Testament. War is referred to more than three hundred times in the Old Testament. Biblical figures such as David are portrayed as fighting the battles of the Lord (1 Sam. 18:17; 25:28). God is often portrayed as a consultant about war (Judg. 1:1; 20:18) or even as a warrior (Ps. 24:8). The slaughter of the idol-worshiping Israelites is described as taking place at the direct command of God (Ex. 32:26–28), and the victory over the pharaoh's armies is understood as a victory of God, not of the Israelites (Ex. 15:1–18). Even the laws given for keeping war within some moral limits sound harsh (Deut. 20:10–18). There is, however, eschatological imagery of a time of peace when, contra Joel 3:10, swords shall be beaten into plowshares (Isa. 2:4; Micah 4:3), and the wolf shall lie down with the lamb (Isa. 11:6). And a fundamental rule for all human society is found in the Sixth Commandment (Ex. 20:13).

New Testament. Jesus' Sermon on the Mount looms large in any consideration of issues of violence or war—blessed are the peacemakers (Matt. 5:9), do not resist evil but turn the other cheek (Matt. 5:39), love your enemies (Matt. 5:44). Yet Jesus failed to condemn the profession of military men (Luke 3:14; 7:1–10) and himself used force to drive the money changers from the Temple. There are also several positive biblical images of political authority (Rom. 13:1–7; 1 Tim. 2:1–2; 1 Peter 2:13–17), giving at least implicit approval of the state's functions of providing order, security, and justice. These must be seen in conjunction with negative images about the misuse of political authority (Revelation 13; 1 Cor. 2:6–8; 6:1–6; Acts 5:27–29) and other relevant passages such as Mark 12:13–17 and John 18:33–19:11.

Options for Preaching

On being a peacemaker. Does being a peacemaker rule out the use of force and violence for Christians? The Christian tradition has usually said no, so long as humanity is living "between the times." In a time of "wars and rumors of wars" and of widespread domestic violence, what is the meaning of the call to peacemaking (and peacekeeping) in a world not yet conformed to the gospel?

The governing authorities: obedience and resistance. Tensions between God and caesar are legion and always will be. The laws determining when and what forms of force and violence are legitimate are made by "caesar." Unjust laws may be a factor creating conditions that may even foster violence. Just laws may require violence if they are to be enforced. What is the relationship between love of neighbor and the use of force in pursuit of justice? How is the determination to be made concerning what is properly due to God and to caesar? What is the proper role and function of "the governing authorities"?

The Sixth Commandment. The commandment "Thou shalt not kill," or "Thou shalt do no murder," raises a basic issue about the requirements for living in organized human society in a fallen world. A series of sermons on the increasingly neglected Ten Commandments would put this theme in its proper and broader context.

Turning the other cheek. Matthew 5:39 offers an opportunity to explore pacifism as a viable Christian option for responding to war and violence. For pacifists, to whom does the proscription against violence apply? What level of violence is to be excluded? Does pacifism call for nonresistance or for nonviolent resistance?

VOCATION

Donald W. Shriver, Jr.

The term "vocation" refers to a call—a summons to a particular state of being or course of action.

Analysis

The term "call," in the Bible and in common speech, can be objective (emphasis on the source of the call) or subjective (emphasis on the person or persons receiving the call). A call requires a caller and a hearer—and this is the relational assumption behind almost everything the Bible says about vocation.

Biblical Instances

Old Testament. A call, says George Mendenhall of its biblical context, is "a summons issued by one in authority, especially

God, to perform a particular function or to occupy a particular status" ("Call," in *Interpreter's Dictionary of the Bible* [New York: Abingdon Press, 1962], 1:490). This biblical meaning should be carefully distinguished from the modern, often secularized use of "vocation" to mean a job in which an individual earns a living. In the Old Testament one meets One who calls the universe into being with a creative Word (Gen. 1:3), who calls Abram to leave Haran for a destination unknown yet to him (Gen. 12:1), who issues marching orders to Moses as the future leader of the exodus (Ex. 3:4), who calls Hebrew captives to leave Egypt in haste (Ex. 12:41), and who—centuries later—calls them again to leave Babylon (Isa. 40:28; see 49:12–20).

The God of Israel is thus a "calling God," the initiator of worlds, liberations, and "new things." The divine call comes to both groups and individuals in the Old Testament, always for purposes that transcend the immediate wishes of either. Abraham and Moses are the classic instances of prophetic figures who are arrested in their tracks by the authoritative summons of the Spirit of God—precedents that prepare the way for the calls of the First Isaiah (6:1–8), Jeremiah (1:4–10), Amos (7:14–15), and Jonah (1:1–2). All these prophets report experiences of divine calling, which overcomes, redirects, and breaks into any other human vocations they and their societies may have devised for themselves.

The calling-God of the Old Testament does not merely overwhelm the human object of the calling. Humans can resist the divine call, provoking in the divine Caller both the anger of judgment and the grief of love: Hosea 11:1–2; Isaiah 65:1, 12; and Jonah. See also the portraits of "the Servant of God" in Isaiah 42–45 imaging ideal Israel and the ideal faithful human as one who heeds the call of God (50:4–5), who embodies covenant-loyalty (42:6; 49:6), and who obeys the divine call even to the point of death (53:7). Here the terms "call" and "election" merge in the Old Testament, as the patient, powerful, loving Lord of the world takes responsibility, not only for calling humans into faithful covenant but for conferring on them the power to be faithful.

Where, when, and how will this power come to people who heretofore have disobeyed the divine call? This is the great agonized question of much of the prophetic writings of the Old Testament. Equally agonized is the reversal of the question in the books of Job and Psalms: Where, when, and how will God answer the deepest *human* calls? (Job 9:16; 13:22; Pss. 22:1; 91:15).

New Testament. Two remarkable advances come with the New Testament: (1) Unlike Old Testament prophets, Jesus asks followers' help in the performance of his own vocation. They are to be partners as well as objects of his ministry: Mark 1:15; John 1:12. (2) The "high calling of God in Christ Jesus" (Phil. 3:14) encompasses a human community of indefinite inclusiveness. God's purpose to fulfill the great Isaianic prophecy of "light to the nations" (42:6) is now happening. People of diverse nationality are now hearing the call of God in Jesus (Acts 2). Persons high and low in the social hierarchy are coming into community with each other in the church (1 Cor. 1:26), thanks to the sheer grace of God (1 Cor. 1:30; Rom. 8:16–17, 28–30).

In this new Spirit-empowered set of relationships flows a multitude of "gifts of the Spirit" marking the new life of the new "called-out" community—the church. (The English word "church" derives from the Greek *Kyrios*, Lord, so that the church is "the Lord's people." And this people is "called out," the *ekklesia*. (See Eph. 4:1–16; 1 Thess. 2:9–12; 4:7–8; 5:23–24; 2 Thess. 2:13–14; 2 Tim. 1:8–14). To answer the call of God in Jesus Christ is to join the company of other called people, and the "progressive" nature of this call is unfolded as apostles and other new Christians have their sights repeatedly raised to see all humans as potential members of the new called-out community (Matt. 15:21–28; 28:19; Luke 19:9; 23:43; Acts 2:39; 9:1–22; 10:1–11:18).

Vocation in the later history of the church. At least once in the New Testament, Paul uses the term "calling" to refer to a secular occupation or social status—1 Corinthians 7:17–24. Here he advises new church members to "lead the life which the Lord has assigned" to them, whether it be a life of traditional Jewish ritual custom or the life of a slave. This implies a static view of the Christian's occupational slot, in view of the expectation—common in the New Testament church—that the world's end was near at hand anyway. A thousand years later, when the world had not ended, this static view became part of the overarching medieval European view of society as a whole: as a rule, no person was expected to occupy any social status at death different from the one occupied at birth. The one exception to this rule was the call—or vocation—of some people (from any social stratum) to service in the church as a priest or in a monastic order. To this day, in Roman Catholic parlance, vocation is likely to mean a call to such a special churchly office.

Protestantism, inspired by Martin Luther, challenged this notion directly, returning to the spiritual equality (and "priesthood") of all believers that Luther found in Paul's Galatian and Roman letters. At the same time Luther denied all hierarchical measurements of the worth of honest human work. God calls the Christian as much into shoemaking as into the monastery.

As expanded by Calvin, this doctrine of Christian vocation took hold of the Protestant imagination and flourished in the form of zeal for hard work and profit. Max Weber saw this development as a contribution of Protestants to "the spirit of capitalism," in which work for money becomes an end in itself and therefore an idolatry.

Options for Preaching

No good work lacks dignity in the sight of God. In a day when "vocational education" often means "training for low-level jobs," it is important to remind Christians that "with God there is not respect for persons"—or for their place in a hierarchy of a workplace. Ethically, this means urging Christian workers to take notice of the humanity of their neighbors high and low, to love their neighbors as themselves in the workplace too.

God's call is not first of all to a career but to service to the world. Christians are required to ask if their jobs and professions serve their calling from God. In obedient pursuit of *that* calling, they may change jobs and professions. A calling from God is an invitation to a journey, and only step by step does one discover where the call will lead.

All human "work" depends radically on the works of God. Sermons on the doctrine of creation should link the Genesis images of God as Creator to modern environmental problems, which are sins against the Creator more than mere "problems." If humans stood more in awe of the Creator's work, they might repent of their destructive, careless work, which currently endangers the "garden planet."

The call of God redeems human work, using it for larger purposes than our own. In the biblical view, human effort can serve the purposes of God, and this is the highest compliment ever paid human effort. *Any* job done in love for one's neighbor has its place in the "economy" of God's work in the world (Esth. 4:14; Rom. 8:28–30). On the other hand, even socially prestigious work can degenerate into boredom, emptiness, and futility if not seen in the context of some large and good purposes, beyond "all that we ask or think" (Eph. 3:20). Christians, too, sometimes experience in their work a sort of practical atheism: no Holy Spirit to call them to work each day, nothing holy in the work, no "author and finisher" (Heb. 12:2, KJV) of the work, fragmentary as it always is. Here, as in every other part of their lives, Christians look to Jesus as the one who perfectly answered the call of God but who, in doing so, offered up his own fragmentary life, with the words, "Into thy hands I commit my spirit." It was his last act of obedience to the Divine Caller, an act whose perfection every one of his followers can imitate.

WEALTH

R. Alan Culpepper

Wealth is the possession of an abundance of material goods.

Analysis

While wealth is generally measured in terms of property, possessions, and money, these do not always bring to the possessor the intangible benefits of joy, fulfillment, and peace. The challenge for those with wealth is to receive their abundance as a gift and trust from God to be used for the benefit of society, and especially the poor. While wealth is not inherently evil, it brings temptations of materialism, pride, and self-centeredness.

Biblical Instances

In the early period of Israel's history, wealth consisted in the possession of cattle, slaves, gold, and silver (Gen. 24:35). Houses at early Israelite sites were all about the same size. Later a ruling class with more land and larger houses emerged. Wealth was viewed as a sign of God's blessing (Deut. 28:1–14). Wealth was of little use, however, if one had no descendants. In the Old Testament, the patriarchs, Job, and Solomon are singled out as wealthy (Gen. 13:2; Job. 1:1–3; 42:10–17; 1 Kings 4:26–27). Wealth can lead to injustice and social irresponsibility. Amos, for example, condemns those who "lie upon beds of ivory" (Amos 6:4–7).

Jesus embraced the poor and warned the rich that their wealth would destroy them (Luke 4:18; 6:20–26; 16:19–31; 18:18–30). Nevertheless, repentance is possible. The rich should use their wealth for the benefit of the poor (Mark 10:17–27). Zacchaeus (Luke 19:1–10), Joseph of Arimathea (Matt. 27:57), and Barnabas (Acts 4:36–37) provide positive examples. Paul urged those with means to give generously (2 Cor. 9:6–10). James (5:1–6) and the pastoral epistles (1 Tim. 6:9–10) warn against the temptations and vanity of riches.

Options for Preaching

Middle-class American Christians are caught in a double bind. They have a hard time making ends meet and maintaining their standard of living, yet they are rich when compared to the poverty of millions in the world. Sermons on wealth can develop a number of different themes, such as:

Living simply so that others can simply live.

Accepting abundance as God's gift (Eccl. 5:19).

Gaining independence from materialism.

The preacher's aim should be to help those who are struggling to reconcile their style of life, and their ambitions and desires, with God's call to be a good steward of one's possessions and generous toward the needs of others. In a materialistic society, even those who struggle to get by often live beyond their means and succumb to an idolatry of possessions.

WHOLENESS

Glenn H. Asquith, Jr.

Wholeness refers to the state or quality of being whole, entire, or complete. When applied to the human person, wholeness calls for attention to all aspects of the self. In holistic theory, individual decisions and actions are viewed with consideration for how they impact, and are impacted by, the spiritual, physical, intellectual, emotional, and social dimensions of life.

Analysis

A holistic view of life stresses the interrelationship of and the need for balance among these various dimensions. For example, a holistic approach to health requires treatment of all these aspects alongside the physical. Some historic and contemporary churches have stressed spiritual healing without regard to the knowledge and practice of medical science. The scientific revolution of the twentieth century has led others to a purely physical view of health without regard to the spiritual dimension.

Biblical Instances

Wholeness is an important biblical theme. Deuteronomy 6:4–5, the *Shema* (Hebrew: "hear"), a passage of central importance in Jewish worship and tradition, calls for the worship of God with all of one's heart, soul, and might. In Hebrew psychology, "heart" (*leb*) is much more than a physical organ; it is the seat of the emotions, the intellect, and moral life. Likewise "soul" (*nephesh*) is not separate from the fleshly body as in ancient Greek thought but is the source of life, vitality, and strength of the self. Used together, these two terms certainly refer to the "whole being" in Hebrew understanding; "might" is added to reinforce what is already implied.

Jesus reaffirmed the necessity of holistic love for God by referring to the *Shema* as the greatest commandment (Mark 12:28–30). Further, the second commandment is to love the neighbor as the self, which implies wholeness in relationships. Love for both God and neighbor is also called for in 1 John 4:20–21.

Options for Preaching

1 Corinthians 12:12–30 is an important commentary on wholeness from a variety of perspectives. Just as the physical body must operate as an organic, interdependent whole, so the church as the body of Christ witnesses under the concept of wholeness. Each member is gifted in a particular way. While each gift is necessary for the total witness of the church, no one gift is more important than another. Ephesians 4:11–16 affirms that the whole body grows and develops in love when each part is working properly.

Romans 7:13–25 shows Paul struggling with the concept of wholeness. He recognizes that there is a sinful, "carnal" part of himself, frequently unconscious, that makes him "do the very thing I hate" (7:15). The good news is that God in Christ accepts, redeems, and uses all aspects of the self for the glory of God.

WOMEN'S ISSUES

Edwina Hunter

Women's issues are any issues that affect humanity because women constitute more than half the world's population. More narrowly, women's issues as a theme for preaching may be defined as the denial to women and people of color of their full humanity and equality in the sight of God and in the church, and the use of scripture itself as a tool of subjugation to keep women as second-class citizens in the church and in the world. Women are the majority present in most worship services; however, because of their awakening to centuries of sermons that ignore the everyday reality of women's lives and preachers who cite scripture to deny women their wholeness as persons made in the image of God, many women now perceive the Christian church, the Bible, and God as patriarchal and oppressive. Many women are leaving the church and the faith of their childhood, and many feel great pain and a sense of homelessness.

Analysis

Theology sensitive to women's issues will begin with the stories of women, taking a creative and imaginative approach. Images are essential in order to take into account women and their stories as well as the traditions, races, and cultures from which they come.

Theology that values women as created in the image of God is concerned with justice for all peoples. It responds to injustice as reason for personal involvement and action on behalf of the unjustly treated. The language of racial and gender inclusivity is a practical outworking of such theology. In addition, the church must understand that there is a deeply perceived connection between spirituality and sexuality. Women theologians are addressing the abuse of sexuality as it occurs in exploitation of, and violence toward, women.

A foundational concept for women's issues is that theology is and must be relational and develops in dialogue. This is consonant with the life of Jesus in the Gospels as he talked with his friends, engaged the woman at the well in a theological discussion, and yielded to the challenging request of the Syrophoenician woman (Mark 7:24–30; Matt. 15:21–28).

Taken seriously, such an approach profoundly impacts the

act of preaching. Relational, dialogical preaching becomes the norm. The possibility for collegial sermon preparation becomes practical reality. The preacher, as an act of justice, speaks inclusively of humans and of God.

Any preacher who seeks to address women's issues should discover the wealth of books by women theologians, ethicists, preachers, historians, and biblical scholars. This may well be essential, because the preacher is asked to embrace a new biblical hermeneutic, to read the Bible with a new set of lenses, to employ new interpretations of such texts as 1 Corinthians 14:33b–36 (the "women should keep silence in the churches" text), a new reading of the creation story in Genesis, a rethinking of such sayings as "pride is sinful," and a deepened sensitivity to women's stories throughout the Bible. The presence and role of women as the last of Jesus' followers at the cross and the first at the tomb will be a story told over and over so that female children may see the courage, steadfastness, and worth of their scriptural foremothers and, perhaps for the first time, experience pride in their femaleness as a gift from God.

Biblical Instances

Old Testament. Resources are available from both Euro-American and African-American women biblical scholars to reexamine the stories of Hagar in Genesis 16:1–16 and 21:9–21, of Tamar in 2 Samuel 13:1–22, of the daughter of Jephthah in Judges 11:29–40, of Vashti and Esther in the book of Esther, of Lot's wife and her daughters in Genesis 19, and of an unnamed woman in Judges 19:1–30 who experienced such violence any reader must recoil. The stories of these women raise issues of women's oppression, the sexual exploitation of women, women used and misused as property, and women as scapegoats.

At the same time, women such as Ruth and Naomi, and Shiphrah and Puah (the wonderful Hebrew midwives of Ex. 1:15–22), can be lifted up as models of strength and ingenuity.

Fresh reading and the assistance of biblical scholars can free the creation texts from the misinterpretation that "women brought sin into the world." Correct and comparative translation of the Hebrew will reveal that "help meet" (KJV) or "helper fit" (RSV) of Genesis 2:20 is not a suggestion of woman's inferior position but is correctly understood to bear the same meaning as the word translated "help" in Psalm 46:1: "God is our refuge and strength, a very present help in trouble."

A new reading and appreciation for Joel 2:28–29 ("your sons and your daughters shall prophesy") recognizes that God is moving in just this way in the present as women are responding to God's call to ordained ministry and churches are validating their call.

New Testament. Jesus in relation to women in the Gospels has been explored by many women scholars. Jesus' relational, dialogical approach in John 4 to the Samaritan woman who then became an evangelist is but prelude to his relation to women followers who went with him to the cross and returned to the tomb. According to John 20, Mary Magdalene was Jesus' messenger and witness to resurrection.

Most troubling for many women, however, are the writings of Paul. Galatians 3:28 ("there is neither male nor female; for you are all one in Christ Jesus") can be cited with great rejoicing, but what about 1 Corinthians 14:33b–36? Perhaps even this often-quoted "women should keep silence in the churches" has been misinterpreted. After all, there are no marks of punctuation in the original Greek. And Paul's style of writing in this epistle is to quote from the letter received from the Corinthians and then to respond with irony or rebuke, as in 1 Corinthians 6:12–20. It is possible he is again employing this device in chapter 14: that verses 33b–35 are to be read as a quotation from the letter written by the Corinthians, and that Paul's reply is found in verse 36. It is known by translators that the "you" of this verse is masculine. It may then read, "What! Did the word of God originate with you [men], or are you [men] the only ones it has reached?" Some scholars believe this is, indeed, the correct rendering.

The list of Romans 16 makes it clear that Paul considered women as equal co-workers or co-ministers with him in the faith. Of the more than thirty persons mentioned, eight are women.

Options for Preaching

In memory of her. Here is a story that is told in one form or another in all four of the Gospels: Matt. 26:6–13; Mark 14:3–9; Luke 7:36–50; John 12:1–11. These texts certainly contain differences, but each depicts a woman anointing Jesus. Not yet realized is Jesus' promise in Mark 14:9: "wherever the gospel is preached in the whole world, what she has done will be told in memory of her."

Jesus and women. This may suggest a sermon series drawing on such stories as the following: "Jesus and a Woman of Questionable Character," from Luke 7:36–50; "Jesus, a Woman, and a Girl," from Mark 5:21–43; "He Was Talking with a Woman!" from John 4:1–42; "He Is Alive and He Called My Name!" from John 20:1–18; "Choosing the Better Part," from Luke 10:38–42. This latter is all the better taken in the context of verses 25–31, where Jesus has just told the story of the Good Samaritan to illustrate love of neighbor. The story of Mary, a woman, sitting and learning at the feet of Jesus, a rabbi, may be seen as illustration of how to love God.

Seldom told tales: (1) "What About Hagar?" A retelling of Genesis 16:1–16 and 21:1–21 from Hagar's point of view gives the preacher the opportunity to speak on behalf of all oppressed women, particularly women of color. (2) "How Can Such Things Be?" Judges 19:1–30 contains one of the most horrifying stories in all of the Bible—a story of a woman brutally gang-raped, killed, and mutilated. There are parallels in the present. (3) "Dishonorable Honor." In Judges 11:29–40 Jephthah's daughter pays the price with her life for her father's unnecessary and faithless vow. He did not fully believe God's spirit was with him and so he bargained with a vow that he felt his honor demanded he pay. That meant the sacrifice of his daughter.

WORD OF GOD

Bernhard W. Anderson

The motif "word of God," which pervades the Christian Bible from Genesis (1:3) to the Apocalypse of John (1:2; 19:13), bespeaks God's self-revelation. It signifies the outgoing manifestation of God's being and therefore the expression of God's will, purpose, and concern. The God who speaks seeks to enter into relationship with, and to communicate with, human beings so that they may "know" (acknowledge) God (Ps. 46:10) and walk humbly and responsibly before their Lord (Micah 6:8).

Analysis

Speaking and hearing. The metaphor is derived from the human experience of an "I-thou" relationship in which speaking and hearing is the bond of communion and communication.

Created in the image of God, human beings are constituted for relationship with God; consequently God may speak to them and they may respond in prayer and praise (Psalm 8). In the Bible, with a few notable exceptions (e.g., Ex. 24:11; Job 42:5; Matt. 5:8), human beings do not see God (Ex. 33:20; John 1:18), but may hear God's "voice" articulated by prophets, sages, and apostles. The New Testament announces that God, who has spoken by prophets in various ways, has spoken supremely through a Son, Jesus Christ (Mark 9:7; Heb. 1:1–2).

God's desire to speak to human beings, however, encounters obstacles. Sometimes it is the "hard-heartedness" of people who are so trapped in a false way of life or a deceitful ideology that God's word, spoken by a prophet, cannot get through (Isa. 6:9). At other times, people are so victimized by oppressive powers or chastened by suffering that God seems to be absent and there is a "famine of hearing the words of the Lord" (Amos 8:11). In such situations, persons of faith must "wait for God"—until God's presence is manifest and God's word is heard again (Ps. 130:5; Hab. 2:1–4).

The word of judgment and mercy. In the divine-human relationship, the word of God cuts incisively like a surgical knife, exposing inner thoughts and motives to God's inescapable judgment (Heb. 4:12–13; Psalm 139). False prophets are exposed as those who heal the wounds of the people superficially, while God's prophetic servants are called to a critical task. The negative impact of God's word, however, is part of the larger redemptive purpose of building and healing (Jer. 1:10).

When human confidence is shattered and there seems to be no hope for the future, God speaks a word of consolation and promise. Change and decay are all around, but God's word "endures forever" and is the ground of hope (Isa. 40:6–8). Further, God's word of forgiveness emancipates people from the bondage of past failure and makes a "new covenant" that cannot be broken (Jer. 31:34; Isa. 54:7–10).

The sovereign word. At the human level, the power of a spoken word depends upon the prestige and status of the speaker, as in the case of a patriarchal blessing (Gen. 27:26–29). Analogously, God's word is fraught with holy power that arouses awe and evokes praise. By the word of God, the cosmos was created (Gen. 1:3; Ps. 33:6). God's promissory word is like the rain that falls from heaven, gently and irresistibly accomplishing the divine intention (Isa. 55:10–11). In a Wisdom writing that paraphrases the exodus story, the word of God is personified as the powerful executor of God's will to save (Wisd. of Sol. 11:5–19:22). In short, the word of God is the dynamic power at work in creation and history. In the New Testament this theme is transposed into the announcement that Jesus Christ is the Word of God, through whom the cosmos was created and a new creation has been inaugurated (John 1:1–4; Heb. 1:1–2; Rev. 19:13).

Biblical Instances

The word as message. The word of God is a communication from God. In Old Testament prophecy this aspect of the divine word is especially prominent: the prophets are regarded as messengers sent from God to proclaim a message, usually of divine judgment. Even when these "words of God" (Jer. 1:9) were put into writing, they had a shattering impact (Jeremiah 36). Moreover, the word of God is often identified with God's torah, that is, the guidance or teaching that God gives the people. By treasuring God's word in the heart, people may know how to live (Ps. 119:9–16). Thus the spoken word of God finds expression in written words (scriptures) that are the basis for meditation, exhortation, or proclamation. In this sense the Bible is often called the Word of God, for it is the "enscripturated" message of salvation and the written version of the unfolding drama of God's purpose.

The condescending word. The word of God finds expression in human words. This paradox discloses both its majesty and its humility. In former centuries some Christian interpreters stressed God's accommodation or condescension to the limitations of human speech. Just as a parent gets down on the floor and speaks baby talk to a child, so God condescends to the human level of speaking. God does not meet humans in some ideal world or speak to them in the tongues of angels but rather meets them in this world, under the social and cultural limitations reflected in scripture. Therefore in interpreting scripture it is necessary to understand the circumstances of God's speaking: the original idiom of language, the patriarchal limitations of society, the social setting of the message. This is actually the doctrine of the incarnation, broadened out to include the whole of scripture.

The word of God as preached. Theologians have summarized the subject by delineating three major aspects of the word of God: the Bible, Jesus Christ, the preaching (*kerygma*). In all of these senses the word of God is not locked in the past: its power is felt in the present as each generation is called to hear anew. In the Old Testament the contemporaneity of God's word is evident especially in the sermons of the book of Deuteronomy. In Moses' preaching, the contemporary generation of the people are summoned to stand again at Mount Sinai and to respond anew to "the word of the LORD" (Deut. 5:1–4). Similarly, apostles of the New Testament engaged in "preaching the word," that is, telling the good news of the gospel that centers in the story of Jesus (Acts 8:4). Thus the word of God is the "living word" that lies within and beyond "the sacred page." When the interpreter, faithful to the biblical tradition as handed on in the community of faith, preaches effectively to the life situations of a congregation, then the word of God may be mediated anew through the human words of our time and place.

Options for Preaching

Each of the above themes offers rich material for preaching.

Made in God's image, people are called to respond to God's word with their human words (Hos. 14:2), such as the various types of prayers found in the Psalter: hymnic praise to God who is Creator and Lord (Psalm 8); laments or cries of distress "out of the depths" (Psalm 130); songs of thanksgiving for demonstrations of God's amazing grace (Psalm 116).

God's word is "sharper than any two-edged sword" (Heb. 4:12), cutting through humans' rationalizing defenses and ideological justifications and exposing them to God's searching judgment and healing forgiveness. God desires not only a "pure heart" (Ps. 51:6–12) but a society in which justice flows like a never-failing stream (Amos 5:24).

God's word of promise "endures forever" (Isa. 40:8) because it is grounded in God's faithfulness and sovereign power (Isa. 55:10–11). Through Jesus Christ, the God who is faithful is fulfilling the promises made to the people of God (Rom. 4:13–25).

God's word "lived" (or "tented") among us. This christological announcement (John 1:14) has implications for the whole of scripture, in which God condescends to meet humans at their own level, speaking in very human words.

The word of God is not imprisoned in the past but addresses each generation with new power and meaning. As the Sinai covenant was not made just with Israel's ancestors but "with us, even us, who are all of us here alive this day" (Deut. 5:3, KJV), so in the Eucharist God's people are invited to hear anew God's word spoken by his Son (Mark 9:7) and to reexperience the saving power of Christ's sacrifice. Preaching at its best contemporizes the biblical story, so that it becomes the story of our life.

WORK

Glenn H. Asquith, Jr.

Work is purposeful activity, labor, employment, or occupation; that which is done to produce a product, accomplish a goal, or perform a task. In theology, "works" are moral acts, distinguished from faith.

Analysis

For many, work is a primary source of meaning and self-esteem, often lost upon retirement or sudden unemployment. Thus a spiritual task for many is to reframe the sense of self apart from one's work role; God accepts people for who they *are* rather than for what they *do*.

Psychologists have generally viewed ability to work as one criterion of mental health. However, overwork or addiction to work at the expense of other aspects of life can be a psychological defense against fear of mortality or a method of avoiding intimate relationships.

Biblical Instances

In Genesis 1 the *word* of God is also the creative *work* of God, a theme cited later in Psalm 33:6. Judges 2:7, 10 refers to the great work the Lord had done for Israel. The mighty and creative works of God are also a frequent theme in the psalms, notably 8:3; 102:25; and 104:24.

The priestly creation narrative concludes with the concept of Sabbath, in which God rested (Hebrew: *Shabat*) from the work of creation on the seventh day and blessed it as such (Gen. 2:2–3). The Fourth Commandment requires that the Sabbath be kept holy and devoted to God (Ex. 20:8–11). Genesis 3:17–19 portrays toil as the only way humanity can bring forth food from the ground following Adam's expulsion from Eden. Humans working from sunrise until evening is part of God's ordering of creation (Ps. 104:23). Ecclesiastes 1:3 and 3:9 question what the worker gains from such toil, given the repeated cycle of time and events that God has ordained.

John 1:1–18 recounts the theme of the creative *work* of God's *Word*, which became incarnate in Christ, in whom is seen the works of God (John 5:36; 6:28–29; 10:25). In John 9:1–17, Jesus interprets a man's blindness as an opportunity for the works of God to be made manifest; the works of God in Christ transcend the Pharisaic tradition and laws of the Sabbath (John 9:25).

Options for Preaching

The contrast between works and justification by faith is a primary theme for preaching. Ephesians 2:8–10 proclaims salvation through faith, not works, which are the result of salvation; this is also seen in Romans 3:20; 9:11; and 11:6. This theme is addressed from a different perspective in James 2:14–26, which defines faith as sound doctrine (2:19) and works (defined as acts of charity) as necessary for a vital faith.

The parable of the householder (Matt. 20:1–16) uses the image of differing amounts of work for the same pay to teach that God's grace is extended equally to all believers—Jew and Gentile alike—regardless of "length of service."

WORSHIP

William H. Willimon

The Hebrew word for worship in the Old Testament means "to bow down, to prostrate oneself." Worship is the bending of the believer to the will and the ways of God. While it has the same meaning in the New Testament, "worship" is also used there to translate Greek words signifying service or pious actions.

Analysis

Christians speak of a "worship service." Worship *is* service in that it is the work that is done, not for oneself, but for God. The more formal word, *liturgy,* stems from the Greek *leitourgia* which was used in antiquity to designate taxes owed by individuals to the state. Worship is service, both inside church and out, in word and deed, in public and private, to the God who first loved and is therefore loved in return. The English word "worship" stems from the Old English "worthship." Worship is ascription of worth, designation of what is most worthy in life. In worship Christians reach out to God, believing that, in worship, God reaches out to humanity.

Biblical Instances

Old Testament. Israel's worship involved animal sacrifice as gifts to God in recognition that all of life is a gift from God.

While ancient Hebrew worship involved sacrifice and burnt offering, similar to worship practices of its pagan neighbors, a unique aspect of Hebrew worship was its strong ethical dimension. Israel's prophets asserted that true worship involved obedience. Israel's God was insulted by a people who honored God with their lips but not with their lives (see Isa. 1:11–17; Amos 5:21–22).

The synagogue practice of gathering to read and study scripture on the Sabbath probably began during the exile when the people of Israel gathered apart from the Temple. People in exile, far from home, gather to tell the old story, to recite the major tenets of the faith, to pass on their beliefs to the young, and to sing the songs of home. Jesus is depicted as a faithful participant in the worship in the synagogue (Luke 4) as well as in the Temple. After the destruction of the Temple in A.D. 70, the synagogue became the sole location for Jewish worship.

New Testament. Early Christian worship duplicated many of the features of synagogue worship, though at an early date Christians began gathering on Sunday, the first day of the Jewish work week, the day of Christ's resurrection, rather than on the Jewish Sabbath.

Christian writers (Heb. 9:11–12, 24–26) interpreted Christ as the perfect sacrifice, the perfect self-giving of God, so that now no more sacrifices were needed. The church itself was now the temple and all believers constituted the holy priesthood (1 Cor. 6:19; 1 Peter 2:9).

Three public rituals appear in the New Testament: baptism, the Lord's Supper, and the laying on of hands, though no explicit instructions are given for any of these. The New Testament seems more interested in the meaning of these rites than in details for their performance. Baptism was the rite of initiation into the church. The Lord's Supper was probably held each Sunday when the church gathered for worship. The laying on of hands was associated with empowerment by the Holy Spirit and commissioning for special work for the church (Acts 9:17; 13:2–3).

Options for Preaching

Worship is fellowship. In 1 Corinthians 11–13, Paul speaks of the need for the church to embody, in its gatherings, the fellowship, the unity, of those who are united with Christ. Whenever the church gathers, this is the body of Christ taking visible form in the world. Therefore, if there are divisions within the congregation, Christian worship is jeopardized (1 Cor. 11:17–18, 20–22, 28–34). Thus the strong ethical emphasis that characterized Hebrew worship characterizes Christian worship.

Worship is exuberance within God's presence. Psalm 150 is characteristic of the believer's experience of unrestrained joy upon entering "the house of the Lord." Worshipers are glad to be gathered in God's presence (Psalm 100). The Westminster Confession speaks of the "chief end" of believers as that of "glorifying God and enjoying God forever." In worship, in Sunday exuberance, worshipers experience the simple joy of being with the One who has loved and is therefore loved. They are given strength and vision that enable them to meet life's challenges, and they are sent forth renewed and reborn.

Worship is responsive. Christian worship responds to the God who has first reached out to humanity. One's praise is reflexive. Today, when many conceive of their relationship to God as mainly a matter of what they do, think, or feel, worship is a reminder that one speaks to God because God has first addressed humanity. The Creator asks, "Where are you?" (Gen. 3:9), "What have you done?" (Gen. 4:10). Divine initiative evokes human response.